From clinician to manager
An introduction to hospital and health service management

From clinician to manager

An introduction to hospital and health service management

SECOND EDITION

James S LAWSON
School of Health Services Management
University of New South Wales

Arie ROTEM
School of Public Health and Community Medicine
University of New South Wales

with

Ian O'Rourke
Institute of Clinical Excellence, Sydney

Kevin Forde
School of Public Health and Community Medicine
University of New South Wales

Phillip W Bates
University of Newcastle

The *McGraw-Hill* Companies

Sydney New York San Francisco Auckland
Bangkok Bogotá Caracas Hong Kong
Kuala Lumpur Lisbon London Madrid
Mexico City Milan New Delhi San Juan
Seoul Singapore Taipei Toronto

First edition 1996
Reprinted 2002, 2003

Text © 2004 McGraw-Hill Australia
Illustrations and design © 2004 McGraw-Hill Australia Pty Ltd
Additional owners of copyright are named in on-page credits.

National Library of Australia Cataloguing-in-Publication data:

Lawson, James S.
From clinician to manager: an introduction to hospital and health service management.

    2nd edn.
    Includes index.
    ISBN 0 074 71484 8.

1. Health services administration – Australia.
2. Hospitals – Australia – Administration. I. Rotem, Arie. II. Title.

    362.10680994

Published in Australia by
McGraw-Hill Australia Pty Ltd
Level 2, 82 Waterloo Road, North Ryde NSW 2113
Acquisitions Editor: Thu Nguyen
Production Editor: Sybil Kesteven
Editor: Sharon Nevile
Proofreader: Tim Learner
Indexer: Diane Harriman
Designer (cover and interior): Jenny Pace
Illustrator: Alan Laver
Typeset in Melior by Jenny Pace
Printed on 80 gsm woodfree by Pantech Limited, Hong Kong.

The authors

James S Lawson is Emeritus Professor and past Head of the School of Health Services Management at the University of New South Wales, Sydney, Australia. He has extensive experience as a clinician, particularly in the field of child health, and as a senior health service manager. He has been a hospital medical director, the head of a state health department and a director of a state health policy and planning division. He is an international health service consultant for the World Health Organization and the Asian Development Bank. He has published widely. In 2003 he was made a Member of the Order of Australia.

Arie Rotem is Professor in the School of Public Health and Community Medicine at the University of New South Wales, specialising in health development. He is an international consultant to many governments and international development and donor agencies, including the World Health Organization and the World Bank. Many of his consultancies focused on capacity development, institutional strengthening and leadership development in health systems. He has published widely in the fields of workforce planning, management of human resources and health program evaluation.

Ian O'Rourke is past Professor of Surgery at Flinders University and has had extensive clinical and managerial experience. He has commenced a new role as the inaugural Chief Executive Officer of the Institute of Clinical Excellence, which is based in Sydney. The purpose of this new institute is to promote high standards of patient care. He is responsible for the chapter on quality.

Kevin Forde is Lecturer in Health Economics and Healthcare Financial Management in the School of Public Health and Community Medicine at the University of New South Wales. He has published widely in the field of financial management. He is responsible for the chapter on health service finance.

Philip W Bates is visiting Professor of Law at the University of Newcastle in New South Wales, Australia. He is an international consultant to the World Health Organization. He is responsible for the chapter on health service law.

Contents

Preface

Since the first edition of *From Clinician to Manager* was published in 1996, the field of health service management has witnessed dramatic changes to the standard and quality of patient care. This new edition gives much greater emphasis to this issue, and includes a chapter on quality of care. The reason for this emphasis on quality of patient care is the realisation that the ever-increasing introduction of new technology has also increased the complexity of patient care and subsequently the risk of error.

In addition, the book has been generally updated in accord with advances in the field of health service management while continuing to provide essential information on management principles in the health services sector.

Readers have responded very positively to the practical approach adopted in the first edition. Clearly, clinicians of all types—doctors, nurses, therapists and clinical scientists—have valued a book which introduces them to health care management in Australia.

The rationale behind this book is that the management of hospitals and other health service organisations requires more than just education or clinical skills. Clinicians—doctors, nurses and other health care professionals who care for patients and their families—who find themselves in the management role need more than the clinical knowledge and skills they acquired during their training. However, others entering the health service management field will also find this book useful.

The complexities and unique features of health services demand a capacity to cope with responsibilities beyond those associated with the care of individual patients. These include, among other things, the capacity to develop and maintain harmony and teamwork among staff and an ability to set priorities and allocate scarce resources, to manage conflicting demands, to make decisions and take action promptly, to work within a budget, to undertake strategic planning and to organise the work for others.

The authors of this book aim to bridge the gap between the domains of the clinician and the manager in a practical and informative way. They bring to the project many years' experience of health service management. The intention is not to produce another authoritative text; rather it is to provide sound practical advice and relevant anecdotal experience that encapsulate many of the essential management issues the clinician is likely to meet as manager. In particular, there is a deliberate aim to increase the reader's understanding of the major issues that influence the organisation and management of health services, both nationally and internationally. Where appropriate, case studies and personal experience are used to illustrate the practical application of the information provided.

Many chapters suggest topics for reflection. The idea is to encourage readers to review their own experience as managers, to explore the application of the material of their own workplaces and to identify the potential for improvement.

The book has been organised in such a way as to help readers identify with the unique features of being a manager, understand the organisation in which they work and the external pressures affecting their performance and identify the management principles underpinning the successful organisation and management of health services. It also provides guidelines and practical tips on how best to supervise staff, improve working relationships and perform as a manager.

Chapter 1 introduces the notion of becoming a hospital and health service manager. The authors describe what is special about managing health services and provide an overview of the skills required to be a successful clinical manager. A key message is that to be effective, the new manager initially must recognise his or her own strengths and weaknesses and accept that some basic skills can be improved.

In Chapter 2, the authors describe some of the major issues and challenges facing hospitals and health services since the mid-1990s. Some of the issues are so large and so daunting that the individual manager might find it hard to see their relevance to day-to-day workplace management. The authors suggest strongly that an appreciation of these issues is an essential component not only of strategic planning, but also in the successful resolution of many of the problems facing health services. The message is that we do not work in a vacuum.

The need to understand health care organisations is explored at some length in Chapter 3. While there is no way a book of this size can encapsulate their complete historical development, an attempt is made to address the development of the different facets of the health services in sufficient detail as to provide useful guidance on how they should be organised and managed. This chapter also contains some thoughts on the people who work in health care organisations and how their development as health professionals has and still does impact on health service delivery. Prospective health service managers need to have a good grasp of the big picture of health care delivery in terms of both where it has come from and where it is heading. Not least is the need to understand the power and influence wielded by the different professional groups over time and the way their respective needs and expectations will continue to shape the provision of health services.

Chapter 4 presents practical advice on planning and managing health services. It starts with a brief overview of what managers do and then provides a logical framework for planning and management. The authors highlight the paradox between the apparently disjointed and interrupted way in which the typical manager works and the need for structure so that systems and procedures are streamlined and coordinated. The critical point is made that to be effective, managers must ensure that a carefully developed means of evaluating the performance of their organisation is built in at the initial planning stage and carried out consistently as part of routine operations.

The next section, Chapter 5, explores the skills required of health service managers. The authors initially look at the 'managerial personality' and some of the characteristics of a good manager. No perfect mix is presented, as readers are challenged to assess the right balance for themselves. The authors do, however, make a clear statement about the critical importance of leadership. This is a chapter that condenses the whole gamut of qualities required of a manager into a succinct summary of key features; much is good advice based on many years' experience. The need to be a good people manager underpins the text whether read in the context of teamwork, motivation or the deceptively simple art of communication. By way of summary, the authors provide at the end of this chapter some practical tips for health service managers that, as they say, are based on hard-won experience.

Chapter 6 is a completely new chapter on quality issues that has been prepared by Ian O'Rourke, who is the inaugural Chief Executive Officer of the newly created New South Wales Institute for Clinical Excellence. This institute is responsible for raising awareness and improving quality of patient care. This chapter covers the establishment and implementation of guidelines and safety procedures for effective quality of care.

No discussion of management would be complete without advice on managing money. Chapter 7, revised by Kevin Forde, covers the vital issue of health service finance and seeks to answer the teasing questions of why hospitals and health services are so expensive and what can be done about this. Clearly the authors identify with the fear the typical clinician has when given responsibility for the financial affairs of a division, department or unit and asked to prepare a budget for the first time. Some helpful hints are offered. More disturbing is the advice on defalcation and the need for the health service manager to be 'squeaky clean' when it comes to financial matters.

Chapter 8 encompasses discussion of health service management in different contexts. In particular, the authors highlight the differences between managing in the public and in the private sectors. This is a useful summary for any clinician contemplating moving into management. In the broader context, there is a section on managing health services in international settings that will be of particular interest to readers from other countries or to those thinking of working in other countries. Finally, some practical advice is offered to clinicians contemplating managing public health services. This section highlights the quite different challenges of addressing the needs of populations.

In Chapter 9, Philip Bates offers an introduction to legal matters that are of direct concern and interest to clinicians who are becoming responsible for managing health services. The purpose of this summary of legal matters is to familiarise readers with the issues and with some legal terms. In a subtle manner Philip Bates is offering caution to readers, indicating that there may well be legal consequences of decisions taken by health service managers and that we should think before we act. The chapter also demonstrates that the law as we know it is not the only legal system that influences events; there are long-established Islamic, Chinese and Japanese legal systems that are totally relevant to an increasingly international world view.

Chapter 10 starts with the vitally important issue of information. At best, it is a brief outline of some of the most critical concerns. There is also an overview of total quality management and the increasing emphasis being placed on customer satisfaction. The intent is to highlight the increasing importance of systematically evaluating the quality of care and service provided in hospitals and health service organisations, and to identify some of the key issues that managers need to address.

Trends in management of health services are discussed in Chapter 11. This chapter not only presents current trends, but also provides a framework for considering the future direction of health service management. The chapter gives brief sketches of the trends in the management of health services that have largely developed out of the need to control costs; for example, casemix, purchase–provider split, health outcomes, benchmarking and best practice. The potentially frustrating brevity of the discussion of these various trends is partly explained by the authors when they say that 'trends are just that … they come and they go'. Prospective managers are well advised to do their homework before introducing a change that may well turn out to be only a passing fad.

As the title suggests, the aim of this book is to provide helpful advice for people making the transition from clinician to manager. The content is practical, concise and potentially useful. Ultimately, acceptance of its value is up to the reader: to read and reflect on the material, supplement the advice with relevant readings, and put the advice into practice.

Simple approaches to concepts and problems are often best, particularly in fields of human activity that involve status, power and territory. Writings on management often reflect the high status and power involved by becoming very complex and detailed explanations of the obvious. The evidence for this is the continuous stream of published texts on management in which writers purport to offer new approaches but in reality market old ideas as new breakthroughs. Among the many books on the subject, the authors could find only one, *Management for Nurses* by Marjorie Cuthbert, that they would recommend to introduce clinicians to management.

Hence, this book. It is deliberately brief. It is as simple as possible. Above all, it is an introduction.

Give it a go, evaluate your progress, seek continuous improvement—and good luck.

Becoming a hospital and health service manager

Few hospital and health service managers have deliberately planned careers in management. Most start their careers as health professionals; others study arts, psychology, accounting or economics. Due to a combination of circumstances ('someone has to manage') the majority of health service managers evolve into the role. As Torrens puts it, the transition from clinician to manager is:

> a change from a life of objective, scientifically based diagnosis and treatment of disease in individual patients to a life of subjective, often manipulation of emotion-based groups of people in an organisation.[1]

The story of one individual, Dr Harry Symons, is typical.

When Dr Symons was first promoted to become a staff medical officer, he made the common assumption that because he was a good physician he would automatically be a good manager. But the management role, which involves the ability to plan and organise, requires certain basic qualities and skills that must be learnt and continually improved upon. It is a constantly changing field in which new concepts and strategies are being developed, tested, modified and eventually applied. Traditional approaches to management have often been found less useful than was once thought.

The effective manager needs first to recognise his or her own strengths and weaknesses and then to accept that basic skills can be improved.

As a first step, we suggest that you consider your own experiences and difficulties as a manager in relation to the story told by Dr Symons. If you can identify with this situation, you are likely to find useful suggestions in this book. Dr Harry Symons was essentially able to recognise some of the weaknesses in his managerial role and he developed an enviable reputation as an excellent health service manager.

case history

I suppose I never really considered any field besides medicine. My high school teachers used to say I had a natural talent for the sciences and my family encouraged me to consider medicine. Although I certainly wasn't a star pupil in medical school, I enjoyed caring for the patients and was lucky to be assigned after graduation to a busy health post in a town not far from home. I was transferred quite a bit, and for a short period worked as an assistant to the director of clinical services at the central hospital. That was my first real exposure to management.

A few years later I was appointed as a staff medical officer in a district hospital. I was delighted to be promoted, but by then I'd become terribly frustrated by so many administrative obstacles that limited what I could do for the community. I suppose my predecessor had done what he could, but I was tired of the constant cost-cutting that led to the closure of beds, restriction on operating theatre times and the consequent waiting lists for surgery and appointments. In addition, my favourite and experienced nursing colleagues were often assigned or transferred without any apparent reason.

I was very pleased that as a staff medical officer I'd have a chance to improve things. The first thing I wanted my staff to know was that I was going to resolve our operational problems. During my first few weeks I visited nearly all the wards and departments in the hospital and talked with the staff about their problems. Each day my list of problems kept growing, and quick solutions were hard to find. The few problems I was able to solve seemed to take all my time, no matter how many extra hours I put in. What was worse, I soon found that what seemed to be an ideal solution to the hospital administrator only created more headaches at the wards. It seemed I was only putting out small fires and not doing much to really improve the services.

The best decision I made was to force myself to take a good, hard look at the list of problems. My second useful step was to look at how I was using the resources available to me, especially the amount of time I was spending on 'putting out fires'. Were we contributing to better health care? We were certainly very busy, but what were we producing? Apparently I was keeping myself and my staff busy trying to solve problems, but was not anticipating or preventing them. A lot of resources, including time, were being wasted.

I made time to study what the health problems and service needs were and took a fresh look at whether or not the hospital wards were really responding to those needs. In many cases they weren't. Many changes were needed; some services were costly to run and had little effect, and the administrative office produced a lot of paperwork but did little to support the staff. The list of needed improvements was long—far too much for me to handle. I had to learn to delegate these tasks to appropriate people. For the most part, my staff proved quite capable and needed only occasional supervision, leaving me more time to respond to those issues that demanded my direct involvement.

I made many difficult decisions at that time. Staff had to be reorganised, the distribution of supplies and equipment had to be changed; the entire budget was restructured. I was encouraged to find that by relying on competent staff, carefully managing my own time and helping them to manage theirs some positive results were slowly appearing. Most importantly, I made sure that what we were doing was, in fact, directly linked to the most important problems facing both staff and patients in the hospital.

I learnt that it wasn't up to me to try to resolve all the problems; as a manager, I had to get tasks accomplished through others and also to first decide on future policy and then reorganise the available resources of time, staff and material to carry it out. We were finally working as a team—no longer just trying to put out fires, but actively planning better ways to provide services to the community.

What is special about managing health services?

Health service management has a range of characteristics that distinguish it from many other forms of management. These characteristics include knowledge of hospitals and health services, their values and their culture.

Knowledge of the field

To have knowledge of health service problems and issues is an obvious advantage. To have some knowledge of the relevant technical language also helps towards understanding and planning. In addition, knowledge of epidemiology and its concepts is very useful for the development of priorities and plans.

Nevertheless, government leaders and others continue to insist that knowledge of the health field is of little advantage. They believe it is managerial 'know-how' that counts. We do not believe this to be true. Take, for example, our experience of participating in regular meetings of senior health service officials responsible for managing services for a population of 5.5 million. For many years, not one health issue was discussed; the meetings were confined to budgets, staff matters and the need to reorganise. Attempts to explore spending priorities according to need, health status outcomes or even changing demographics were doomed to failure. Regrettably, this is not an isolated experience.

It should not be assumed, however, that those who are knowledgeable about health services are also knowledgeable about finance and management. They may or may not be. Hence, there is considerable value in the encouragement and development of 'teams' of people from an appropriate range of professions and experiences. Provided such teams are led and managed in a productive manner, they can be very effective.

Facility planning provides a concrete example of the value of teams. Few physicians and hospital managers have experience in the planning and construction of hospitals; similarly, few architects have current knowledge of the needs and developments in modern medicine. However, when a multidisciplinary team is created that contains people with the required range of knowledge and experience, the outcomes can be both exciting and sound.

We are arguing the obvious: namely, that health service managers should have relevant knowledge. This implies that health service managers should be accountable to the community they ultimately serve. Such accountability is greatly enhanced if the community is aware that their health services are managed by skilful, knowledgeable professionals.

Values

Hospitals and health services operate within a sophisticated value system that crosses religions, races, governments, friends and enemies. The central value is a humanistic one; namely, that the best possible care shall be offered to all in need.

This value differs fundamentally from that of the world of business and the marketplace, where the essential values are competition, the need to make a profit and, above all else, survival. Businesses do operate within their own system of values and ethics, but the central health service value leads to a different style of management. In a practical sense, this health service value leads to the belief that 'patients come first'. Doctors and nurses are conditioned to this goal and thereby offer care to individuals regardless of cost, energy or time; they pay secondary regard to overall consequences to the community. For the health service manager, this can present a major dilemma. On the one hand it is good to encourage devotion and commitment by the staff, but on the other hand there is the ever-present need to ensure that the hospital or the clinic remains financially viable.

Other values concern the nature of the health service workforce. The medical profession is the key group. Medical graduates are used to competing and performing at the highest academic level; their life goal is to achieve. In addition, and most importantly, they have been trained and have become accustomed to making important decisions every hour of their professional lives. As a consequence they cannot be 'managed' in any traditional sense. In fact, the key decisions affecting hospitals, clinics and health are frequently made by individual clinicians and not by management.

Health service staff are also members of professions. Where these professions, such as medicine and nursing, have long-standing traditions and are of high status, the loyalty of individuals will most often be to the professional group and only secondarily to the hospital or health service. This is a radically different value from most other organisations, including the public service. So powerful and influential are such professional organisations, and the commitment of health care professionals to them, that very often when managers may be seeking to introduce management reforms such as development of standard treatment guidelines, health care staff will respond by saying: 'That is a professional matter, not one for the hospital'.

Culture

Organisations often develop characteristics that can be regarded as a 'culture'. Historically, this has been most frequently observed in military organisations. While there is a culture common to most hospitals, individual hospitals may have their own particular culture.

The culture common to all hospitals is hard to describe, except to say that all hospital workers are aware of it. It is characterised by the staff becoming members of a special group who tend to speak a common quasi-technical language; for example, using terms such as 'the theatre' and 'cas'.

The culture is hierarchical and the social stratification well defined: doctors on top, nurses second and therapists and scientists third, followed by the clerical, catering and cleaning divisions. All consider themselves superior in status to equivalent ranks who work in other organisations.

The hospital culture also has a 'religious' feel about it. With the important exception of the surgeons, who need to dominate the centre of any building, staff—and certainly, visitors—tend to walk quickly but quietly along the sides of corridors rather than down the middle. Staff tend to speak to each other in confidential tones, and when discussing a patient's condition with relatives, tend to be quietly condescending.

These hospital cultures appear to be universal, with similar characteristics in all countries. Hospitals in the United States, the United Kingdom, Australia and even Japan, China and Cambodia are familiar places to all hospital workers.

However, some hospitals and health services develop their own cultures in addition to the general one. A hospital can become an innovative centre where to be creative is encouraged and admired. The University College Hospital in London provides an example where highly innovative intensive care of newborn infants has been developed. Other hospitals are the opposite, regarding conservative values as traditions to be upheld; the Royal Melbourne Hospital is typical of this. Some hospitals are known for being warm, friendly and secure places in which to work; for example, Melbourne's Royal Children's Hospital. Others are difficult, cold and insecure for staff.

Many years ago, Revans analysed this phenomenon in the United Kingdom (UK).[2] He demonstrated that hospitals with a tolerant, altruistic culture had fewer postoperative wound infections, less staff absenteeism and more efficient care than did 'unhappy' hospitals, which were characterised by high staff turnover, relatively poor patient care and long inpatient stays.

Finally, culture can change. For example, Launceston General Hospital was known throughout Australia as a leading hospital during the first half of last century. It declined in reputation for several decades, but has gradually risen again.[3] These fluctuations tend to come about from a complex combination of factors including leadership, conflicts among key staff and changes in government policy.

In summary, hospitals and health services are very different organisations from almost all others. Perhaps the only parallel is the university, which also is dominated by highly educated, individualistic staff who can make crucial decisions independent of senior management. An understanding of and empathy with the values, traditions and culture of hospitals and health services is a basic requirement for their successful management.

The clinical manager

Most of the management of hospitals and health services is conducted by men and women with clinical backgrounds: for example, doctors, nurses, physiotherapists, occupational therapists, speech pathologists and social workers. Such clinicians have been educated and socialised into giving priority to individual patients and clients with respect to care, resources and emotional support. While clinicians are pleased to belong to a hospital or health service, they will most often give the organisation secondary priority after the patients. Therefore, many have difficulty in undertaking management, where the expectation is that the organisation, not the individual, has priority.

In addition, clinicians have a number of fears: first, about managing money (including their own); second, about managing people (they fear loss of friends and colleagues); and third, about entering a field where power is exercised over territory and status. Finally, they fear they have no language or knowledge about the management game.

While nothing takes the place of experience, it is helpful to examine the similarities between managing a patient and managing a health care organisation.

To illustrate this important matter, in Table 1.1 we have shown the similarities and differences of management approaches with respect to a patient with suspected tuberculosis (TB) and the organisation and management of a tuberculosis service.

While the language of the clinician and that of the manager are similar—problem identification, situational analysis, planning, implementation, evaluation (even the word 'diagnosis' is used by both)—the problems of implementation are very different. Clinical decisions can be made and implemented without difficulty provided that the patient is compliant—and patients usually are compliant. The clinician is very much in control of the management of the patient.

The management problem in organisations is much more difficult. The manager usually does not have the control of the external environment that, using the above example, is necessary if housing and nutrition problems are to be solved. The cooperation of a range of people and organisations is required. This

Table 1.1
Similarities and differences—managing a patient with tuberculosis and managing a tuberculosis service

		The patient	The tuberculosis service
1	Identifying the problem	Cough, loss of weight	Many people with TB
2	Situational analysis	Unemployed, transient worker	Overcrowded living conditions in the community
3	Information	X-ray, pathology confirming diagnosis	X-ray, pathology confirming person-to-person transmission of TB
4	Development of plan and objectives	Antibiotics, rest, cure	Vaccination of community Economic development Community free of TB
5	Implementation of plan	Visiting nurse	Intersectoral action between government and private agencies
6	Evaluation	X-rays, clinical examination	Achievements against objectives
7	Period of time	Twelve months	Five years
8	Difficulties	Patient compliance	Lack of investment Political priorities Departmental priorities

may include the affected community, the housing department and industrialists. Even the economy of the nation is relevant. Territory and power are factors that must be considered and influenced.

It also needs to be remembered that if managers of such organisations do not keep the goodwill of their superiors, they may well lose their jobs—an unlikely outcome for the clinician.

Few clinicians have the time to devote to prolonged education in management. Most will learn 'on the job' and it is difficult to organise education and appropriate experience in management for them. In our view a reasonable approach is for clinicians to read this introductory book, to participate in seminars that consider the various topics and issues, to share experiences with their peers and, finally, to evaluate and assess both their own performance and their places of work.

What do health service managers actually do?

Finally, in this introductory chapter, we present some observations on what the managers (that is, potentially you!) of hospitals and health services actually do. We suggest some of the skills that a clinician might acquire when making the transition from clinician to manager. Of course, depending on circumstances, such a clinician can be both a manager and a clinician at the same time. These roles are not mutually exclusive.

Increasing numbers of health professionals—medical and nursing graduates, social workers, physiotherapists, dentists—are entering the field of management as directors and managers of hospitals, health services, wards, clinics and departments. This has not always been the situation, as in the past many health services have been managed by people with administrative, accounting and other backgrounds.

Our studies,[4] confirmed by others,[5] show that there are practical difficulties in making the transition from clinician to manager. The main area of difficulty is to find the right balance between the requirement of managers to place the welfare of the organisation as their highest priority and the conditioning of clinicians to place the patient as the highest priority. Indeed, for many clinicians this focus on the individual patient is a major ethical priority. Personal comments from clinicians who have made the transition to that of manager are very revealing.

'Despite being a manager for over five years, I find my interest has remained with individual patients. Therefore, the limited time spent on organisational objectives has been inappropriate.'

'The need to cut costs caused hardship for clinical peers. My new role caused difficulties with old colleagues.'

'I had problems with status issues and the social isolation that can accompany senior management roles.'

'I became isolated in my own managerial role from usual staff relationships. I did not like the loss of clinical skills and loss of respect from fellow clinicians.'

Careful discussions and a period of transition appear to help ameliorate these difficulties. On the other hand, many clinicians savour their own managerial roles, as the following comments illustrate.

'I just loved the opportunity to influence events on a global instead of an individual scale.'

'I was able to solve problems that had been upsetting me for years.'

'The opportunity was there for me to make this a much better hospital service.'

Geoffrey Prideaux is the director of a successful health service management education program based in Melbourne, Australia.[6] He has drawn together key findings from Mintzberg's work[7] and supplemented these with a major study by Boyatzis,[8] and with other studies of competencies required of managers in health settings. This work suggests that a health service manager needs to develop skills in:

‹ leadership
‹ interacting with peers
‹ information processing
‹ conflict resolution
‹ resource allocation
‹ decision making and understanding ambiguity
‹ goal setting and action management
‹ directing subordinates and in the use of power and authority
‹ managing human resources, including managing group processes.

In addition to these basic skills, the successful health service manager needs to develop quite sophisticated strategic and service-planning skills. The terms 'strategic' and 'service' need more explanation. *Strategic planning* refers to preparation for the long term. Strategic plans tend to be developed as principles rather than as details. They tend to take into consideration possible changes in the external environment—such as political, economic and demographic changes— plus scientific developments. *Service-planning* skills, however, refer to the development of concepts, organisational framework, resources, staffing and the needs for particular health services, such as a geriatric service. Service planning demands sound knowledge of the service required.

For an up-to-date review of innovation and trends in Australian hospital management we suggest reading the excellent analysis by Dwyer and Leggat.[9]

EXAMPLE
Sidney Sax was a most sophisticated health service planner—the classic strategic thinker. As the creator of one of the first health service planning units he reviewed the distribution of population and health services in Sydney. He documented the stark fact that half of Sydney's population lived in the western suburbs, but 90 per cent of hospitals and specialist services were in the eastern half of the city. He developed a strategic plan that, in summary, provided for a wholesale transfer of resources from the east to the west. This plan had major political, economic and service implications, all of which were considered and included in the Sax strategic plan.

The implementation of the plan has taken over twenty years—but it has happened.

With respect to service planning, the Sax strategic experience provides an excellent illustration. While the plan was entirely appropriate in the 'big picture' (that is, in strategic) terms, it was lacking in detail. As a consequence, where allocation of resources included the development of well-known facilities such as hospitals, there was no problem. New, good hospitals were built in the west. However when it came to new concepts, such as providing community-based health promotion or mental health and geriatric services, detailed knowledge of service planning and management was not available. As a consequence, the development of such services fell well behind those provided elsewhere.

We have previously referred to the great difficulty 'outsiders' have when they need to manage health services. Despite this worldwide experience, it should not be concluded that only health professionals can become health service managers. There are many highly successful health service managers who do not have backgrounds as health professionals, particularly in the United States. However, what these former accountants, engineers and general managers do not have is experience and education in the specific field of health service management. For an 'outsider' to become an 'insider' requires training and experience similar to that acquired by people with a health profession background.

There is a recent example from the private health sector of the great difficulty 'outsiders' may have. Under the leadership of Dr Barry Catchlove the general transport and security company, Mayne Nickless, entered the health service field. A range of health service facilities including hospitals, pathology laboratories and even pathology waste services were purchased. Mayne rapidly became one of the largest operators in the field. The financial rewards were considerable and the share price leapt upwards. After a period, Catchlove and the experienced team of health managers he had recruited left to pursue other interests and managers from the finance sector took their place. In less than twelve months Mayne's highly successful initiatives into the health sector had failed and financial disaster threatened. Why? The financial managers had been very successful in other industries but when they applied traditional management controls on hospital expenditure they ignored the powerful culture of the referring doctors. This culture demanded of the doctors that their patients' interests were paramount, not the financial interest of the owner of the hospital. The financial managers and the doctors were in open conflict and the doctors simply referred their patients elsewhere, which of course led to empty, non-profitable hospitals. Mayne was forced to sell off its hospitals and largely to leave the health sector.

Reflections for the reader

Who are you?

At the present time, those of you who are entering the field of health service management are almost certainly from a health service profession. This is in contrast to the situation in the past, when most entrants to health service management were from a financial, managerial or administrative background.

> Some of you will be medical clinicians who have evolved into roles entailing both clinical and managerial responsibilities—for example, as directors of surgical, medical, obstetrical, geriatric or mental health divisions.
> The majority of you will have nursing as your major discipline. You will be seeking to become nurse unit managers or directors of hospitals, particularly in the private sector.
> A smaller number of you will be physiotherapists, social workers, medical-record administrators or health-information managers, health inspectors, or health technicians of various kinds.
> A few of you will be accountants, administrators, teachers and people from other backgrounds.
> Some of you will be full-time career managers, but will have medical or nursing backgrounds.
> Regardless of where you fit, we trust all of you are seeking to learn how to improve your ability to plan and manage hospitals and health services.

What is your current role?

A small proportion of you will already be occupying senior management positions. However, you may not be very confident in that role—hence your need for both education and experience.

Most of you will have had some experience in a management role, whether it be as a supervisor, a member of a planning team or a member of a committee. A few of you will have absolutely no management experience. However, you may be seeing management as a possible career option.

What preparation have you had for management?

Even if you have not had any real responsibility as a manager, most of you will have had the experience of working with managers. Even those of you who have been clinicians since graduation will have experienced the activities of deans, medical directors, registrars and heads of departments.

You will have formed opinions about the management skills of these people; were they good, bad or indifferent managers? We can all learn about management by such experiences and observations.

What difficulties are you experiencing as a new manager?

When we surveyed student health service managers, we found remarkably consistent experience of the difficulties.[10] Many reported experiencing a conflict between the priorities of the organisation as compared with the priorities of the patients. The whole educational experience of health care professionals is directed towards care of individual patients and their families, and there can be enormous emotional turmoil when priorities for care have to be determined in the interest of the hospital or clinic. On the other hand, some students who had been quite senior clinicians experienced no such conflict. They even referred to themselves as 'organisational animals', and expressed satisfaction at being able to achieve influence on an organisational scale.

Nevertheless, a great many student managers had difficulty in losing their perceived status as clinicians when they became full-time managers. They reported feeling a great sense of loss at no longer 'belonging' with former colleagues.

Interpersonal conflicts were also a frequent difficulty. Many respondents said they had trouble when they had to discipline staff, particularly clinical colleagues, for poor adherence to clinic times, budgets or productivity.

Regardless of these problems, however, most student managers (average age, 36 years) were excited about the challenges and possibilities that come with management roles—in particular, the possibility of resolving longstanding problems and of influencing events on a much wider basis than is possible as clinicians.

The purpose of this book is to help you achieve your ambition to become an effective and contented hospital and health service manager. We encourage you to read on.

2

Major hospital and health service issues and challenges

The provision of health services is becoming increasingly complex. In global terms, there is a considerable shift away from the cure of individuals presenting for service and towards the prevention of illness in populations and the strengthening of the community's capacity to deal with its own health. It is a shift that requires re-evaluation of the fundamental paradigms of professionalism. For doctors, nurses and allied health professionals, it asks whether health care is something we do for people or something we do with people.

For the manager, this shift is but one of a range of trends and developments having a significant impact on health service delivery.

The World Health Organization (WHO) has sought to identify the main factors 'driving' changes in health services.[1] Regardless of differing national cultures, these 'health drivers' are remarkably similar for all nations. They include:

‹ cost constraints
‹ ageing populations
‹ the impact of advances in technology
‹ the desire for improved health outcomes, and increased consumer knowledge and expectations
‹ changes in the health task—from acute to chronic conditions.

In addition, there are the health system reforms that are part of broader political and socioeconomic agendas; for example, reforms such as 'internal markets' in the United Kingdom and New Zealand which have been mainly driven by broad political agendas.

A detailed examination of these health drivers is important for health service managers so that they can understand the social and economic environment in which they, in turn, must make more local adjustments and decisions. Health service managers may have little influence on this external environment, but if they develop an understanding of the major drivers they will be in a position to offer appropriate education to their staff and to work together to make more correct and appropriate decisions. Those who do not develop such insights and understanding may find themselves and their organisations outdated, irrelevant and, finally, closed down.

Cost constraints and matters of finance

It was in the 1960s that, for the first time, the cost of caring for a patient for one day in hospital exceeded $100. There was universal alarm and concern. How this cost would ever be met was the question commonly put forward at professional conferences.

Even allowing for changes in the value of money, years later this figure seems absurdly low when the cost of caring for some patients can currently exceed $3000 to $4000 per day.

Why are hospitals and health services so expensive?

There are three basic factors to consider in assessing why health services are so expensive.

1 Health services are labour-intensive, and in economically developed countries labour has become very expensive. Labour costs dominate the budgets of hospitals and health services and account for over 80 per cent of total expenditure.
2 The availability and the cost of health care technology are expanding. Virtually every patient admitted to a modern hospital is subject to some form of technology, whether it be an X-ray, a blood test, intravenous medication, an anaesthetic or surgical intervention. While each separate test may not of itself be very expensive, when the costs of all the tests and treatments offered to a particular patient are added they can be twenty times the cost or fee of the attending physician. In addition, the cost of some specialised investigations is high; magnetic resonance imaging, for example, can be over $500 per scan.
3 There are increasing expectations on the part of citizens for improved health status at the expense, if necessary, of the state.

The cost of health services has become so great (up to 15 per cent of the gross domestic product in the case of the United States) that the problem has become a major economic issue. In recognition of the importance of cost to managers of health services, financial issues are considered in greater depth in Chapter 7.

Ageing of the population

Australia, in common with other countries with advanced economies, has an ageing population. By the year 2020, approximately 20 per cent of Australians will be 65 years of age or over. However, of greater significance is the increased proportion of the 'aged aged'; that is, people aged over 80 years. Use of hospitals and health services increases rapidly with age; persons 65 years and over consume up to five times the volume—and hence, the cost—of health services consumed by younger adults.

In addition, aged persons develop chronic and debilitating diseases such as senile dementia, osteoarthritis, and loss of visual and hearing ability, which inevitably lead to increased demands for long-term care.

Aged persons are often unable to afford private health insurance. This places increased demands on the public sector.

It can be validly argued that, of all the factors impinging on health service provision, the ageing of the population will have the most profound effect. At the very least, an ageing population will lead to:

‹   increased demands on the health services
‹   a change in the range of health facilities—for example, a greater need for long-stay accommodation and community-based services
‹   changes in ethical traditions—in particular, the right to a high-quality life and not necessarily a long life.

The brevity of this section should not detract from the importance of the issue of ageing. We have been brief because the issue is well known among health service managers and is comprehensively covered in the literature.

The impact of advances in technology

The profound impact of technology in the provision of health services has previously been mentioned. The impact of technology is all-pervasive.

Technology influences all facets of the health services; for example:

‹   diagnostic investigations such as X-rays, biochemical tests, use of radioactive isotopes and magnetic resonance imaging
‹   treatment procedures such as laser technology and keyhole and open surgery
‹   transplant procedures
‹   pharmaceuticals
‹   rehabilitation and the use of artificial limbs
‹   cataract lens replacement.

Even death can be the subject of major technological applications, with the monitoring of the brain to determine the moment of brain death, the identification of suitable donors and recipients for transplantation and the freezing of body parts for future use. Then there is also the antithesis of death—reproduction, which now occurs in a complex technological environment including techniques ranging from technical contraceptives to hormone maintenance, artificial insemination, surgical births and surrogate wombs.

Health has become a technological wonderland, but at a cost in terms of both money and the emergence of a whole new range of ethical concerns.

Technology is therefore a major influence that has to be recognised, understood and managed by the health service manager.

The desire for improved outcomes

Probably as a consequence of improved standards and the expansion of education, consumers' expectations of improved outcomes from health services are continually increasing. A good example is the modern expectation that birth should be relatively painless, with a perfect outcome for both mother and baby. If such a perfect outcome is not achieved, there is every prospect of litigation against all concerned.

Hong Kong provides a good example of health reforms that have been driven not by economics, but by the increasing expectations of citizens for improved hospitals and health services in terms of quality and convenience. These are paralleled by similar expectations in housing, education and welfare.

The issue of equity has also emerged in recent years. Equity has a philosophical basis. In the context of health services, it implies equality of access for all citizens to health services, plus a fair allocation of resources according to need. The philosophical underpinning of this expectation is illustrated by the lack of a similar outlook with respect to food, housing and transport.

The increase in consumer knowledge and expectation is illustrated by the demand of patients to have detailed information about their health problems, to transfer decision making from the doctors to themselves and to have freedom of choice about methods of treatment, attending physicians and other health professionals. This interest in and high expectation for effective health care is seen daily in the increasing media coverage of health issues, backed up by the ready access to information via the Internet.

In addition, communities as a whole have an expectation of being informed and consulted about the provision of health services on their behalf. Particular examples include Australian Aboriginal communities, new suburban communities and isolated mining communities, but also include citizens living in suburbia. These communities demand information concerning the provision of hospitals, clinics and medical services. They also demand information about current health problems such as coronary heart diseases, drug abuse, diabetes and motor vehicle accidents—not only in the interest of individuals, but also so that they, as communities, may influence events and not remain at the mercy of all-knowing governments and health care professionals. Take, for example, the community concern at nuclear waste facilities, exhaust stacks for vehicle tunnels and genetically modified foods.

Changes in health tasks—from acute to chronic conditions

The new epidemics include HIV/AIDS, severe acute respiratory syndrome, coronary heart disease, trauma and cancer. The old epidemics were mental ill health, diabetes, and drug and alcohol abuse.

Finance has become such a dominant issue that in many countries it has diverted attention from the health status of the population. To the average citizen, it would seem extraordinary that the cost of running a hospital occupies 90 per cent of management's time while the remaining 10 per cent is reserved for industrial and other issues. Literally no time at all is given to the consideration of whether or not citizens are dying, or becoming sick from conditions in which scientific knowledge allows for effective prevention and treatment. An important exception is the growing concern about the quality of health care offered in both hospitals and clinics. In part this has been driven by medico-legal issues, with doctors becoming increasingly concerned about being sued by their patients. However, quality issues have also evolved because of increasing awareness that avoidable errors in patient care are a problem. These matters will be given detailed attention in later chapters.

Despite the many pioneering public health initiatives aimed at reducing the rising incidence of stroke, heart disease, cancer and trauma, these have often been fringe activities compared with the main game of controlling escalating expenditure. Throughout the world, governments and health service managers have battled to close obsolete hospitals; health departments have been reorganised and people's careers thrown into turmoil. Regardless of these efforts the cost of providing health services continues to rise and there is precious little evidence that any of the cost-cutting measures have had any effect.

Perhaps the most important pioneers to address the new public health epidemics have come from the scientific research community.[2] Throughout the 1950s and 1960s, predominantly in the United States, solid data was gathered about the nature of heart disease and stroke and the link between tobacco consumption, air pollution, lung cancer and respiratory disease. These issues were recognised by the famed epidemiologist Sir Richard Doll in the United Kingdom and by others in the United States. There was also increased realisation within various traffic authorities that improved engineering in vehicles, including the fitting of seatbelts, and an epidemiological approach to traffic and to crash prevention could pay handsome dividends.

The use of mass media to educate populations about health services was shown to be effective by Maccoby and Farquhar, working at Stanford University in California.[3] These experiences were used in the United States, Australia and New Zealand for a broad range of prevention activities. Together with better control of high blood pressure and diabetes, these types of initiatives have proved their value; death rates for atherosclerotic heart disease have fallen dramatically. A multidisciplinary or intersectoral approach in applying this new knowledge was developed in a number of countries. It was perhaps best documented in Finland, where heart disease had reached such alarming proportions that the widows of men who died of heart disease formally approached their government to ask for help. This resulted in the North Karelia cardiovascular disease prevention program, another extremely effective pioneering effort.[4]

Nevertheless, public health issues remain a major priority. Apart from cardiovascular disease and a range of cancers, AIDS and malaria have become the most important priorities.[5] Again, led by a research approach, it does appear that in Organisation for Economic Co-operation and Development (OECD) countries—including those in Western Europe and North America, Australia and Japan—the situation with respect to HIV/AIDS is gradually coming under control. Regrettably, this is not the case in Africa where the HIV infection followed by AIDS has reached epidemic proportions and continues to threaten whole populations.

The essential feature of public health is the consideration of the health of whole populations. The priorities for virtually all the OECD countries are the prevention and amelioration of atheromatous cardiovascular disease; lung, breast, prostate and bowel cancer; and traffic accidents and other forms of trauma. Also the amelioration of alcohol and other drug-related conditions; the amelioration of the effects of mental disorders; and the control of a range of conditions as varied as diabetes and cancer of the skin.

A major investment in continuing research will be required in order to advance the control of some of these conditions—in particular, of AIDS and mental disorders. For many of the other conditions knowledge is well advanced, but the application of this knowledge requires the allocation of funds and a commitment to place public health issues high on the health agenda.

EXAMPLE
A good example of the adverse consequences of neglecting such public health approaches is the United Kingdom where, in contrast to the Unites States and Canada, Australia and New Zealand, deaths due to atheromatous cardiovascular heart disease (coronary heart disease and stroke) continued to rise and remain at much higher levels than those in comparable countries during the 1970s and 1980s.[6] During this time the National Health Service was organised and reorganised, and while territorial battles were fought and all manner of irrelevant priorities pursued, the citizens literally ate and smoked themselves to death.

It is only quite recently that improvements in health status have belatedly begun to take place in the United Kingdom.

While these 'public health' issues have particular relevance to specialist public health physicians and scientists, health service managers can have an extremely important influence in this field. The reasons are simple.

‹ Hospital and health service managers have considerable control over the allocation of financial and staffing resources.
‹ Such managers can have a major influence on the objectives of a hospital or health service organisation.
‹ Managers can counsel and adjudicate between competing clinical interest groups.

For example, control of finance has allowed the development in many parts of Australia of specialised health service programs, in fields such as diabetes, geriatrics and heart disease, that contain major preventive elements. Health service managers, usually clinical directors, have been able to include the concept of clinical epidemiology in the work of heart and cancer services. This has led to an examination of the effectiveness of treatments and a reorientation of activities. Adjudication of territorial clinical disputes has allowed the creation of new hospital and clinical divisions, such as imaging services, in place of competing radiology, ultrasound and nuclear services.

Even traditional managers of hospitals have learnt to adopt public health approaches. These include examining workers' compensation trends and subsequently taking action to reduce back injuries in hospital staff; developing guidelines and education programs to reduce accidental wounds by needles and other instruments (the 'sharps' programs); developing effective waste-disposal methods, particularly with respect to infected waste; and reducing postoperative wound infections by developing standard practices and monitoring compliance and outcomes.

Reflections for the reader

The issues outlined in this chapter will be familiar to those in both senior and junior management levels of the health services. It will be tempting for such readers to avoid these issues, because they are so large and daunting. Issues such as AIDS, ageing of the population and ever-increasing costs come immediately to mind.

When confronted with such immense problems, it is helpful to break issues into smaller, potentially manageable parts. Take, for example, the ageing of the population.

1   A population that is healthy enough to reach advanced age should be regarded as a major success. Many early tragic deaths have been avoided. This is a major historical advance and should be recognised as such. You, the reader, can take some credit for this. What has been your contribution—as a participant in immunisation campaigns? as a prescriber of medication to lower blood pressure? as a cancer surgeon? as an ambulance officer? Having identified your contribution, there is an argument for informing the community about what can be done—this is health education.
2   Conduct a situational analysis of the needs for and provision of services for sick and disabled aged persons in your community. Having gathered the information, you can commence negotiating for the creation and allocation of resources to fill the gaps. This may take many years—therefore, it is better to have an early start.

Another example is cost escalation. The action you might consider is as follows:

1   Consider the costs in 'manageable' portions—cost of a single hospital, costs of pharmaceuticals, costs of staff.
2   Consider these current costs against a background of having a free hand to allocate resources according to need and without heed to current allocation
3   Plan to redirect resources according to your assessments.

Consideration of these major issues is necessary not only to find solutions, but also to allow the external context to be considered when you are developing strategic and service plans. Your local plans and management cannot be developed in a vacuum; they must be created in a context.

For a challenging view on major hospital and health service issues we suggest you read a series of articles by our colleague, Professor Jeffrey Braithwaite.[7]

3

Understanding health care organisations

The provision of modern hospitals and health services has been part of our historical evolution from agrarian to industrial societies during the past two centuries. The creation of hospitals, in particular, has been very dependent on the evolution of technology. During the nineteenth century, however, individual hospitals tended to be established according to an assessment of needs by a group of citizens, very often with medical-practitioner involvement. Thus began the voluntary hospital movement in which a board of governors was established, funds were raised through community fund-raising activities, staff were employed and the first patients were admitted. In most cases, the premises were large, converted domestic dwellings.

As these hospitals grew in size and complexity during the nineteenth century, they also became more expensive, and accordingly the governing boards sought financial help by charging fees to patients and by seeking government subsidies. With the passage of time, government subsidies became an increasing proportion of the budget and gradually laws were enacted to ensure the proper expenditure of public funds. In this way, charitable hospitals gradually became quasi-government institutions, and by the middle of the twentieth century almost their entire funds came from government sources in one form or another.

For specific services, such as those for persons with serious mental disorders, the patient group was not sufficiently attractive to secure the interest of the community. Governments were therefore forced to develop, fund and manage special institutions, which became the mental asylums of the nineteenth century. A similar evolution occurred with other special types of patients, particularly those with contagious diseases such as typhoid, tuberculosis and cholera. In addition, the women's movement of the early part of the twentieth century led in many countries to the development of hospitals for women, run by women but financed to a large extent by governments. These women's hospitals have been an essential part of the women's movement because in them it was possible to recruit female medical graduates and others who could not gain access to the mainstream hospitals.

The social reforms that took place in Europe, the United States and Canada during the nineteenth century had a major influence. This was the time of European domination of world affairs, and anything European—particularly British, German or French—was seen to be desirable. Accordingly, patterns of hospital and health care that evolved in continental Europe and in the United Kingdom spread throughout the world. It was not until the epidemics of smallpox and other contagious diseases occurred at the turn of the century that formal government health departments were created. These have since evolved into major bureaucracies charged with a myriad of activities.

The financing of health services has also been an evolutionary process. As the cost of providing health services has increased with the advancement of technology and the employment of trained health professionals, government funding has become universal to a greater or lesser extent. In more recent times, it has been found necessary to develop various forms of insurance arrangements to protect citizens at least from the costs of catastrophic illness and injury. In virtually all countries there are now universal funding mechanisms to protect citizens from otherwise insurmountable health and financial problems. The exception is the United States. The most common and effective method of financing health services has been to combine direct government subsidies with a form of compulsory health insurance. This combination is now the key feature of health care systems in countries such as Canada and Australia; it is also widespread in continental Europe, Japan and South Korea.

The operation of hospitals

In many countries, including Australia, non-government agencies own and manage hospitals. Commonly, these organisations have religious affiliations that determine to varying degrees the underlying values and policies of their hospitals. The best known example in Australia is the Catholic hospital system, where the values preclude the conduct of sterilisation and abortion. Most public general hospitals in various countries are governed by boards of management, either appointed by governments or elected in some way by citizens. Non-government hospitals may operate as either public or private organisations. Most private general hospitals are governed by boards of directors of a commercial company who rarely have a local interest in the management of the hospital, a function almost always delegated to a financial manager.

Governing authorities of hospitals almost always exercise a good deal of delegated authority over the detailed running of the hospitals, despite their almost total dependence on government financial subsidies. The traditional internal organisation of hospitals, whether public or private, has been along a tripartite line of administration, nursing and medical services, each with its own hierarchy. Heading the administrative hierarchy of the hospital has been the business manager, directly responsible for the general service departments such as accounts, engineering, clerical administration, stores, catering, building maintenance and grounds. The area of nursing services has traditionally been headed by a senior nurse. Invariably, nursing services constitute the biggest hospital department, employing around 40–50 per cent of the total hospital personnel. Completing the tripartite structure have been the medical and other health professional services, traditionally headed by a medical graduate. Contrary to the custom in the nursing division, the head of the medical services may be quite junior. This apparent contradiction evolved as part of the 'honorary medical staff' system, in which all senior medical staff were part-time and were not paid for their services to public patients.

This situation is gradually changing, and senior surgeons, physicians and obstetricians are accepting full-time hospital positions that include major management roles. This is a beneficial development as management and leadership of hospitals becomes of even greater importance. In the majority of hospitals, the chief executive officer or general manager has responsibility for the global management of the hospital. However, because of the complexity of the needs of individual patients and the traditional organisation of hospitals, in practice there are cross-responsibilities for the whole range of activities and services. For example, a surgeon may be responsible for the surgical ward, but a nurse will be responsible for the nursing staff in that ward and both parties will call in services from the full range of other departments as part of the total care of individual patients. This type of organisation is frequently referred to as a 'matrix organisation'.

The senior members of the medical staff of most major hospitals are organised into a formal group. This group provides professional advice concerning the administration of the hospital, with specific reference to the medical care of patients. Potentially a very powerful influence within the hospital, this group meets on its own, rarely involving other key members of the hospital staff, however important they may be.

While it can be argued that the organisation described above has stood the test of time, there are obvious difficulties. Perhaps in part because individual medical practitioners on the hospital staff pursue their own objectives, it has proved to be very difficult for the hospital as a whole to have a clear objective; that is, an individual hospital's role has not been carefully defined. This has often resulted in hospitals carrying out roles that have little relationship to the true needs of the community. For example, it is frequently very difficult to obtain care for an elderly patient with an 'unpopular' condition, such as a fractured thigh bone, because the priorities of the hospital are towards those patients who can be admitted and discharged quickly.

In some cities, elite hospitals have provided world leadership in their activities, but these activities have been totally unrelated to the socially rather unattractive communities that they should serve. In addition, many hospitals have been insular in their approach to care. By this it is meant that they have restricted their activities to the care of those patients presenting to the hospital, while accepting no responsibility for the provision of care for members of the community who do not seek care. Accordingly, many citizens with long-term chronic conditions have no relationship with a hospital. In addition, a great many hospitals do not see the needs of patients as part of the changing

political patronage, a costly legacy

We can offer dozens of stories about political patronage in the hospital system, but a favourite example comes from Australia's deep south where, in the island state of Tasmania, the hospital services of Devonport provide a living memorial to the folly of our political masters. Devonport lies to the west of a river that marks the electoral boundary. It was decided that the area needed a new hospital (which it probably did not). Thus began a fierce fight over the site of the proposed hospital. Should one electorate be favoured over another?

A hopeless compromise was reached—the hospital would be built in two locations; obstetrics and gynaecology in the town, and surgery, medicine and emergencies 15 kilometres away on the other side of the river.

Years later the inefficiencies, inconvenience and high cost are continuing problems.

Similarly, in developing countries there are hospitals—paid for by international donors—that are too large, too expensive and epidemiologically inappropriate. It is said the main hospital in Western Samoa consumes half the national health budget. It was built by an international donor despite advice to the contrary.

There appears to be no answer to this problem, for not only are there displaced hospital dinosaurs in democratic countries where votes are won or lost according to political decisions, but also such follies occur commonly in communist nations such as China.

Perhaps the best approach is to seek the sharing of objective information by both the community and the decision makers.

The painful experience of closing a hospital

For many years it was obvious that there were too many hospital beds in North Sydney. In addition, the surplus had increased because of a political decision to open 450 additional new beds in an expanding teaching hospital—the Royal North Shore Hospital—situated in the same area. The Mater Hospital, managed by a Catholic religious order but financed by the government, was also situated in the area. The Mater was old, a firetrap and poorly sited. Clearly it should have been closed. However, despite the offer to own and run a

new hospital in the needy western suburbs, the nuns refused to cooperate.

Finally, as the government could no longer meet all demands, a decision was made to withdraw all funding from the Mater. This was political dynamite, as the order commanded well-deserved respect and gratitude for nearly a century of service to the community and could potentially influence voting behaviour. However, the hospital did close, patients did not die and resources were freed up for use in deprived areas.

continuum whereby it is necessary to care for patients with chronic conditions, such as stroke or dementia, for many years.

An important organisational issue for hospitals has been the unplanned manner in which they have been sited and developed. Very few hospitals in any part of the world have originally been planned with a population and a role in mind. While such planning has occurred in recent years, historically there remains a legacy of hospitals that were sited according to the availability of land, and where very often the surrounding population has dramatically changed or dispersed. Because it is much less expensive to add to an existing institution than to begin a completely new venture, long-established hospitals have gradually expanded over the years despite their comparative irrelevance to the local population. However, as the economies of health services and whole nations have changed, it has become an economic necessity to plan the closure of these institutions and their replacement with fewer, better-sited hospitals. This has proven to be an extremely difficult political process, as it is very easy for opponents of such plans to gather emotional support and to debunk reformers as uncaring power brokers.

Because of cost factors and changing needs for hospitals, there has been a gradual decline in the number of beds for any given population during the past ten years. This appears to be a universal trend. While it is almost impossible to compare hospital bed-to-population ratios on an international basis, the trend downward has been consistent except in some major countries such as China, where the direction has been the reverse.

The economic need to reduce hospitals to the absolute minimum is dramatically illustrated by some very simple statistics. These relate to the costs of labour in an industry that must provide services 24 hours a day, 365 days a year. In order to keep a 24-hour service in a hospital ward with one nurse, it requires approximately six people; that is, sufficient numbers to cover three shifts a day, including weekends and holidays, plus sick leave and annual leave. Therefore, if it requires ten people at any one time to staff a thirty-bed hospital ward, to maintain the ward on a 24-hour a day basis requires over fifty people. Accordingly, the trends are all towards hospitals becoming gigantic intensive care units, with the only patients actually admitted for care in hospital beds being those who cannot be cared for in any other way. This means that these patients must become increasingly fewer and sicker and the intensity of the treatment and the cost per patient must rise. However, it is seen to be of overall economic benefit if the number of such beds is gradually reduced and the care of patients increasingly exercised in a non-institutional setting.

How should hospitals be organised and managed?

As they differ in size, role, location and economic structure, there is no simple example of the best way of managing hospitals. There are many experiences that can be shared, however.

We have referred to the lack of goals or objectives of many hospitals. Although the purpose of a hospital seems obvious—namely, to treat and care for sick people—close examination soon reveals that the roles of different hospitals differ dramatically. There are general hospitals, such as the Royal Melbourne Hospital in Victoria and the Prince of Wales Hospital in New South Wales which, despite their 'general' name, often only accept patients with medical and surgical problems. Then there is a range of specialist hospitals that accept specific categories of patients: for example, the Royal Eye and Ear Hospital in Melbourne; the Royal Hospital for Women in Sydney (which does not take all women, only those with obstetric and gynaecological problems); hospitals for children only (although age is rarely defined) such as the Children's Hospital in Perth and the Children's Hospital at Westmead in Sydney; hospitals restricted to the mentally ill, present in all states; geriatric hospitals, for the sick and elderly only; and accident and emergency hospitals, as in the United Kingdom and the United States (US). In addition, there are bone hospitals, brain hospitals and heart hospitals, all of which are common in various countries—particularly those with predominantly private hospital systems, such as Japan, South Korea and the US.

Hospitals can also be classified financially: publicly owned and operated; privately owned but dependent on government finance; purely privately owned and operated; and charitable or non-government (usually dependent on government finance).

This extraordinary range of hospitals is but one reason why there cannot be a single best method of organisation and management. The range does, however, lead to a definite need for each hospital to develop a set of very clear roles and objectives. This has been a very beneficial process in New South Wales, where all public sector hospitals have developed not only broad rules, but degrees of specialisation. This has prevented much duplication of services and development of inappropriate activities, such as extensive bone surgery in remote rural hospitals in response to a clinician's interests.

Definition of roles, in turn, has an impact on the objectives of a particular hospital. For example, a district general hospital in the public sector may have roles similar to those of a general private hospital, but the objectives may be very different. The essential objective of the public hospital will be to care for all in need, whether they need admission or not, whereas the essential objective of a private hospital has to be to find and admit patients capable of paying fees. The managers of the public sector hospitals need to be capable of managing as part of a health service. In contrast, the managers of the private sector hospitals must necessarily give priority to commercial survival.

Should the tripartite organisation of hospitals be maintained or changed?

In our view, if the hospital has more than 200 beds, there are advantages in having and maintaining the traditional three divisions—medical, nursing and administration—with one of the three providing the chief executive. The basic reason for maintaining this system is that in most circumstances it works. Also, in a situation where technology is constantly changing, where there is industrial difficulty and where the economic pressures to do more work with less staff are great, there is advantage in keeping the senior management and organisational structures stable. This offers much-needed security for the organisation and its staff.

This support for the tripartite organisation does not mean that improvements are not needed. In our view and experience, the availability of a senior physician to lead the medical division has enormous advantages over the appointment of junior (and therefore inevitably ineffectual) recent medical graduates to this role.

There are many Australian examples where the appointments of such senior medical managers have dramatically improved the quality of medical services (as distinct from 'hotel' services) in hospitals.

Large hospitals—say, over 400 beds—become very difficult to manage. The senior management cannot provide personal support at the ward and theatre level, and morale falls. There are some indications that hospitals over this size become less efficient and more costly to run. This statement is based on broad comparisons of hospitals, although they may not be directly comparable with respect to the types of patients treated. However, our recent studies, which compare teaching with non-teaching public hospitals, suggest that large hospitals (over 400 beds) are about 15 per cent more expensive than smaller ones.

The answer to this problem—loss of staff morale and managerial inefficiency associated with large size—is to divide large hospitals into smaller, independently managed hospitals. This appears to work reasonably well except when, in times of economic difficulty, the divisions are reamalgamated on the spurious grounds of 'efficiency'. This happened in a 1500-bed Sydney hospital where all surgery, including obstetrics, was recentralised. There were short-term financial gains, but long-term losses because of increased postoperative infection rates.

Large hospitals have always been divided into sections: usually surgery, medicine and obstetrics. More recently, as at St Vincent's Hospital in Sydney, completely new divisions, termed 'institutes', have been created to include a 'Heart Lung Vascular Institute', an 'Oncology Cell Biology Institute', a 'Metabolic Orthopaedic and Gerontology Institute', and a 'Neurosciences Institute'. However, it is not clear that there are advantages in creating such allied but competing entities. On the one hand, decentralisation appears to lead to improved decision making; on the other, delegation of financial responsibility appears—as in the case of Sydney's Royal Prince Alfred Hospital—to have contributed to serious cost overruns. There is a serious message in these experiences: namely, that clinicians who are put in charge of decentralised divisions have quite different objectives from those of the hospital as a whole. Inevitably, it seems, they are advocates for their peers and are judged by 'how well they did at the financial bargaining table', not whether they contained expenditure within a budget.

Clearly, if there are to be divisions within a hospital, then the concept of 'loose but tight' management needs to be applied. This means that the decentralised division can make its own decisions within overall policy guidelines, but that finance, quality and activities are very tightly controlled from the centre, which has a managerial objective to achieve a balanced budget as well as a good-quality service.

The experience in Australia with respect to change in hospital management has been analysed by Jeffrey Braithwaite.[1] Most large hospitals in Australia have undertaken extensive reorganisation during the past decade, all in search of elusive economic efficiency. The gains are quite dubious, and many of those endeavours appear to have been quite pointless. Undoubtedly there have been many gains, such as 'multiskilling' whereby catering, porterage, cleaning and other services can adopt more general and thus more efficient roles; also, layers of unnecessary management have been removed. However, radical organisational restructuring of whole hospitals does not appear to have achieved real advantages.

With respect to small hospitals—under 150 beds—the best lessons come from the private sector, where organisations such as Health Care of Australia have demonstrated that 'small is truly beautiful' and have reduced managerial overheads to, basically, a medical or nurse manager plus a receptionist. All other workers operate at the bedside, in the theatre or in the kitchen. The detailed weekly self-monitoring of performance against targets in terms of costs, activities and quality is an interesting and important lesson for the public sector.

The hospital of the future—what will it look like?

Leading international authorities, such as Robert Maxwell[2] of the King Edward's Fund in London[3] and Dominique Jolly[4] of the Public Hospital Bureau of Paris, have separately addressed the issue of 'the hospital of the future'. We have also analysed trends in hospitals from OECD and other countries.

The trends in virtually all countries (the major exception is China, where the concept that bigger is better still prevails) are similar, and are as follows:

1   The length of stay in hospital is falling. The reason is predominantly the introduction of new technology: internal and external metal pins in bone surgery; the use of tubes in place of open surgery.
2   Increasingly complex treatments are being provided to ambulatory patients. The reason is a combination of technology and cost-effectiveness. For example, chemotherapy and radiotherapy for cancer is just as effective and less costly when administered on an ambulatory basis.
3   Hospitals are increasingly being linked to ambulatory service programs and other health service networks, particularly day surgery and treatment centres. The reason is the need to care for the increasing numbers of chronically ill patients associated with the ageing of the population, plus the high cost of inpatient care.
4   Hospitals are becoming smaller. The UK-inspired district general hospital, which provided all services to all patients, has become so large as to be very difficult to manage. Hence, there is a trend to smaller, more specialised hospitals. It is probable that the 1400-bed Westmead Hospital in Sydney will be the last of the 'district dinosaur' hospitals in Australia.
5   The demand for acute hospitals will decline and the demand for long-stay accommodation for the elderly will rise. These trends are in response to changes in disease patterns: the virtual elimination of all serious communicable diseases except HIV/AIDS, plus the ageing of the population.
6   There will be continued advances in all areas of technology. It is likely that three fields will develop particularly rapidly: molecular biology, which will lead to intervention in genetically-based conditions; improved communications, reducing the use of the voluminous, traditional patient clinical record; and the further development of imaging technologies. These technical changes may shift clinical power from the surgeons and physicians to the laboratory-based specialists.

The hospital has been one of the features of twentieth century life, as were the cathedrals of medieval Europe. During the twenty-first century, hospitals will remain as important centres of health service activity. However, they will be smaller, less obvious and more part of networks of district or population-based health services.

The development of district health services

In order to overcome the problems associated with the fragmentation of services and the existence of hospitals without any relationship to a particular community, the concept of district health services has gained credibility during the last twenty years.[5] A 'district health service' is the term adopted by the World Health Organization for a service provided for particular populations or communities. Regions or areas have the same meaning in this context.

District health services are organised on behalf of a defined population; this means that both hospitals and other health services can be planned to serve the needs of a community, whether or not individuals require admission to a particular hospital. In addition, with the creation of a single health authority responsible for all health services in a particular district, whether public or private, a range of services can be developed that extend from the community to the hospital or vice versa. Geriatric, mental health, maternal and child health are typical services in which such networks have been developed with a good deal of success. It is also possible to use such districts to plan the provision of medical, dental, pharmaceutical and other community-based services on a staff-to-population ratio, thus at least having a measure of need that can be put into practice, although with difficulty, using financial and other incentives as well as regulatory devices.

Finally and of equal importance, population-based planning and organisation of hospital and health services allows public health activities, particularly health promotion and disease prevention, to be offered on a community-wide basis. The concept allows a managing body to operate responsibly on behalf of communities and to lobby effectively for access to resources, thereby providing a means of achieving equity across populations of individual countries. This is very difficult to achieve when health services are provided on an individualistic institutional basis and one institution can play off another as part of the political game.

In forming an area or district health service, the optimum size for both urban and rural populations is considered to be from about 250 000 to 650 000. Populations need to be of at least these sizes to allow sufficient throughput of patients so that substantial high-quality services can be provided. It is an advantage to have a teaching and referral hospital in each district or area; however, this is not practicable in many circumstances, and the absence of such a hospital does not appear to be a real disadvantage. This is because teaching and referral hospitals have gradually evolved into central referral centres for populations of 1 million or more, which in most circumstances is too many people for a district or area health service. The major exceptions to such population sizes are those countries with vast populations, such as China and India, where it is impractical and not cost-effective to consider districts with populations of fewer than 500 000 to 1 million.

The population catered for by an area or district health service should ideally have a community of interest in relation to education, welfare and commercial activities. Transport networks are also important. Wherever practicable, area and district health services should have the same boundaries as local government areas, or as combinations of such areas. For planning purposes, it is also a distinct advantage for the boundaries to be the same as those used for statistical divisions.

District or area service planning has been developed with apparent success in the United Kingdom, Sweden, Australia and New Zealand (although in New Zealand, political forces have yet again reorganised the health service). Similar patterns of organisation are evolving in China, the Philippines and, to a lesser extent, Canada. The basic reasons for their apparent success are that population-oriented health services can be planned, a community can be served beyond those who seek care in particular hospitals, duplication of expensive specialised services can be avoided and coordination can take the place of historical fragmentation.

Geriatric services provide the classic example of the advantages to be gained from this type of planning. In economically developed countries they have evolved from a scattered range of services provided through hospitals, nursing homes, hostels, meals on wheels, district nursing, general and specialist medical practitioners and denture services, as well as a range of assessment and rehabilitation programs. All of these services may be owned and operated by different private and public organisations. By creating a district health service within which a geriatric program can be organised, the care of geriatric patients and supporting family members can be maintained through an organised network of services appropriate to the changing needs of patients.

Who will manage the district health service?

The chief executive officer or manager of a district health service needs a considerable range of skills. Perhaps the most important is the ability to lead and motivate staff and to define and pursue objectives. In addition, planning and organisational skills are obvious attributes. In other words, the district health service manager needs the full range of traditional management skills plus specialised knowledge of demography, epidemiology and health services. The acquisition of these attributes will be considered in detail in the sections on management; at this stage, it is sufficient to indicate that the district health service manager will need both education and experience, in addition to relevant personal attributes.

As health services have been historically fragmented, there have been few opportunities for such managers to gain the appropriate experience. Managers with a purely clinical or hospital background need significant re-education and experience if they are to become successful district health service managers, as the role is much broader and more population-oriented.

case histories

Paul Neesbins had spent his career as a fine hospital clinician, designer and finally manager. He had well-developed management and leadership skills. However, when charged with managing a district health service, he concentrated on the hospitals to the neglect of community-based services such as the early childhood clinics and other preventive and health-promotion responsibilities. He 'felt comfortable' visiting hospitals, having discussions over tea and scones, but was quite unable to adopt a broader population-based overview.

In contrast is the experience of three remarkable men: Neville Boyce, a trained hospital manager; Stan Williams, an ex-World War II naval rating but also an experienced hospital manager; and a young medical graduate, Stuart Spring, who had been trained in community health at St Thomas's Hospital in London. These three were put in charge of separate district health services in Northern Sydney, where they flourished. All ultimately achieved special awards from the Australian Hospital Association for leading their hospitals to become part of integrated networks of health services. Of particular interest was the ability of Stuart Spring to change the direction of the Royal North Shore Hospital, a major teaching and referral centre, towards the community it served, including the development of community-based mental health and geriatric services.

Why were these three pioneers successful? Their personal attributes were of major importance. They were kind, caring, trustworthy personalities who wanted to do the best they could for their local communities. They were willing to learn 'new tricks' from each other's experiences and from elsewhere, and were sufficiently confident to pursue objectives against vested interests. It is of interest that age was not a factor, as the age difference between these three managers was over thirty years.

Mental hospital and health services

Mental illness is probably the greatest social problem facing economically developed countries. It ranks in social importance with unemployment and relative poverty. About one-fifth of all hospital beds in developed countries are occupied by patients who have mental disorders, and of these almost two-thirds are occupied by persons suffering from schizophrenia. In addition, studies have shown that approximately 5–10 per cent of adults have some form of mental disorder (neuroses, emotional problems, depression and psychoses).[6]

Mental health services in developed countries evolved in a formal sense in the early part of the nineteenth century. The opening of mental asylums was an enlightened and well-intentioned development. They provided protection for the patient from adverse community elements and protection for the community from severely disordered and aggressive patients. During the latter part of the nineteenth century day centres for people with intellectual disabilities were opened, early treatment hospitals evolved and, in the early 1900s, voluntary patients began to be admitted to mental hospitals. Unfortunately, after this reforming period mental health services throughout the world gradually deteriorated, and by the end of World War II had reached a state of serious disorder. By the 1940s, patients in most developed countries, including Australia,[7] lived in conditions of squalor, filth and horror; no occupational diversions were available for them and many spent their days in straitjackets, some shackled to the floor. This deplorable situation came about in part through deteriorating economic conditions in wartime, but also because of the priority given to acute general hospitals.

Throughout the developed world this situation created a public outcry and governments of the day took the first steps towards action and reorganisation during the early 1950s. It was also extremely fortunate that, at this time, the first of the truly effective psychopharmaceuticals was developed. This was chlorpromazine, a French invention. Psychopharmaceuticals brought tranquillity to severely disturbed patients, allowing for the removal of shackles and straitjackets. The combination of social reform movements and new pharmaceutically-based treatment techniques began to revolutionise mental health services.

The most obvious impact of these reforms has been the dramatic decline in all countries in the required number of beds for mentally ill patients. This has become possible because of the provision of community-based mental health services, strongly supported by the availability of the new tranquillisers.

Debates continue about the way in which mental health services should be organised and how they should be funded. However, some basic principles have become clear. The most important of these is that psychopharmaceuticals should be available on a supervised and continuous basis, even if this requires legal sanctions. The second requirement is that patients with serious mental disorders should have continuous access to formal counselling and support services, such as day centres and specialised accommodation.

From an organisational point of view, it has become clear that the mental health field should be divided into the following three basic categories:

1 patients suffering from serious mental illness
2 persons with serious intellectual disability
3 persons with severe alcohol and/or drug dependence.

These are three clearly separate categories, each demanding a separate organisation. They should not be put together as a single mental health service. It can be argued that services for those with severe intellectual disability need not be associated with health services at all. There is merit in this argument, although such persons should have ready access to modern health services.

Services for the seriously mentally ill

It is convenient to subdivide services for the seriously mentally ill according to age groups: services for children, for adolescents and for adults. The form each of these services should take is dependent on local circumstances and traditions. This is a model that can be followed.[8]

Children's services

Formal services for children should be offered in the context of family-guidance clinics, at which specialised staff support general staff in schools and in general medical practice. It is necessary to support the service with several specialised inpatient units on behalf of populations as large as 4–5 million.

Adolescents' services

It has become clear that the number of psychiatric problems occurring in the adolescent age group justifies the establishment of specialised clinics on a district or area health service basis. Mental ill health among adolescents should be treated seriously. It is frequently possible to offer interventions that can avoid depression leading to suicide and also emotional disturbances that can lead to personality disorders.

Adults' services

The major burden of psychiatric illness comes in the adult years. The key element of health services for patients with serious mental disorders is the provision of services that combine inpatient facilities with community-based clinics and day centres. In addition, the community-based services need to have staff who are mobile and are able to see patients in their own homes. A range of suitable accommodation is necessary. The precise form of the clinics and of the inpatient units is not so important, provided that skilled psychiatrists and support staff are continuously available. It has become fashionable to develop teams of health care professionals who can intervene in a crisis situation and maintain the person in the community, out of hospital.[9] However, we are not convinced that this is necessarily better than a short hospital admission, followed by intensive support care in the community. There is little difference in costs.

Perhaps the biggest challenge in the mental health service field is to gradually return the isolated asylums of the past back into the mainstream of our society. Such asylums probably need to remain in some form, as the tradition of general hospitals by and large precludes them from providing a first-class service for difficult, aggressive patients—particularly those with psychotic illness and those who are prone to aggressive, unpredictable behaviour. Major problems relating to the asylums of the past stem from the fact that they were far too big; they were situated in outdated buildings; and they were very often located in the countryside away from available staff and the patients' relatives.

District, teaching and referral hospitals should all have quite small units for the seriously mentally ill, and these should become part of the responsibilities of the district health authority. Experience at Hornsby Hospital in Sydney strongly suggests that psychiatric units in general hospitals can successfully care for severely disturbed patients. It will take time for this experience to be accepted elsewhere, however.

For non-serious mental illness, but in cases that cause considerable distress, the most appropriate service appears to be general medical practice, backed up by psychologists and, where necessary, specialist psychiatrists.

The quality and range of mental health services have been shown by Hoult to vary enormously.[10] There are several world-class services in Sydney and Melbourne, but totally inadequate services in parts of Queensland.

Despite these many difficulties the provision of health services for the mentally ill continues to improve, primarily as a result of dedicated local health professionals.[11]

The use of institutions for the care of the seriously mentally ill became an established practice during the nineteenth century. These institutions were true asylums in the best sense of the word, where distressed persons could be protected and supported. However, by the mid-twentieth century many mental hospitals had become too large, with patient populations of several thousand. This led in some cases to abuse of both staff and patients, as individuals could rarely be offered personal attention. The modern tranquillisers changed possibilities for care, but traditions die harder.

Dr John Hoult, a young Sydney-based psychiatrist, observed the success of community-based care in several US centres. Accordingly, in North Sydney he began a series of pilot services that ultimately demonstrated that many seriously mentally ill patients could not only be cared for in the community, but also could achieve greater contentment and satisfaction. This type of care has been adopted on a widespread basis even though the costs of community care are comparable with hospital care.

The reason for the success of this initiative appears to be a combination of new technology (psychopharmaceuticals), an informed enthusiast and pilot programs conducted in a measurable manner (offering reliable results), plus a sympathetic management.[12]

Services for the intellectually disabled

Approximately 8 per cent of the total population has some degree of intellectual impairment. However, the most difficult group comprises those who are profoundly or severely retarded; that is, they have an intellectual capacity that does not even allow them to enjoy television. This important group, while comprising less than 0.3 per cent of the population, is nevertheless significant in total number. A full range of services is required for this small group, including institutional services for those who cannot remain in their own homes, a range of community clinics, special domestic-level accommodation and a range of supportive services to maintain persons in their own homes. One of the key elements is to provide temporary inpatient care for people with intellectual disabilities so that relatives and others can have some period of respite from the ongoing demands of caring for such disabled persons. In this way, intellectually disabled persons can be kept in their homes for quite prolonged periods.

Services for the sick and disabled aged

The objective of these services is to assist sick and aged persons to achieve and maintain their maximum physical and social potential. The number of aged persons is increasing in absolute and relative terms in all economically developed societies; the proportion of persons 65 years and over has reached over 16 per cent of the total population in the United Kingdom and other European countries. However, the big change is reflected in the number of very aged persons—those who are 85 years or over—which is increasing in both absolute and relative terms. This trend

case study compassionate care for the intellectually disabled

Any form of intellectual disability is a tragedy. Severe intellectual disability, particularly when combined with physical disability, is both tragic and distressing. Parents are burdened with guilt and siblings resent their lives being dominated by an unattractive rival. All are concerned for the disabled person, who may be abandoned at birth or left alone when parents die. Seriously intellectually disabled persons were frequently admitted to mental asylums until quite recent times, mainly because no other places were available.

Before the more enlightened 1970s, it seemed that possibilities other than continued development of institutions were non-existent. Sympathetic leaders of the New South Wales Health Commission agreed to a pilot proposal to use the funds allocated for a new 250-bed institution for people with intellectual disabilities to purchase domestic homes and develop a network of community-based services. While the pilot was successful, and provides a current model, the difficulties were immense. The main problem was resistance by local communities. Vigilante community groups were established that used all legal avenues to block the scheme. Progress was achieved only by Kevin Stewart, the health minister of the day, who courageously used reserve powers of government to acquire the properties. There was even resistance to changing the role of small community-based hospitals for housing the intellectually disabled.

This experience demonstrates that there can be a proper use of power and authority in the community interest.

is particularly evident in countries such as Japan, where longevity has come about primarily (but not wholly) because of the healthy diets of most Japanese people.[13]

The provision of health services for sick and aged persons is particularly difficult because frequently they do not seek assistance when breakdown occurs. They may have a number of different conditions at the same time, often presenting in unusual ways, and as a result there are often medical, emotional and social needs among these groups that are frequently unrecognised and unmet.

It should also be recognised that there are disproportionate demands made on health and welfare services by aged persons. Persons over the age of 65 years occupy over one-third of all hospital beds, consume one-third of all prescribed medications and are responsible for over one-quarter of all medical practitioner consultations.

Preventive and health-promotion services for aged persons

It is obviously appropriate for us all to try to have a nutritious diet, to take regular exercise before we become aged and to avoid smoking or drinking too much alcohol. There are, however, specific problems associated with ageing, particularly the dementias and osteoporosis. At the present time there is no known preventive strategy with respect to the dementias other than the reduction of microinfarcts or microstrokes, which can be achieved as part of preventive atherosclerotic vascular disease strategies.

case study developing services for the disabled elderly

Scotland has long had a high proportion of elderly citizens. Naturally, some of the model services for care of disabled elderly persons have been developed in Aberdeen and Glasgow. These experiences were used as examples to follow in many parts of Australia. There have been two difficulties: one, the raising of sufficient financial resources, and two, the recruitment and training of key staff. In Australia, we have found the best source of finance to be within existing hospitals. Accordingly, existing buildings have been reused as assessment and rehabilitation units, funds have been reallocated from the acute hospital services and governments have been successfully lobbied to enhance these efforts. However, while these achievements have been summarised in one sentence, in reality they took years of planning with, educating of and bargaining with hospital and health authorities. A key to success has been the realisation that governing boards of hospitals consist of middle-aged people who have experienced the need to care for ageing parents and who are therefore very sympathetic to the geriatric cause. The support of hospital boards has developed to such an extent that in times of severe economic constraint they have closed acute hospital facilities in order to maintain geriatric services.

In addition, as the medical and nursing workforce has increased it has been possible to recruit able and interested people into the geriatric field.[14]

With osteoporosis, it is known that exercise and an adequate intake of calcium before the menopause is of advantage to women. For women in postmenopausal years who are at risk of developing osteoporosis, as measured by bone-density scans, the use of female oestrogen hormones is the most effective strategy available. Unfortunately, the prolonged (over five years) use of such hormones leads to a small, but definite, increase in the risk of breast cancer. Accordingly, great care needs to be taken with the use of oestrogen and other hormones.

Health services for the sick and disabled aged

Services for the sick and disabled aged have evolved in recent decades in most developed countries. They include the provision of a range of private and public services by general and specialist medical practitioners, community-based nurses and home carers, and occupational therapy and home-modification services. In addition, a range of accommodation concepts have been developed that include housing especially designed for the frail aged; hostel accommodation where supervision of elderly persons living independently is offered; nursing homes for those who are bedridden; and rehabilitation services, usually based in hospitals that offer physiotherapy and occupational therapy.

There is a particular need to have links between the hospital or institutional services and community services. This can be achieved by the establishment of a coordinating service with responsibility for the careful assessment of all elderly at-risk persons in the area or district. Such a geriatric assessment and rehabilitation team needs to have power over admission to publicly funded nursing home services in order to ensure that only the most needy are admitted. Apart from the social deprivation of admission to a nursing home, the costs are approximately ten times those of being maintained in the community.[15] Good coordinated geriatric services can be established, in a formal sense, for relatively small populations with a total number of 100 000 persons. The maximum population size appropriate to a single service is probably around the 400 000 to 500 000 level.

Pharmaceutical services

It can well be argued that the availability of modern pharmaceutical products is the key factor in modern medicine. However, it is the combined availability of blood transfusions and surgery, antibiotics, psychopharmaceutical drugs and a myriad of other medicaments that have revolutionised preventive and curative medical practice.

Regardless of the systems of distribution in any given health service, it is important to recognise the absolutely crucial role that market economies have played in the development of new pharmaceuticals. Chain, of penicillin fame, has reviewed the most valuable compounds introduced to medicine since aspirin in 1899.[16] His analyses show that only nine of these pharmaceutical compounds came from universities and research institutes; all the rest were discovered and developed in the laboratories of industries operating within market economies. Not one (to the best of his knowledge) has come from socialist economies.

Offsetting these very significant advantages are problems concerning the cost and side effects of new pharmaceuticals. Accordingly, governments have found it necessary to subsidise their cost in order to ensure equity for all citizens, in addition to carefully controlling their quality and safety as well as their efficacy. The cost of providing various subsidies has become astronomical in both developed and underdeveloped countries. In some countries that do not have a pharmaceutical industry, approximately one-third of the total cost of their health service goes towards the importation of pharmaceuticals. This compares unfavourably with an amount of between 5 and 10 per cent in countries that manufacture most of their own pharmaceuticals.

There is no doubt that pharmaceuticals are overutilised, but their use is extremely difficult to control, particularly as communities have become more legally aware and are willing to sue for any perceived malpractice. Therefore, prescribing doctors tend to 'cover their tracks' by prescribing antibiotics for modest and short-term infections, tranquillisers in place of careful counselling and hypertensive agents instead of encouragement of behaviour changes in persons with modest levels of high blood pressure.

Most countries have adopted systems that provide for private outlets for pharmaceuticals, such as the common corner chemist shop, and public outlets most frequently seen in publicly owned hospitals and clinics. In recent times, it has become inevitable that patients should be required to pay some of the cost of government-subsidised pharmaceuticals; this is because, almost without exception, governments have had to control overuse of pharmaceuticals in addition to facing the enormous difficulty of meeting their ever-rising costs.

Dental health

The objectives for any dental health service are to provide all members of the community with the best possible quality and range of services—to prevent and treat dental disorders within the availability of a trained workforce, knowledge and financial resources, and with acceptance by the community.

Dental decay has been a formidable factor in many societies during this century and it is almost certainly associated with increased consumption of foods that contain high levels of sugar. Because of the ubiquitous nature of dental caries in many communities, it has been realised that prevention, rather than treatment, is the best way of achieving the above objectives.

The key preventive strategy is undoubtedly the use of fluoride. The introduction of fluoride to a community has been successfully achieved through a variety of methods including fluoridation of the water supplies and the use of fluoride tablets and fluoride toothpastes. When fluoridation in any of its forms is supplemented by modification of diet, health education with respect to universal oral hygiene, and the application of dental sealants to fill cracks and crevices, the results have been dramatic. Those who have lived through the dental-decay period, and have witnessed teenagers and young children with badly decayed teeth, have been amazed to see many young adults without any dental decay whatsoever in the post-fluoridation era.

In turn, this dramatic reduction in dental decay has focused attention on other problems, such as overcrowded teeth requiring orthodontic care and diseases of the gum requiring periodontal care.

The success of the fluoridation and other preventive programs has meant that workforce planning has had to be radically altered to meet the requirement of more dental health professionals to undertake simple as well as sophisticated orthodontic care. The need for armies of dentists and dental assistants to repair decayed teeth has passed.

Health transport systems

Health transportation can be divided into two clear categories. One system offers care to injured and sick persons in emergency circumstances and is available on a 24-hour basis to transport the sick and injured to centralised facilities; for example, trauma victims to casualty departments or to accident and emergency departments.

The second system operates to take health care services to consumers in the community. These include home nursing services, child health screening services, and services for elderly and otherwise immobile persons.

Included in the health transport system is the conveyance of patients and others from one part of the health system to another, such as inter-hospital transfers. The ownership of health transport systems, whether private, public or

promoting teeth

Why dental services developed independently of medical services is a matter for historians. However, this accident of history has rendered dental services a status problem, because dentists are left off key health service planning committees. They are asked for advice as an afterthought, and rarely occupy senior management positions in the health service. In part this may be due to the lack of life and death issues with respect to tooth decay as compared with, say, cancer.

Therefore, the development of dental services presents a difficult planning and management problem. A good approach has been to gather relevant information on the incidence in the community of dental decay, malocclusion, periodontitis and artificial dentures. This information can then be matched with the availability of dental services, shortfalls noted, extent of fluoridation examined and future plans developed. Again, because the same authority has responsibility for planning, organising and managing the health services, it is possible to successfully implement these plans.[17]

getting involved with ambulances

The organisation and management of ambulance services differs throughout the world. In many parts of the United States ambulances are managed by the fire authorities; in the United Kingdom often by local government authorities; in Australia often by separate ambulance authorities; and in many places they are managed by hospitals. All these services appear to work well.

Some years ago in northern Sydney ambulance services were managed within the local health services. This worked well, as the leadership of both the ambulance division and the health services developed excellent working relationships and resources; training and communication were all shared. However, individual ambulance staff preferred to be part of a larger organisation and, following industrial agitation, local services were combined with a large statewide service. This does not appear to have detracted from the service, but certainly it has added to the cost.

a mixture of both, does not seem to affect their level of efficiency. However, there does appear to be a need for government intervention if such systems are to be available on an equitable and affordable basis. In most developed countries, this has taken the form of some type of public financial subsidy. Very often the health insurance systems include provision for the cost of health transport.

Occupational health services

Occupational health has come to be regarded as the Cinderella of the health services because the field receives little attention from the formal health authorities and the public in general. Nevertheless, it has assumed increasing

case study developing special services for special circumstances

During recent times, excellent occupational placement services have been developed in large industries. General Motors has, for example, developed highly sophisticated services identifying jobs that can be performed by staff with specific disabilities—such as telephone switchboard operation, which can be managed by blind people, or assembly-line jobs that can be successfully done by wheelchair-bound workers.

Occupational health and safety services for small industries, however, are much more difficult. A good example is farming, where the work is done largely by individuals and where it is usually not feasible to develop a service. In parts of Australia, experience has shown that such farmers are at considerable risk of damaging their backs, of being crushed by tractors and farm machinery or of picking up animal-borne infections. In response, many rural hospitals have developed education programs for farmers that involve the identification and fixing of these problems by visits to individual farms and by holding special seminars.

importance with the realisation that the working environment continues to affect the health and productivity of the individual.

The basic purpose of occupational health services is to protect workers against health hazards that may arise from their work or working conditions. Included in this concept is the contribution of work and the working environment to the worker's psychological as well as physical wellbeing.

At its most sophisticated level, occupational health involves the monitoring and control of toxic substances associated with the working environment; for example, the monitoring and control of the use of plastic materials, the fabrication of asbestos and benzene products. More traditional roles of occupational health and safety include the prevention of hazards to the worker from machinery and from any moving objects, such as railway cars.

The organisation of occupational health services must vary according to the nature of work in any given locality. Personal services can include those offered by industrial medical officers and nurses who work within industrial plants or offices. It has been found to be of advantage in many countries to group together small industries that cannot support individual occupational health services; in this way a good-quality service can be created to the benefit of the total industrial community in any one locality.

To be successful, occupational health services have to involve all members of the workforce who are at some form of risk. Therefore, workers on the industrial plant floor as well as management and unions have to work together to identify problems and seek solutions. There has been a temptation to accept 'risk' money in hazardous industries, such as coal mining and construction work, as compensation for a greater likelihood of receiving occupational injuries. This is an unfortunate practice, as the incentive should be to create safer working places and reduce risks.

A further current problem has been the widespread availability of workers' compensation, usually in the form of finance aimed at compensating workers who become sick or are injured at work. While admirable in concept, experience has indicated that many workers exploit such insurance schemes, and it has been found necessary to tighten working procedures while seeking to change attitudes of the workforce. On the other hand, expensive workers' compensation bills have led to radical restructuring of the workplace. Such trends are to be applauded.

Public health services—prevention and health promotion

Public health services describe those preventive and health-promotion services that are aimed at protecting whole populations from disease and injury. For convenience, they can be broadly divided into three separate areas:

1 environmental health services
2 services that seek to control communicable diseases
3 health-promotion and related services that seek to modify health-related personal behaviour, nutrition and related matters.

The activities of each of these areas need to be based at national, regional and local levels. It is necessary to have a strong epidemiological capacity in order to monitor demographic trends, current patterns of environmental change and current developments in personal behaviour.

Environmental health services

Health services designed to protect individuals from the physical environment have an honoured and traditional place in any modern health service. These services had their formal beginnings in the mid-1800s and have since developed in a most sophisticated way. The areas of activity are very broad. From a public health perspective, they include the supervision of domestic premises (including the keeping of pets and other animals), garbage disposal and the monitoring of milk and water supplies, as well as sewerage services.

Other areas involve the inspection of trade premises including boarding houses, barber shops, restaurants and premises requiring the use of noxious materials; the inspection and sampling of food supplies; the supervision of food outlets (particularly of fast food outlets); the supervision of mass producers of foodstuffs; the supervision of pest control; the monitoring of recreational facilities such as swimming pools and camping areas; and the monitoring of noise, radiation and a host of miscellaneous problem areas, all of which are of direct relevance to the health of the individual. Such monitoring and supervision requires the creation of a well-trained and educated staff in sufficient numbers to both educate and monitor in all these fields.

In accord with modern developments in quality assurance, it has been found more effective to use education and motivation as the means of maintaining appropriate standards rather than much more expensive inspection and policing. Nevertheless, because of the financial incentives involved in both market and centrally planned economies, some form of monitoring and sanctions are necessary.

Control of communicable diseases

Since the mid-1800s, health services have had a formal organisation devoted to the control of infectious and communicable diseases. The principles developed nearly 200 years ago remain valid today. They include careful monitoring of the occurrence of infectious diseases, the relevant circumstances and the geographical locality. This was the method first used by Snow in his attempts to control cholera in central London in the early 1800s.[18] Using such information, modern epidemics of conditions such as legionnaire's disease and AIDS, plus the historical problems of typhoid, tuberculosis and cholera, can be controlled. In addition, the historical practice of tracing contacts in order to prevent the spread of communicable diseases remains valid.

Health promotion

Seeking to encourage healthy behaviour among whole populations has come to be known as health promotion. Health problems differ widely and include obesity, diabetes, atherosclerotic vascular disease, lung cancer, AIDS, some forms of mental illness and skin cancer—most of which can be prevented or ameliorated by changes in personal lifestyle. This requires the mobilisation of resources on both an intersectoral and multidisciplinary basis. For example, the control of tobacco smoking has required the combined efforts of a multitude of professional groups and of many government, non-government and private organisations concerned with the mobilisation of campaigns against tobacco consumption; the raising of taxes to discourage consumption; the conduct of health education programs for the community as a whole and for special groups, such as school children; and legal sanctions against smoking in public places such as schools, shops, theatres and public transport vehicles.

It is relevant to note that health promotion is a long-term endeavour and that the successes achieved with respect to tobacco smoking have been the consequence of more than three decades of activity in all of these areas.

It is also pertinent to distinguish between health education and health promotion. Health education has an honoured place in the public health field, but it is necessarily limited in scope compared with health promotion. Although health promotion does include health education, it extends beyond this to activities such as seeking legal sanctions or taxation reform; and to the conduct of international campaigns, such as those used in Finland, the United States and Australia against heart disease and against AIDS.

According to WHO expert Fiona Kikbusch, Australia has become a world leader in the prevention and health promotion field. It is interesting to speculate why this is so. Perhaps, in a new society such as Australia, there are few conservative traditions and it is not so difficult to introduce new ideas. Australia is economically affluent and can afford new initiatives. There has been strong leadership from both health professionals and politicians. While the approach to HIV/AIDS offers the best example of such leadership, a similar successful action has been achieved in such diverse fields as prevention of traffic accidents, drowning, burns, smoking, heart

The World Health Organization popularised the 'new public health', a term that encouraged a return to the old population-based public health principles of fifty years ago. This has largely been in response to the emergence of chronic problems such as coronary heart disease and cancer.

On a much more local basis in Sydney, there has been a tremendous response by the community to initiatives in health promotion and public health. These initiatives included advice about nutritious food, the need to increase exercise and improved parenting; the development of group activities for isolated mothers of newborn infants; screening for high blood pressure and blood fats; and anti-smoking programs. These initiatives contributed to a marked reduction in deaths due to heart disease, stroke and, latterly, lung cancer. (Caution is required with respect to the cause and effect of health promotion programs. While it is almost certain that the decline in tobacco consumption is related to a range of health promotion actions, it is quite probable that the decline in deaths due to coronary heart disease is due to technical interventions.)

In addition, and most importantly, the AIDS epidemic has been the stimulus to re-establish a capacity in scientifically-based prevention and management of communicable diseases.[19]

disease and stroke. Public health has become so fashionable that there is a current epidemic of master of public health graduates from twenty-one universities.

Medical services

The provision of medical services in Australia is well known and need not be considered in detail in this book.

Specialist medical practitioners work in both a full- and part-time capacity in public hospitals and in private practice. Contrary to the pattern in Japan and in parts of the United States, private hospital medical services are provided by visiting private medical doctors, who charge patients fees that are separate from the hospital charges. Private hospitals seek to attract doctors who will use their hospitals—as distinct from attracting patients.

General medical practitioners (GPs) are almost wholly employed in private practice. There is no planning mechanism for the distribution of either GPs or specialists, nor is there any detailed planning mechanism for the provision of numbers of doctors.

To a large extent GPs in urban areas no longer provide services in hospitals, which have become the domain of the specialists.

There are several key issues with respect to the provision of medical services in Australia:

‹ the maldistribution and shortage of some specialists, particularly orthopaedic and ear, nose and throat specialists, eye surgeons and psychiatrists

< the generation of costs by doctors

< the separation and alienation of some specialists and most GPs from the public hospital and health system.

These issues have been considered by governments over the years without any significant resolution being reached. There have, however, been some gains. Attempts have been made to introduce 'best practice' guidelines. GPs are being encouraged to join divisions of general practice in an attempt to reduce their professional isolation and to re-introduce them to hospitals.

However, the essential problem of alienation remains. The major adverse consequence is the difficulty in coordinating services between the public and private sectors, plus the difficulty in the control of costs.

Governments could theoretically reduce the problem of area supply and maldistribution with financial incentives; however, no government to date has been willing to tackle this task.

Health professionals

The role of different health professionals, such as doctors, nurses, therapists and scientists, has been fairly clear for most of this century. Since the late 1970s, however, demarcation disputes have been increasing. The most important of these disputes refers to the demand by nurses for greater recognition. This is hardly surprising. It is inevitable that all professionals, as they gain additional education, will seek to develop careers of higher status and income. In turn, this becomes more costly to the community and causes demarcation disputes.

In addition to the situation in the nursing profession, there is the classic example of the educational curriculum for medical students compared with that of chiropractic students. The modern chiropractic educational curriculum is virtually identical to the medical curriculum and is just as long in terms of years. The only exceptions are in the treatment area and the extent to which diagnostic services are used. As a consequence, chiropractors are increasingly referring to themselves as doctors, while continuing to undertake more and more activities. This type of evolution applies to virtually all the health professions.

Another interesting example is the expanding role of podiatrists. Podiatrists began by specialising in the clipping of toenails and care of the feet; that is, as chiropodists. They are now gradually claiming more of the body, and at the present time attend to legs as well as hips. Some podiatrists also diagnose and advise about a whole range of orthopaedic problems. In some parts of the world, particularly in some parts of the United States, they have begun surgical interventions—an area previously reserved by law for medical graduates.

It can be argued nevertheless that nurses, together with medical practitioners, are the most important professional group in the health area and that it is natural for them to seek to expand their roles—for example, into diagnostic activities and the application of more complex treatments, including intravenous therapy and the administration of anaesthetics. This expansion, however, is creating conflict by bringing them into the territory historically occupied by medical graduates. There is no obvious solution to this problem except for all parties to keep in touch with each other and to refrain from allowing their differences to erupt into warfare. In addition, all parties have to recognise the economic consequences of the drive for higher status and higher pay. Inevitably, it leads to other groups having to be employed to do lesser tasks at a reduced cost; these tasks, undertaken by nursing assistants and enrolled nurses, are vital, but are more mundane than modern nursing tasks.

Experience in the United Kingdom, and in particular at Guy's Hospital in London, suggests that nurses and doctors can work in parallel. First-hand observers indicate, however, that despite the rhetoric, the real situation is one of considerable tension and competing interest groups in that famous old hospital.

Furthermore, in our view, the most significant consequence of the continuing drive for more education, status and pay is the increasing length of the training programs. It is now literally true that some medical specialists are not fully trained until their early thirties. They may not enter full independent practice until that age—after which, with luck, they may give the community some ten to twelve years' hard work before 'burning out' and seeking alternative ways of earning their living. It is extremely hard to control this phenomenon. Again, economics and the laws of supply and demand prevail and lesser trained persons are employed to undertake the basic duties at much less cost.

Also involved in staffing issues is the need for increased productivity. It is very expensive to have health care professionals looking after individual patients on a one-to-one basis. It is far less expensive if they can care for groups of patients. This is particularly applicable to the various therapies; for example, a speech pathologist can be just as effective in caring for ten children at the one time as in the traditional one-to-one situation. The productivity gain is tenfold. Likewise, it is expensive to have a physiotherapist guiding stroke patients with paralysis down a hospital corridor, but to have the physiotherapist supervise a group of much lower-paid aides carrying out this task is far more cost-efficient.

How do you manage health professionals?

In virtually all countries, hospitals and health services were mercifully free of serious industrial relations problems until the 1960s. In that decade, however, the first doctors' strike occurred in Saskatchewan in Canada, and during the 1980s doctors and nurses went on strike for the first time in many other countries. Considerable bitterness developed between health care workers and governments and between different groups of health care professionals. For the first time, nurses confronted doctors over issues concerning roles, female affirmation, prestige and pay. At the same time there emerged among doctors, particularly specialists, a gradual dominance over their much lower-paid and lower status colleagues, the general practitioners.

Why do people with comparatively high and secure incomes and status seek to advance their own ends by disrupting essential services? There appears to be no obvious answer. It seems that there has been a breakdown of values, in the sense that service to others is not a priority above service to self.

While there is no easy way forward, the use of quality as the basic goal directed towards patient care provides a means of encouragement. Although

The implications of these strikes and industrial disturbances have been profound. Services to patients have been disrupted, previously sound working relationships have been compromised, and morale (which is very important in the health field) has deteriorated. The bitter and adverse consequences of doctors' strikes cannot be overestimated. This is illustrated by an event during 1917 in Tasmania. In 1917—the year of the Battle of the Somme, when half of the world's men were fighting to the death—a key group of specialist doctors in Tasmanian hospitals withdrew their services; that is, they went on strike. The issues prompting this behaviour were the inadequacy of their recognition and their pay.

This seems strange nearly a century later, because these doctors were not paid at all. They were known as 'honoraries' and gained goodwill from their hospital work that enhanced their private practices. The strike continued until the outbreak of World War II in 1939. Tasmanian doctors showed that attitudes can be inherited from one generation to another, because the sons of the 1917 striking doctors again withdrew their services in 1973, nearly fifty years after their fathers' strike and over precisely the same issues. Fortunately, however, they did not remain out for two decades; they returned to work after two months.

A major doctors' strike also occurred in New South Wales in 1983. Based upon complex issues ultimately associated with finance and status, it has left a bitter legacy. From the patient's point of view, the distinction between a public and a private patient has been enhanced, with public patients being increasingly cared for by junior doctors and private patients by senior doctors. In addition, key specialist groups such as orthopaedic surgeons, who have a monopoly regarding the number of practitioners joining their group and who have restricted their numbers, have disrupted services to the public for nearly a decade. This has caused resentment not only between these particular groups and their peers, but also between them and other health professionals, especially nurses.

As for the nurses, it is also unfortunate that in many countries they have felt the only way to advance their cause is by the use of strikes. This has happened in widely differing countries such as the United Kingdom, Hong Kong and Fiji, as well as in many of the OECD countries.

quality assurance programs can be threatening, they do involve a multidisciplinary approach; participants have to collaborate and get to know each other. In addition, loyalty to the team becomes as important as loyalty to a professional group. If quality can be linked with self-interest, progress may well be possible. A positive outcome of payments to hospitals by diagnostic related groups (DRGs) in Victoria has been a group self-interest in the survival of clinical units and hospitals. This has, in many instances, brought previously warring parties together in a common cause.

Reflections for the reader

A comprehensive survey of the full range of health services does not allow for their examination in detail. Prospective managers working in the various sections of the health services are encouraged to review and read the literature on their particular service. While standard service patterns have emerged on a worldwide basis with respect to some services, such as geriatrics and mental health, the opposite is the case with respect to hospitals, public health and medical practice. It may be that readers can develop 'model' services, evaluate their key features and publish the results.

Readers should remember that conservative approaches are often best. Compulsive, male-driven, repeated reorganisation of hospitals has, for example, often been responsible for disruption, increased cost and reduction in quality. In today's society, rewards and recognition go to those who develop new ideas, new services and new organisations—whether good or bad. Very often it is the courageous person who has the stamina to maintain good structures, to maintain and enhance quality and to provide stability in an environment of rapid technical change.

In other words—think before you leap!

4

Planning and managing health services

What do managers do?

To understand what managers in health services really do, it is necessary to make a number of observations. First, we need to recognise that effective managers do not necessarily do what the experts advise. The gap between what management is expected to do according to some expert prescription and what they actually do is well documented.

Second, the appropriateness of what managers do depends on the situation in which they work. Management is essentially an adaptive process, contingent on many factors. These include the type of organisation, its stage of development and its position in the system, access to resources, social support and the unique opportunities and constraints it is facing.

Third, we note that managers at different levels of the organisation respond to different agenda and terms of reference. Senior managers are required to be more strategic, political and policy-oriented than mid-level managers, who are responsible for supervision of staff and compliance with policy directives.

Fourth, the focus of management may shift in time and across situations. In different situations, managers may be required to manage themselves, manage functions, manage relations, manage the organisation and/or, most importantly in this day and age, manage change.

If we add to these distinctions the complexity inherent in the health system, with its myriad of functions, customers and operators, it is not surprising that the uninitiated manager tends to become very confused.

Our purpose in this book is to convey in simple terms the essence of management. At the same time, we wish to clearly indicate that management occurs within a complex context that must be understood. The effort of managers is affected by many forces, which often pull and push in different directions. To understand the management function, we need to become familiar with these influences and to consider optional ways of response.

There is a popular belief that managers are dynamic, scientific, rational beings whose highly organised days revolve around decision making, followed by a social round among peers. The reality is startlingly different. Mintzberg, in the United States, has observed that the working day of the manager, particularly at senior levels, is constantly interrupted; issues are handled superficially and managers work at a range of different locations, spending up to 90 per cent of their day in discussion with other people. Mintzberg and other commentators have also observed that much of the manager's role is 'invisible', leading to the notion that they are removed from the 'real world'.

ANECDOTE

A personal experience confirms this rather superficial impression of the manager's day. JSL's daughter, Harriet, spent her student work experience with him when he was a regional director of health. At the end of the week, she noted: 'You have a lovely job. You arrive in the morning, greet your friends for an hour or so, then join them for morning tea, telephone some more friends, have lunch with even more friends, then go to a meeting where the main talk is about football; then you go home and tell Mum about the long and difficult day you have suffered. Why don't you treat some patients or make something? That's real work.'

Mintzberg's seminal contribution includes classification of the managerial functions into ten roles, which can be clustered into:

‹ interaction with others
‹ handling information
‹ making decisions.[1]

Luthens, also working in industry, has observed that successful managers engage more often in conflict management, interact more with outsiders, participate in more exchanges of information, make more decisions and are actively involved in training and development activities.[2] In addition, Luthens found noticeable differences between the activities of successful managers at various organisational levels.

The work of our colleague at the University of New South Wales, Peter Degeling, further emphasises the role of managers in negotiating with and influencing others.[3] His analysis, based on case studies, surveys and observations, reveals that senior managers behave in a partisan way, using political means to promote their own standing and their view of the world. In the same way they develop coalitions and partnerships with colleagues to advance their own careers and credibility. Degeling also observes that managers' opinions may well differ with respect to identical facts when they occupy different positions and specialisations within the organisation.

Degeling sums up the situation in the following terms:

The activities in which managers engage, such as mobilising, co-opting, mediating, networking, broking, structuring, and contesting, are not neutral in content or intent. Rather these activities are oriented towards shaping and sustaining existing systems of order and sustaining the manager's own position within and external to an organisation.

Indeed, personal survival is a necessary part of the game. If views are offered that are unacceptable ideologically or for other reasons, the manager at worst will be shot, as in Stalin's era, banned from work, as in the McCarthy era, or left languishing in a back office, as in Margaret Thatcher's era.

These observations of seemingly unconnected random activities of managers have been replicated among high school principals, physiotherapists and health service managers.[4] The findings are broadly similar.

‹ Managers typically spend their time talking to people—not thinking, writing, analysing or deciding.
‹ Most managers' time is spent working in groups.
‹ Managers spend a large share of their time interacting with subordinates and peers rather than with superiors.
‹ The working day of the manager comprises brief, highly fragmented encounters, most of which are not planned in advance.
‹ Managers rely more heavily on oral information than on formal, routine reporting procedures.
‹ Managers use a variety of different channels of information, never relying solely on formal channels.

To understand the purpose of these seemingly superficial and interrupted people-centred encounters, we turn to our own study.[5] Lawson observed that successful managers do not waste their time. They use these processes to influence events, to exert authority, to allocate resources, to gather information, to gain support and to mobilise action. In other words, they are continuously negotiating and, in particular, negotiating for the adoption of their plans and objectives. They are using these interactions to find out, to condition others and to prepare people for action and change.

Changing perception of management

Emerging from these studies is a notion of management as a dynamic set of functions and processes associated with pluralistic expectations, uncertainty and complexity—a shift in emphasis from order, regularity, predicability and control to continuous adjustment and change.

The metaphors used to describe organisations also change. The organisation is increasingly perceived as a living organism continuously changing and adapting to maintain its equilibrium, to defend itself against threats and to take advantage of opportunities. In contrast, the 'mechanistic' organisation is viewed as a sophisticated engine with many specialised parts, programmed to perform well-defined tasks in a relatively certain environment.

Corresponding to these images are two very different types of managers. The latter, known as an administrator, is seen as a skilled driver able to efficiently reach predetermined destinations using detailed maps, and at the same time to look after the vehicle and keep it ready for further trips. The former performs as a leader, is seen as an explorer in uncharted waters, navigating towards new and promising territories with all the turmoil, uncertainty and risk of adventure.

Ability to perform well in one capacity does not guarantee success in the other. Administrators may be extremely well educated, highly intelligent and hard working and yet lack the vision of leaders and the ability to mobilise people and resources in new directions. Similarly, leaders may fail to create appropriate systems, to translate their ideas into clear and realistic operations and to monitor aspects of implementation.

Clearly, we need both. Management is a set of complementary functions, all of which must be performed to achieve good results. The common attribute of both effective leaders and effective administrators, at all levels, is the commitment and sense of responsibility for the success of the organisation and its operations. They perform as conductors creating music by integrating the contribution of players and promoting harmony.

A key feature of effective leaders is their strong focus on results. As Ulrich and his colleagues suggest, leaders who focus on results clearly and specifically communicate expectations and targets to the people with whom they work.[6] They influence everyone around them to achieve agreed results by creating and communicating clear directions and by creating processes that promote a sense of ownership and commitment. They use results as a test for continuing or implementing leadership practice and determine what they need to do personally to improve results. They ensure that their subordinates and colleagues perceive that their reason for being a leader is the achievement of positive results, rather than personal or political gains. They measure the standards they set and, most importantly, they constantly take action—results won't improve without it.

Having placed the managerial function in its dynamic context, we turn now to the review of the specific tasks involved in managing and the required skills (see Chapter 5).

The specific tasks involved in managing

Specific tasks are the elements of major functions. To review in specific terms the actions of managers it is useful to relate to some of the common tasks they perform. The process starts logically with a careful analysis of a given situation leading to the determination of broad directions, which are in turn transformed into specific objectives and targets. During this process, priorities are set and decisions are made concerning time frames, resources, anticipated constraints and contingency approaches.

The detailed plan includes specifications of systems and procedures designed to streamline and coordinate efforts. A sound plan will clearly indicate roles and responsibilities, and arrangements for information flow, communication and reporting. These arrangements will then be considered with regard to staff requirements and ways to enhance their skill and commitment. Last, but not least, the plan will include indicators and methods for monitoring and evaluating the program and services, from inception to completion.

This logical way of describing the functions and their component tasks may seem naive in the light of the dynamics of what managers actually do, as described in the previous section. The functions are linear inasmuch as one step logically follows the other. We therefore trust that this order is a convenient way to review the tasks, but caution against the presumption of a smooth and uninterrupted journey. More likely than not, managers can expect to be required to go back to the drawing board to reconsider targets and methods in the light of changing conditions and requirements often imposed by people who have little idea of or sensitivity to what has taken place.

Having emphasised the bounds of rationality and the disjointed nature of planning and management, it is useful nevertheless to provide some guidance and sequence.

Deciding what to do

Determination of directions is based on analysis of what is needed and what is possible. Managers are expected to respond to perceived problems, but are well advised also to identify and take advantage of opportunities that may present. It is not uncommon to observe solutions triggering the perception of needs rather than the other way around. The availability of new technology, for example, often leads people to seek problems to which it may be applied. Hence, developments in the capacity to diagnose certain conditions trigger the development of services to accommodate new demands for treatment.

In determining directions, it is essential to consult stakeholders and to involve people whose cooperation and support is required for success. Clarity and acceptance of collective goals is critical to the creation of team efforts. People can hardly be expected to contribute to something they either do not understand or do not agree with.

A narrow perception of the issues and challenges we face—without adequate consideration of the perspective of stakeholders—often leads to misconception of problems and solutions. In dealing with complex situations we must not be satisfied with one perspective, compelling as it may be. Bolman and Deal, in their important work on re-framing organisations, suggest that we should apply different filters to the organisational issues we address as managers.[7] Problems may be addressed from an organisational, cultural, political or human resource perspective. Each perspective may yield different concerns and at times different opportunities for moving forward. We need to be conscious that what meets the eye may only be the tip of the iceberg and may require further exploration in greater depth.

At the same time we need to remember that in managing situations, we need to keep moving forward. Analysis should not lead to procrastination and decision paralysis. Often, further information may come to light in the course of implementation and action. On other occasions the whole context may shift, requiring further review of political, financial, legal or other aspects of the situation. Thus we recognise the never-ending nature of decision making, which requires continual review of what is done with a view to revising and doing better or differently in the future.

Analysing the situation is a basic requirement. Data, information, field visits and discussions with colleagues are all required. As managers for many years, we cannot recall a wasted field visit. Without exception, there is always something to learn about morale, the quality of the service and facilities, and new ideas that can only be observed and assessed in the field.

Situational analysis allows the development of priorities for action, identifies gaps in services and encourages the development of particular objectives.

ANECDOTE

In attempting to understand the high rate of maternal and child mortality in a developing country we noted the low utilisation of the local health facilities. Our analysis revealed that mothers were not accessing the available services for a variety of reasons, including: logistic difficulties such as geographic distances and inappropriate opening hours; lack of appreciation of the importance of professional support; lack of trust in the capability of health staff to help; and many more. Clearly this kind of analysis reveals many interrelated issues that need to be addressed through education and service development.

Unfortunately there are times when a manager has to take decisions in a vacuum; that is, without a thorough understanding of the health conditions and the cultural and economic environment. The factors to be considered are complex and the decisions are difficult. By identifying some of these factors and putting them in sequence, we offer you an approach to help you decide what needs to be done.

Gathering information and analysing the present situation

In analysing the situation in which you operate, it is useful to take a broad perspective. It is easy to fall into the trap of perceiving only what you want to see and hear. The danger of 'tunnel vision' is greatest when you do all your planning from behind a desk on the basis of limited information given by people who tend to agree with you. To understand the opportunities and constraints inherent in each situation, you must look at it from different angles. One of the reasons for tragic loss of life during World War I was that the military leadership on all sides traditionally remained aloof from the action; that is, remote from the foul and dangerous trenches. Had they made regular visits, it is most unlikely that they would have continued to order repeated, purposeless charges into the full and fatal face of machine guns.

In order to evaluate both the health problems of the population and the resources that are currently available, you should observe the following procedures:

case history

Mary Rodonekus was a conscientious health officer. She had spent over ten years operating a health centre in a large urban community. To her great disappointment, conditions over the previous three years had been deteriorating rather than improving. Worst of all, the community support of which Mary and her staff were so proud had been dwindling. These disheartening developments took place at a time when Mary and her staff felt they had been working harder than ever. What had gone wrong?

On advice from a senior colleague, Mary Rodonekus decided to review the situation. She talked to her staff and requested information on the work they did and the difficulties they encountered. She talked to old residents and newcomers about their expectations and needs. The picture that emerged made Mary very angry with herself for neglecting to previously review the situation in her community.

In essence, she discovered a gradual but significant change in the demographic make-up of her community. Steady immigration and changing economic conditions had created substantial unemployment. The health services offered in the past had failed to reach the newcomers and to respond to their needs.

As expected, Mary felt frustrated. Like many health service managers, she had limited control over problems associated with migration, housing, employment and other welfare issues.

She did not even have control over health service issues, such as the amount of resources allocated to various service areas. These were determined at higher levels. Yet Mary knew that the problems would not go away by putting the blame on others. The first task, clearly, was to determine the best way to use her limited resources.

❮ Gather statistical data to show predominant trends in morbidity and mortality from:
   – the ministry of health
   – the national institute of statistics, or similar organisations
   – the international agencies involved with health policy (for example, WHO, UNICEF, the World Bank, private not-for-profit agencies)
   – schools of medicine and public health
   – hospital records, health centres and local government statistical and planning offices (for area data).

In considering the information provided by the various organisations, you should check whether the data makes sense. In order to look for inconsistencies and to take account of the nature of the organisation, its probable biases and its reputation, you should take the following steps:

❮ Review the national health plan to learn of priorities and trends. Examination of the relative funding levels of various projects and services over recent years will often provide as much information as the narrative portion.
❮ Gather information pertaining to health services that are currently provided or are being planned by the Department of Health, with particular concern for:

- the number, types and locations of hospitals and health centres
- their stated purpose (for example, service areas, types of services, population served)
- their staffing pattern and material resources
- how the various services are expected to interact and support each other, both in theory and in practice.

‹ Gather similar information concerning other bodies providing health services from:
- the Australian Hospitals Association (AHA)
- the Australian Private Hospitals Association (APHA)
- local medical associations
- public health societies (such as Diabetes Australia and the Alzheimer's group)
- nursing associations
- medical laboratories
- traditional healers and birth attendants
- religious groups.

‹ Visit the health service facilities to evaluate the services provided; interview staff (for example, physicians and health workers) and users of the service, and compare this information with the stated purposes of the facility.

‹ Discuss health and socioeconomic conditions with community organisations (especially women's groups), teachers, religious leaders and political figures.

A careful compilation and review of this information on health conditions and services may still not provide all the information you need. It may, therefore, be necessary to undertake a survey in your area. Before beginning, you should proceed as follows:

‹ Identify precisely what you need and know how you will use the additional information gained. Information about the current situation may also be required for assessment of progress.

‹ Seek assistance from experts in designing a survey; for example, from the sociology faculty of the local university.

‹ Decide who will be the best source of information. Usually some combination of health professionals and the potential users of services is most appropriate.

‹ State survey questions simply and directly, and in such a way that the responses will provide the specific information sought.

‹ Select a sample of the population that will adequately represent all segments of the community, including people who have not previously used the available health services.

‹ Ensure that resources are available to tabulate and analyse the collected data.

‹ Field-test any questionnaire and analyse the results before starting a large-scale survey, with the object of answering the following questions:
- Is the method providing the information efficiently?
- Are there alternative methods that would be quicker or less costly?

- Do responses suggest that there are other issues to be raised, or that some of the questions are unnecessary?
- How easily can information be tabulated and analysed?

Based on this information, you should then:

❮ consider whether or not the services you are now providing are the most appropriate
❮ prepare a list of alternative approaches to providing services
❮ keep an open mind about new, innovative approaches
❮ list all possible alternatives before deciding which are feasible and which are not.

Setting priorities

Once the needs and resources are known and a comprehensive list of alternatives has been developed, some method of establishing priorities is needed. Unfortunately, it is not unusual to find high-cost, high-technology services being selected for the benefit of a small segment of the population while the common (and perhaps less 'interesting') ailments go untreated.

EXAMPLE
During recent years enormous pressure has been placed on hospitals and governments to develop neonatal intensive care units. These units are costly to develop and run (approximately $2000 per bed per day!). While there is no question of the benefit to many premature infants, it is also probable that there are too many such units and that the outcome for some infants with extremely low birth weight is so poor that the expenditure is difficult to justify, particularly when few resources are available to solve the problems of impersonal, overcrowded antenatal clinics.

Clearly, the concept of seeking the most benefit for the largest number of people is not always pursued in determining priorities.

Rigid selection criteria cannot be set in a uniform manner. The importance given to any particular criterion must often be based on past experience. Bear in mind that preventing disease is preferable to treating disease; however, both prevention and treatment must be offered as a package in community health services. A specific project focused on measles prevention, for example, should be linked directly to services that also provide treatment.

When reviewing the information gathered, you may ask certain questions in order to help formulate priorities. For example:

❮ What are the major health threats to the population?
❮ What is the number of persons at risk, or the number suffering from the illness?
❮ Where are the gaps in services currently provided?

The next steps are to:

❮ break down the different health threats according to the population groups that are most seriously affected:

- age and sex group
- geographical location (how accessible are they?)
- economic status

‹ compare the seriousness of different diseases in terms of whether or not they are life-threatening, whether they are acute or chronic and whether they produce only mild symptoms or are seriously incapacitating

‹ consider how susceptible the various illnesses are to prevention and treatment efforts

‹ assess the adequacy of current service provision.

An important consideration in establishing priorities is the relative cost of the various alternatives. Estimate costs for the major alternatives.

‹ Estimate, in general terms, the staffing required and its costs, including training requirements.

‹ Consider the cost of materials, including maintenance costs and the availability of replacement parts of necessary equipment.

‹ Determine the availability and cost of transportation of staff and equipment, and the cost of storage facilities.

‹ Consider what resources can be shared with the existing services.

‹ Include the cost of mounting an outreach campaign to encourage community interest and participation.

‹ Allow for the additional costs of establishing a new administrative and operations unit for any services or project that cannot be incorporated into existing units.

‹ Make a realistic estimate of the number of community volunteers who will be willing to assist in providing services.

‹ Include selection, training and administrative costs when planning to use volunteer staff. Volunteers usually mean a high turnover of staff, especially when no social or monetary benefits are offered. A heavy emphasis on volunteer staff should usually be avoided in the initial stages.

‹ Continually keep in mind that there will be opportunity costs related to whatever services are given highest priority: $5000 devoted to a vaccination project automatically cancels out $5000 that might have been applied to another area—perhaps health education—or used for a highly specialised piece of equipment versus a continuing education opportunity for staff.

All health services, no matter how well designed, will have little chance of success without the community's attaching some priority to them. In setting your own priorities, take into account the interest of the community. This can be achieved by discussing the alternatives with community leaders, local organisations, church groups, members of the medical community, and individuals representative of the different social groups in the community.

All services must, to some degree, rely on other agencies and organisations to be successful. Before making a final decision:

‹ ensure that the proposed services match the current trends within the national health plan

‹ discuss the alternatives with other service providers to evaluate their degree of support, particularly in terms of services that would become part of a referral system

‹ evaluate probable interest among political groups, ensuring that they approve the priorities and will provide the necessary official support.

Establishing long- and short-term goals

When priorities have been set and you know the general areas to which you will direct your efforts, it is necessary to formulate specific goals and targets. Long-term goals state precisely what you expect to accomplish in a certain period, usually over several years. They might deal with broad services, such as providing maternal and child health services (prevention and treatment) for the 12 000 residents in a particular area, or with a single project, such as reducing the incidence of diabetes in the community.

Long-term goals set the overall direction of the services and provide a framework for intermediate goals, which are the steps that will be necessary in reaching the final goal. In the case of improving maternal and child health services, intermediate goals might include the renting of a church hall and the visit of an early childhood nurse already on the staff for, say, two days a week.

In setting goals, you should:

‹ prepare a concise statement of exactly what the project is expected to accomplish in a specific period—for example, to reduce non-insulin-dependent diabetes by 10 per cent within two years by conducting a nutrition and health promotion campaign

‹ clearly identify who the project is going to benefit—for example, adults from over 35 years of age

‹ estimate accurately the number of beneficiaries, how they will benefit and when—for example, in the first year 1000 people will attend nutrition classes

‹ produce a statement of goals that can be easily understood by all concerned with the project

‹ form the statement in such a way that it will be possible to evaluate the goal—that is, so that progress can be measured.

Since the long-term goal will usually be set several years in the future, the use of the intermediate goals will allow you to organise the project's daily operations within a more manageable framework. Properly planned intermediate goals are especially valuable for evaluation purposes. During the project's first year or so, you will probably not be able to evaluate the final goal directly, but whether or not the project is reaching the intermediate goal is a good indicator of its eventual success.

The following things should be done when establishing intermediate goals.

‹ Identify all the steps that must be accomplished before reaching the final goal; for example, the first six months will involve recruitment and training of health trainers, preparation of teaching aids and initial contact made with community groups.

- Ensure that reaching the intermediate goal will, in fact, lead towards the final goal; for example, final success depends on the community recognising the importance of nutrition.
- State the goals in such a way that they can be readily assessed, either directly or indirectly. Forming goals that can be measured should not, however, produce goals that are easy rather than goals that are important to achieve and/or statements that are difficult to communicate.
- Consider the interdependence of the goals; that is, the side effects one goal may produce that will help or hinder the attainment of others. For example, women who have successfully adopted good diets may encourage their spouses or male partners to participate.

EXAMPLE

A current example of the importance of goal setting relates to the 'waiting list' problem. Due to many factors, but in particular to the rising cost of private health insurance, the demand on public (free of cost) services in Australia has increased, perhaps by as much as 20 per cent. This has led to the rationing of some services and the creation of waiting lists as long as two years for non-urgent problems such as hip replacement and cataract surgery.

As a first step in the amelioration of this problem, a situational analysis was conducted. The analysis confirmed the reality of the problem, but also revealed that it was exaggerated because many patients were on multiple waiting lists and others needed to wait for the optimal time relevant to their condition; in other instances, operating theatres were inefficiently managed.

Accordingly, intermediate goals were defined, steps were taken to improve the accuracy of the waiting-list information, and productivity was enhanced. Despite the improvements, however, a substantial problem remained. Further reduction in the waiting-list problem has been achieved through payment to hospitals according to DRGs (diagnostic related groups) which, in turn, has improved productivity and reduced waiting times by 20–40 per cent in Victorian hospitals. The problem is still not fully resolved, however.

Developing a plan

Having set the goals defining just where you wish to go, you must decide how to get there. In other words, you must prepare a specific plan. This is the plan of action or strategy. There is always more than one way to reach a destination, and the manager's task is to select the most feasible, efficient and economical route. The plan of action should be centred on the intermediate goal. When preparing the plan or strategy:

- confer with colleagues about successes and failures of similar strategies in other districts and in similar organisations
- take great care to involve staff members
- consider innovative or novel ideas that could be tested on a small scale in your project
- adapt successful efforts in another hospital, clinic, community or country to your situation (considering the social and economic factors)

- keep the plan flexible, to allow for modifications as experience is gained and evaluations are analysed or the situational context changes
- plan for future growth in the same area, or for a repeat of the project in a new hospital or area
- attend regular meetings of staff and community groups
- invite community representatives to staff meetings when appropriate
- continue your dialogue with staff and the community to encourage their continuing input—this is most important
- develop a timetable for action—not too fast and not too slow, but quite specific.

Developing working policies and procedures

From the project's overall plan, specific activities will now be identified. A chart of working procedures will allow the manager to group these activities into a logical pattern. The chart not only describes the way the project is set up for operations, but is also a helpful tool in visualising how the units and sub-units are expected to interact. It also helps to clarify responsibilities and establish lines of authority and communication. As a staff training device, it will help staff to recognise their role in working towards the project's goals.

If you are developing a new project or service, you will have relative freedom in designing the chart of working procedures 'from the ground up'. Alternatively, it may be necessary to insert new responsibilities into an existing structure. Probably it will be a combination of these two possibilities.

In designing working procedures, you should:

- ensure that the working procedures encourage and facilitate two-way communication, vertically between supervisors and staff as well as horizontally within the unit
- limit the number of staff that report to each supervisor, in order to provide the supervisor with:
  - time to guide and monitor the activities of subordinates
  - time to communicate with subordinates
  - ease of coordination between key units.

A reasonable number of subordinates is six to eight, though this will vary according to the nature of the task and qualifications of staff.

When using the chart of working procedures:

- use it as a training resource when orienting new staff
- ensure that each individual clearly understands how his or her activities are to be coordinated with those of others to achieve the project's goals
- ensure that each individual knows how and when to communicate with others
- modify the chart according to changes in the organisational structure or growth of the organisation, and communicate these changes to the entire staff.

While the work chart helps to clarify what kinds of operational units are needed and how they will interact, written policies will be needed to describe the functioning of the units. Your written policies should:

‹ specifically state the responsibilities of each unit and sub-unit
‹ identify when and by whom decisions are to be made—for example, when each committee meets, when budget proposals are approved
‹ identify who will make the decisions
‹ specify the channels of communication between units and within units
‹ define the authority of each unit.

Preparing a budget and reporting system

The first step in preparing a budget is to review the goals of each unit and to determine how they relate to the goals of the organisation. A fairly new approach to budgeting, referred to as 'zero-based budgeting', requires that each unit must justify its entire funding each year, and includes the presentation of alternative means to reach the goals. This is a departure from the more traditional approach, which assumes that each unit will require the same funding base as in the previous year, plus increases for inflation, new responsibilities and so on. In the previous case history, a zero-based system would probably have allowed earlier identification of the problem and checked the irrational growth of the administrative unit.

Having reviewed the goals of each unit, its function, and how it relates with other units, it is possible to identify an appropriate staffing pattern and to estimate the materials and equipment required. At this point, it is important to collaborate with the senior staff of each unit to ensure not only that the funding level will be well estimated, but also that the staff will view the budget as partly a result of their own planning effort, rather than as a dictate from management. The degree of emphasis on this collaboration will obviously depend on the training and experience of the individual staff.

Once the total funding level is determined, it is not necessary to be overly detailed in the budget itself. For example, in order to estimate the cost of educational material, it is necessary to determine the current prices of each item required (plus an allowance for inflation, if needed). The line item in the budget, however, can simply state the total cost under the heading 'educational materials'.

When preparing budgets:

‹ Identify a clear and direct relationship between the functions of the unit and the goals of the organisation.
‹ Ask each unit manager to prepare a preliminary budget and then work with him or her to produce a final budget—this can be a valuable opportunity for staff development.
‹ Consider alternative methods that might produce the same results at lower cost.
‹ Review the types of equipment needed, the level of technology that is appropriate, and any special staff required.

When Dr Albert Rogers was assigned to take over management of the area office of the health services, he made a careful review of the existing information system, including the budget and related financial reports. He was surprised to see that the administrative unit had been assigned the highest percentage of the total operating budget. The area office had control of two hospitals and six small community health centres, but in each one there was at least one clerk assigned to purely administrative functions, in addition to the large administrative staff in the regional office. On further study, he found that earlier budgets had been quite modest in terms of administrative costs, and that while the number of community health staff had grown in small increments each year, the cost of the administrative unit had somehow grown by leaps and bounds. True, the staff were well-qualified and a lot of information was being produced, but how valuable was the information and how necessary was it in terms of the objectives of this area office?

On reflection, it appeared that previous managers had placed an excessively high priority on the reporting system, perhaps under the delusion that more reports justify the existence of the office itself. In particular, they wanted to ensure that the data they passed up to the central office was complete and fully detailed, even if its value was questionable.

Rather than seeing the administrative unit as a means to an end (a supporting service to the office's goals), the expansion of the unit and its functions became ends in themselves. The new manager now had the very difficult task of reviewing all functions of the unit, suppressing those that were not really appropriate to the goals and redesigning or streamlining the other functions to ensure efficiency. Staff had to be retrained, and in some cases dismissed; a major restructuring was necessary before full attention could again be paid to the overall operations of the area office.

❮ Consider the full cost of each item, such as:
 – cost of recruiting replacement staff and training expenses to allow for regular staff turnover
 – maintenance and replacement of equipment
 – contingency funds for unexpected needs
 – a fair estimate of the effects of inflation, including salary adjustments.
❮ Avoid unnecessary detail and group expenses under manageable headings.
❮ Establish clear guidelines for the expenditure of funds and specifically assign financial responsibility to unit managers.

Before implementing the budget, it will be necessary to prepare a reporting system that will allow a comparison between the predicted budget expenses and the actual expenses incurred. In each case where there is a discrepancy, an analysis is necessary to determine the reason and take appropriate action. For example, it may be found that the pharmacy services are spending much less than was allowed. Investigation may show that the purchase of hypertensive drugs was much less expensive than predicted. This prediction was based on a successful campaign to identify new cases for treatment. The problem appears to be that either some of the planning assumptions were incorrect (such as the estimate of the number of unreported cases in the community being too high) or that the campaign needs to be overhauled. The point is that the financial reports, if efficiently designed and carefully reviewed, not only are a valuable tool with which to control the use of funds, but also represent a method of monitoring the effectiveness of operations.

The number and format of the reporting documents and the frequency of their preparation will depend on local circumstances. Care must be taken to ensure that the information produced actually helps staff reach their goals (avoiding the situation in the first example, where many unnecessary reports were being produced) and yet is still not too expensive to produce.

Check that the financial reporting system:

❭ provides only the amount and kinds of information that are useful for conducting and monitoring the programs
❭ presents the information in a logical pattern and at appropriate intervals, to detect areas of concern
❭ avoids excessive detail
❭ provides a method by which staff are encouraged to search for the most cost-effective strategies as part of their day-to-day responsibilities.

When the reporting system identifies substantial differences between planned expenses and actual expenses, you should:

❭ review the situation with staff members, to analyse the cause before taking corrective action
❭ consider whether the problem may have been in the estimates made during the preparation stage rather than the result of inefficiency during the implementation
❭ refer again to unit goals and make adjustments based on their relevance to the overall goals of the organisation.

EXAMPLE

Table 4.1
Pharmacy department budget—small hospital

Planned 1st year expenditure	Planned monthly expenditure	Actual last month expenditure	Actual total to date expenditure (say, 6 months)	Annual trend
$	$	$	$	$
2 000 000	166 667	198 000	1 150 000	2 300 000

This budget presentation is a summary of much more detailed data that are normally collected.

The key feature is the predicted annual trend; that is, the likely outcome if expenditure continues at the rate of, say, the first six months of the year. The prediction is for an over-budget expenditure of $300 000. (*continued*)

The development of a system that provides information about trends is essential for managing even quite small and uncomplicated budgets, as it allows the manager to have time to analyse the situation and to take remedial action before a financial crisis develops.

Selecting and developing staff

An important factor in assessing your performance as a manager concerns your ability to match staff to individual assignments. During the recruitment and selection process, you should:

- prepare a job description that:
  - describes precisely the primary and secondary responsibilities of the position
  - establishes minimum levels as well as desirable levels of education and experience
  - makes it clear to whom the person reports and the number and type of staff that report to the position
  - identifies other staff and units with which the person will cooperate
- make the vacancy known within the organisation and encourage appropriate junior staff to apply
- ensure a large pool of candidates through wide advertising
- short-list candidates according to predetermined selection criteria—this is particularly important where there are many and varied applicants
- allow adequate time and a relaxed atmosphere in which to conduct interviews of the most qualified applicants and, whenever possible, have other senior staff interview the applicant and include their evaluations in making the final decision
- control the interview by determining in advance just what additional information you need from the applicant, and plan the discussion accordingly
- remember your EEO (equal employment opportunity) obligations.

In assessing how well you have selected existing staff, the following points should be considered:

- Do staff have the appropriate educational backgrounds and experience for the job—neither overqualified nor underqualified?
- Is there a high turnover of staff that may suggest assignments have been inappropriate?
- Has allowance been made for staff to be temporarily assigned to other units for both relief purposes and career development?
- Is there excessive dependence on any one staff member whose resignation would seriously disrupt operations?
- Are there clear paths for promotion?

Delegating tasks

The time available to a manager to respond to all the issues brought to his or her attention never seems to be sufficient. Often, however, this is because the manager has failed in the primary responsibility: to delegate tasks to others. The manager's staff is the most important single asset available, but staff—like money—will be wasted if not properly organised.

Your success as a manager is judged not only by how well you perform your own tasks, but also by how effective you are in organising the work of others. This includes delegating authority. Final responsibility, however, remains in the hands of the manager, and this means that some risks are involved. A good manager will not shy away from these risks, but will be able to minimise them through careful delegation.

Delegation not only saves time for other duties, but allows routine decisions to be taken quickly by field staff and avoids long delays in waiting for approval from higher authority.

To determine whether you are undertaking tasks that could appropriately be delegated, you should:

❬ periodically list your daily activities, to consider whether your direct involvement is required
❬ analyse the tasks you intend to delegate, to determine the minimum qualifications needed to perform them.

In considering to whom tasks should be delegated, you should:

❬ appraise the abilities of staff currently available to you, and match abilities to tasks
❬ ensure that current assignments are sufficiently challenging and draw fully on each individual's abilities
❬ whenever possible, give staff the opportunity to assume more demanding tasks on a trial basis, the better to judge their potential.

When delegating, you should:

❬ provide staff with the appropriate resources and authority to carry out the tasks efficiently
❬ describe carefully what is expected, and explain the limits of authority
❬ ensure that other relevant staff are aware of each assignment, and will respect the authority of the responsible individual
❬ avoid interfering with the person's performance unless required
❬ accept that some mistakes will inevitably be made and use them as a learning experience.

Developing an appropriate style of leadership

Leaders are not necessarily 'born'. Leadership is a skill that can be developed and improved. Perhaps the best single way to assess your own skill as a leader is to ask yourself: 'Do I make a difference?'. Can you think of a case in which your skills allowed you to select a particular course of action that proved more successful than otherwise might have been possible?

In assessing your ability to provide the necessary leadership that will ensure a properly coordinated team effort among project staff, you should:

‹ provide a strong example or role model that will encourage staff to develop similar traits
‹ make decisions without unnecessary delay and readily accept responsibility for them
‹ interpret personnel policies consistently and without bias
‹ encourage frank discussions when conflicts arise and provide fair arbitration to resolve disputes
‹ ensure that each member of the staff understands clearly what is expected and the importance of what he or she does for the total operation.

In general, it is important to involve in decisions people who may be affected by them and/or who can contribute to the process. The leader should also consider whether he or she needs to consult staff or is required to make a decision alone.

In making this choice, you should consider whether:

‹ you need advice from your staff concerning a particular issue
‹ the decision is truly open for staff influence or has already been made by yourself or others.

Effective leaders know that there is a time to ask for advice and a time to tell or instruct. The effective leader considers the particular situation and determines who can help and in what way. It is better to be honest and tell the staff when a particular decision has already been made than to create an illusion that their opinion is welcome. It is easy for staff to become cynical when democratic procedures are not genuine.

Motivating staff

In the example opposite, the senior technician had correctly decided to use a rather humanistic approach to the problem. There would have been other alternatives, of course. He could have followed the clinic director's suggestion of threatening Robert with dismissal. He could also have told Robert that his work was unsatisfactory and then sat back until Robert decided either to change his attitude, resign or be dismissed. These are all examples of what some experts have described as democratic, autocratic or laissez-faire styles. What we need to recognise is that one style will not be appropriate to all situations or to all people. For example, if Robert had been less concerned with his image and less oriented towards achievement, he might have responded quite well to the authoritarian approach in which he would simply have been threatened with dismissal if his work did not improve.

Knowing what will motivate individual staff members in particular situations is a key to managing staff efficiently. Reflecting on your own position, it will be clear that it is not simply the salary for which you are working. To varying degrees,

case history

Robert had worked for nearly three years in the laboratory of a large health centre. He had been trained directly by the senior laboratory technician, took his work quite seriously, and was a positive influence on new staff. Lately, however, the senior technician had received a surprising number of complaints from the physicians, all of which related directly to laboratory tests that Robert had done. In reviewing this situation, it was clear that the quality of his work had dropped seriously, such that the clinic director advised the senior technician to discharge Robert.

The senior technician realised, however, that he had an investment in Robert and that normally he was capable of reliable and efficient work. He arranged a meeting with Robert, during which he made it quite clear that the situation was becoming serious and could not be allowed to continue. At first Robert was obstinate, not even defending himself. The senior technician continued to probe patiently until he got to the root of the problem.

Simply put, Robert had lost interest in his work. He felt less appreciated than he once did. What he personally considered to be consistently high-quality work was no longer eliciting praise from his colleagues and senior staff. Explicit recognition was very important to him, but the staff had over the years become accustomed to Robert's reliability and now took it for granted. Robert felt he had lost their respect.

A rather lengthy conversation followed, during which the senior technician realised that Robert was ready for a new challenge. His present duties had become too routine. He helped Robert to investigate which evening classes in basic sciences at the university might provide him with some of the skills that were a prerequisite to further advancement. He also arranged some minor restructuring of tasks within the laboratory that would give him the opportunity to assist senior staff in more complex work, and thus further develop Robert's practical skills.

people are also interested in such issues as personal fulfilment, self-esteem, recognition, prestige, social contacts and so on. Recognising the interests and needs of your staff will allow you to provide an atmosphere in which people feel they are recognised as individuals and will reach a high level of job satisfaction. Staff who enjoy their work will almost certainly work as productive team members and will better accomplish the unit's objectives.

In motivating staff, you should establish the following policy.

‹ Consider them as individuals, attempt to understand their needs and concerns and respond appropriately.

‹ Ensure that each person understands and accepts his or her role in reaching objectives and sees them as personal objectives.

‹ Encourage open communication and ensure that staff feel they can approach you easily. Bear in mind that the formal channels in the organisation are designed for job-related communications and that informal channels must be actively developed to discuss anxieties, personality conflicts and so on.

‹ Adapt your approach to personnel matters according to the situation as well as the individual, using such strategies as discipline, praise and guidance as appropriate.

‹ Recognise individual abilities and assist staff to realise their full potential.
‹ When considering changes in staffing patterns and assignments, ask for the views of the individuals who will be affected. Often the employee has a better grasp of day-to-day operations and, if properly motivated, may be a key resource in making decisions.

Evaluating staff

How well your staff are performing their individual assignments is one issue in deciding how well you are achieving the overall goals that have been set. Here, however, we are concerned with using personnel appraisals as a means of motivating staff. Regardless of the position one holds in an organisation, receiving feedback on performance is critical to job satisfaction—as Robert's experience, related in the previous section, illustrates. Regular personnel appraisals ensure opportunities to discuss problems frankly and to guide the individual towards overcoming them. They are equally important as opportunities to recognise special achievements.

In planning for personnel (performance or staff) appraisals, you should:

‹ ensure that each job description clearly describes the tasks the individual is expected to undertake
‹ explain to staff what measures will be used to evaluate their performance
‹ identify who will be responsible for the formal appraisal (usually the immediate supervisor) and who will review the results
‹ recognise that routine or informal appraisal is at least as important as the formal, yearly appraisal, and take regular opportunities to discuss strengths and weaknesses with staff—this is especially important for new staff or when new responsibilities are assigned.

When preparing formal personnel appraisals, you should:

‹ see them primarily as opportunities to open doors of communication and help each employee to achieve his or her potential
‹ ensure that unit supervisors understand the importance of appraisals, guide the supervisors when necessary, and review the results
‹ allow sufficient, uninterrupted time to discuss personally both the positive and negative sides of evaluations
‹ leave aside any personal prejudices, and evaluate each individual fairly and honestly on job performance
‹ provide the opportunity for employees to make written comments on their evaluation, including this as part of their permanent personnel records
‹ follow up on the goals set at the previous appraisal (where applicable).

ANECDOTE
Despite the rhetoric and the general view that 'staff appraisals' are a good and rewarding activity, few health services or other organisations have successfully established appraisal systems of long-term value. There are several reasons for this.

1   Staff appraisals are time-consuming and managers very often have other priorities more directly relating to the care of patients.
2   Any formal evaluation of staff almost inevitably becomes part of the power and status game, which may be helpful to those who conduct the appraisal but not to the appraised (many of whom see themselves as victims in this context).
3   Conversely, many managers lack the confidence and expertise to conduct staff appraisals.

Evaluating and monitoring organisational performance

In simple terms, evaluation is a process through which the manager obtains information to help him or her make better decisions. Although the need for evaluation seems obvious, it is often given a low priority by managers simply because they may feel that a particular operational problem or a personnel issue requires an immediate response. The evaluation system is temporarily pushed aside. All too often, however, the result is that staff and funds continue to be invested in a strategy that is not efficiently accomplishing the set goals. Proper evaluation can identify possible solutions.

To be effective, a carefully developed means of evaluating organisational or program-specific performance must be an integral part of the initial planning process and must then be carried out consistently as a part of the routine operations.

Planning for evaluation

The development of a logical evaluation system rests on clearly expressing what it is that you expect to accomplish, and then measuring progress. During the planning stage of a project, you should:

‹   prepare a final goal statement that expresses precisely what the project is going to do in a given period, who will be affected, how, and when
‹   plan interim goals (steps to be accomplished in order to reach the final goal) that can be broken down into measurable tasks that identify who will do what, when, and at what cost
‹   plan for an evaluation system that:
    –   provides information at monthly or at least quarterly intervals
    –   identifies problems or areas of concern
    –   provides feedback early enough to allow corrective action to be taken
‹   keep in mind that the evaluation system must be easily understood by the staff who are responsible for day-to-day operations of the project
‹   involve these staff members in the development of the evaluation program.

case history

Dr Judith Day had long been concerned about the high levels of infant and child morbidity in the early childhood health centre where she was medical director. She knew that a large part of the problem was related to over-nutrition and that this, in turn, was due largely to the fact that many young mothers were switching to the more popular use of bottle-feeding their babies rather than breastfeeding. Clearly, these women did not understand the importance of breastfeeding. She decided to start a breastfeeding campaign as a logical solution.

Her goal was to improve the nutrition status of the 2200 children under two years of age in the centre's service area. Since the cause (bottle-feeding) and the effect (obesity) were so clearly linked, she saw no reason to spend time and money in regular evaluation.

The campaign began with much attention from the local news media and was an important topic of conversation during the initial months. Through seminars and workshops health workers were retrained in how to teach mothers the importance of breastfeeding and the proper techniques to be used. Classes were held once a week in the health centre and were very well attended. By the end of the second year, however, the budget was tight and there was not sufficient money available to increase the number of classes, which were growing in popularity. It was decided that the evaluation could be postponed and the funds devoted to increasing the number of classes. It was only after three years of operation that a survey was finally done, comparing the current level of breastfeeding with the levels determined during the baseline survey.

The results were depressing. The level of breastfeeding was largely the same as it had been three years earlier, and in some of the poorer areas the situation was actually worse.

What was happening here was that many mothers were attending classes simply because they had become a social gathering place that provided a break from the week's routine. They listened to the lectures, but felt that the demands of their urban lifestyle simply made it too difficult always to have the younger children with them. Anyway bottle-feeding was the 'modern' way.

Three years and a substantial amount of funds had been devoted to an unsuccessful strategy. The goal was appropriate, but the means to achieve it were not. Some knowledge was being passed on during the classes, but no changes were being made in child-feeding practices.

This situation could have been avoided if, right from the planning stage, an ongoing evaluation process had been included in the campaign strategy. If that had been done, the community health workers might have used their home visits to discuss and also monitor the feeding practices in each home. Recording the progress of each child and periodic weighing would have helped to identify children at highest risk. These families could then have been singled out for more frequent home visits and an attempt made to identify any special problems. Periodically collecting and analysing data about the women who had changed their feeding practices and those who had not would have helped keep the effort on the right track.

The campaign had been based on the erroneous assumption that once a woman was told that breastfeeding was best, she would automatically adopt the practice. It was also assumed that women from all economic levels of the community would be attending the classes. Without regular evaluation, these assumptions could not be tested.

Selecting indicators to measure progress

Indicators will need to be developed to measure progress towards both the long- and the short-term goals of the project. Whenever possible, they should measure progress directly. For example, in a measles-reduction project an indicator might be the percentage of children in a certain population who have been immunised each month. This is a simple, direct and quantifiable way to measure progress. Other types of project might have to use indirect means. Education projects are typical of these: an indirect measure might be to record the number of students coming to classes or, still better, to check on the practices of the students after completing the training courses.

Collecting information

During the planning stage, it must be decided what information is to be collected, when it is to be collected, how it will be reported and who is to be responsible for the system. In planning the collection of information, you should observe the following procedures:

- ❬ Ensure that the information will be reliable:
    - the staff who collect the information are adequately trained
    - standardised forms and guidelines are used so that each person collects the same information in the same manner
    - allowances are made for language differences and levels of literacy when interviewing service recipients.
- ❬ Collect information sufficiently often to ensure that problems will be identified early enough to take remedial action.
- ❬ To avoid duplication, examine the existing information system of the local health offices, statistical institutes and other local agencies to determine what information is already available.
- ❬ Collaborate with other agencies or service providers to see what possibilities exist to share staff and facilities.
- ❬ Consider alternative ways to gather information that would be less costly, especially in terms of staff time.
- ❬ Consider in advance who will use the information:
    - Who will be able to use it?
    - What type of adjustments might this lead to?
    - Will the information gained be fed back into project operations?

Comparing results with objectives

Once the information has been gathered, and when you are comparing it with the objectives that were set during the planning stage, you should proceed as follows:

- ❬ Present the information in such a way that comparison can readily be made with baseline data. Graphics help.
- ❬ Determine what additional information might be necessary to analyse fully any shortfalls and, if necessary, discover how and where to get it.

- Review the results with your staff. A poor evaluation can be an important learning tool and a positive evaluation can be a chance to reinforce good work habits.
- Review the indicators and the information-gathering system to ensure that they are functioning efficiently and are the most appropriate methods, in view of experience gained in the operational stage.
- When experience shows that the indicators are not the most appropriate measuring devices, modify the system. This may be necessary for indicators that are consistently met and now need only occasional spot-checking.

Taking corrective action

No matter how well planned the evaluation system, its value rests with the manager's ability to use the information gained to keep the operational unit on the right track. After reviewing the results, you should:

- decide which shortfalls will require immediate corrective action and which may only require closer monitoring before taking specific action
- review current literature and discuss the problem and possible solutions with colleagues, other providers and senior health officials (similar to the steps taken in the initial planning process)
- prepare a list of alternative solutions and consider how each alternative will have an impact on:
  - staffing patterns
  - other units of the organisation
  - budget
  - material resources.

EXAMPLE
Even the smallest hospital cannot function efficiently without a simple data and information system. For example, a small fifty-bed hospital would require at least the following data and information.

Table 4.2

	Planned monthly activities	Actual monthly activities	Variation
1 Patient activities			
Occupied beds	45	40	−12%
Number of separations	50	45	−10%
Surgical procedures	40	35	−12.5%
2 Costs in $			
Staff	100 000	95 000	−5000
Food	5000	4500	−500
Pharmaceutical and surgical supplies	5000	4500	−500
Power	1000	1000	0
Other	2000	1800	−200

The above example is simplistic However the principle—having a planned estimate of activity and cost so that actual performance can be compared with a target, plus a measure of variation from that target—applies equally to vast, complex and enormously expensive teaching and referral hospitals.

Reflections for the reader

The practical advice in this chapter has value only if you put it into practice in your place of work. It is a frequent experience that managers undertake extensive and expensive management education programs but have great difficulty in converting new knowledge into practice. Various reasons are given to explain this common experience. Perhaps the most obvious is that most people participate in management education programs as individuals and not as groups from a single organisation. Therefore, in their respective organisations they are the only ones with the new knowledge and so have difficulty in persuading their colleagues to change their methods of work. It is for this reason that many organisations arrange for management education to be considered for groups from the same workplace.

Other reasons include the resistance to change by many people. Therefore, the manager returning from an education program 'with fire in his belly' may be regarded at worst as a threat and at best as a nuisance.

Accordingly, having read and considered the advice in this chapter, please stop and think how you might implement some of these ideas. Implementation is an art form—it requires great care and skill. Perhaps a beginning is to put yourself in your colleagues' place and assess what would be your reaction to these ideas and what would be needed to gain your support. Seek to identify the specific problems of implementation, then explore and discuss them, and cajole your colleagues into accepting change. Above all, do not precipitate change that can be blocked or that will cause offence, as to do so will lead to long-term loss of morale and long-term difficulty in bringing about additional change.

Note: Parts of Chapter 4 are based, with permission, on A Rotem & J Fay (School of Medical Education, University of New South Wales), *Self-assessment for Managers of Health Care*, World Health Organization, Geneva, 1987.

Further reading

There is a range of recent publications which relate to the issues explored in Chapters 4 and 5. See references 6 and 7 for this chapter and the following publications:

‹ MG Harris et al., *Managing Health Services Concepts and Practice*, MacLennan and Petty, Sydney, 2002.

‹ J Arlopia, G Andrewartha, H Armstrong, D Whetton & K Cameron, *Developing Management Skills: A Comprehensive Guide for Leaders*, 2nd edn, Prentice Hall, Australia, 2001.

‹ DC Dunphy & D Stace, *Beyond the Boundaries: Leading and Recreating the Successful Enterprise*, 2nd edn, McGraw Hill, Sydney, 2001.

‹ V Iles & K Sutherland, *Managing Change in the NHS Organisational Change: A Review for Health Care Managers, Professionals and Researchers*, National Co-ordinating Centre for NHS Service Delivery and Organisations R&D, 2001. (This publication by Valerie Iles and Kim Sutherland is a review of models of change management to help managers, professionals and researchers find their way around the literature and consider the evidence available about different approaches to change. The full document can be downloaded from the web at http://www.sdo.lshtm.ac.uk/whatsnew.htm)

‹ LaFond, Brown & Macintyre, 'Mapping capacity in the health sector: a conceptual framework', *International Journal of Health Management*, vol. 17, 2002, pp. 3–22.

‹ NSW Health Department, *A Framework for Building Capacity to Improve Health*, NSW Health, 2001, at www.health.nsw.gov.au

‹ W Wake-Dyster, 'Designing teams that work', *Australian Health Review*, vol. 24, 2001, pp. 34–41.

‹ PM Senge, *The Fifth Discipline: The Art and Practice of the Learning Organisation*, Double Day/Currency, New York, 1994.

The skills required of health service managers

To be successful, a manager needs to master a range of skills and then learn to apply these skills in an effective manner. Texts on management separate the skills of management for purposes of clarity and for teaching. In the real world, however, management skills are deployed in combinations, such as planning combined with power, objectives combined with persuasion and education, counselling combined with supervision and discipline and analysis combined with data collection. The emphasis is on specific skills being dependent on circumstances, both within and outside the organisation. In addition, these skills may be applied in various combinations and intensity over time.

Clearly, management is an art form that requires judgment and maturity, plus particular skills. For most people, both theoretical and experiential learning are required to master the art of management.

Personality and management

Most of us are aware that some people have what might be termed 'managerial' personalities that may lead them to become organisers and managers, and may also determine whether or not they will be successful in a managerial role. The discussion of such personal traits is extremely sensitive, however, particularly when power and authority are involved. Nevertheless, we are all aware of the bright, hard-working, well-educated colleague who is hopeless in a managerial role and who is constantly sent off to undertake managerial courses not to improve his or her performance, but to give everybody—particularly the chief executive officer—a rest.

In order to systematically draw some conclusions about management and personalities, we reviewed the personal characteristics of fifty senior public service managers. They were the heads either of major public organisations such as a department of education, health or welfare or of hospitals and schools. Their overall

case study the Peter Principle

There was a very senior physician who was successful as the director of a sexually transmitted disease (STD) program. He coveted and subsequently gained the role of director-general of health services. He was a disaster—he caused great anxiety among subordinates, allowed gross overspending and could not and did not plan for the future. Finally, he had to be removed.

In retrospect his appointment was, of course, a mistake. As director of the STD division he had a relatively defined role; the existing director-general carried the diplomatic and planning responsibilities and he was not required to make any important independent decisions.

He was a classic example of the Peter Principle, whereby people are promoted to their level of incompetence.

success was measured on a scale of 1 to 10 according to the achievement or otherwise of the objectives of the organisations for which they were responsible (presuming these were achievable within the existing circumstances). Ten key characteristics were identified, and again assessment on a scale of 1 to 10 was awarded according to the possession of these characteristics. The characteristics were:

- a desire to be successful at a senior level
- the capability of developing objectives for the organisation
- knowledge about the relevant activities of the organisation
- confidence
- interpersonal skills
- ability to delegate authority
- capability of changing management styles according to changing circumstances and needs of the organisation
- commitment to the organisation
- stamina
- charisma.

Those judged to be outstanding managers had several key attributes: the ability to successfully develop and achieve objectives; high levels of expertise in the activities of the organisation; and high levels of trust by their peers as well as their subordinates. The outstanding managers had varying levels of interpersonal skills.

Those managers who were good, but not outstanding, had lesser attributes in each of the above areas and did not necessarily have high levels of expertise. This perhaps indicates that managers can succeed without such expertise, but are certainly not outstanding. These good managers did not necessarily have high levels of interpersonal skills, but when they did it was of help. Again, the good managers had a high level of trust by their colleagues.

Neither the outstanding nor the good managers were necessarily good delegators; some were, while others controlled events from a personal level.

In unsuccessful managers, a key factor was found to be lack of confidence in competence—that is, in the appropriate skills relevant to the nature of the organisation. However, much more important was the lack of trust by subordinates and peers in the behaviour of the senior manager, which exhibited itself in a range of ways. Perhaps most important was the creation of a state of high anxiety among many members of the organisation that frequently led to a lack of confidence in their ability to make decisions and get on with the job.

It was concluded that the concept of 'a managerial personality' is a reality, even among the most senior public sector managers. It was also found that the 'Peter Principle' applies, in which a person may manage quite successfully as a subordinate, but fails when put in charge (see the case study opposite). This failure is generally due to a lack of confidence and trust by colleagues.

Being a leader

Leadership is crucial, despite the comment by the famed writer on management, Peter Drucker, that: 'Leadership is all hype. We have had three great leaders in this century—Hitler, Stalin and Mao—and you see the devastation they left behind.'[1]

There have been many studies of the various types of leadership. Collectively they lead to the rather obvious view that different kinds of leadership are appropriate at different times. Arguably the best example in modern times is that of Winston Churchill, the famed wartime leader of Great Britain, who was voted out of office immediately after the war was won in favour of the self-effacing Labour leader, Clement Attlee. The British people had not judged Churchill harshly; they had made a mature judgment that the requirements for leadership were profoundly different in times of war compared with times of peace.

One of the most famous studies of leadership, power and politics was that of the Florentine renaissance man, Machiavelli, who found it necessary to write his findings in the form of the fable, *The Prince*. The book is still in print today and is required closet reading for any aspiring manager.

Holle and Blatchley have defined five leadership styles: autocratic, which is authority-centred; bureaucratic, which is rule-centred; democratic, which is group-centred; parental, which is individual-centred; and laissez faire, where the manager deliberately abstains from direction or interference.[2] The highly skilled leader uses each of these styles according to the timing and nature of the situation. For example, in the management of universities the tradition has been that of democratic laissez faire, but from time to time university leaders need to be autocratic, particularly when distributing resources among a group of world-famous authorities.

None of these five styles deals with the motivation of the leader. Undoubtedly, the motivation comes from the leader's life experiences, from genetics, traditions of a family, traditions of a particular society and culture and, in addition, from situational circumstances.

Miner has identified a range of attitudes common among leaders.[3] These include a good relationship with more senior staff; a desire for competition by both the leader and the leader's staff; an assertive personality combining a capacity to make decisions with an ability to take firm, disciplinary action and to protect other members of the group; a desire to exercise power and the ability to back up words and actions; a desire for success and recognition; and, finally, a sense of responsibility.

case study the late professor Vernon Collins— a leadership role model

Most of us have a role model, most often someone older and with desirable but seemingly unattainable attributes. Vernon Collins was such a person. He was a very tall, dignified and highly intelligent paediatrician who was the medical director of Melbourne's Royal Children's Hospital. He was the person primarily responsible for developing that hospital into a modern centre of excellence. His leadership characteristics were obvious. He was extremely competent, always cool, calm and collected, ever the diplomat though never afraid to pursue proper but difficult objectives such as attaining payment for young medical staff in place of the patronising 'honorary' system (for which he was labelled a communist during the McCarthy period). He could and did develop clear objectives, and could conceive and pursue long-term plans.

In his later years he became less flexible, but even had insight into that problem and accordingly moved from a management into an academic role. In each of his major professional roles—physician, manager, academic—he was extremely effective. In short, he was a model leader.

To this range of attitudes can be added the abilities to subjugate personal ego and pride and to extend recognition to others; to take a personal interest in the work and affairs of staff; and to exercise power and authority with maturity. Additional virtues include stamina and patience with perspective, recognising that many major advances take years, rather than months, before they are realised.

Power and authority

An essential attribute of the successful manager is the ability to attain, retain and use power. Maximillian Walsh is a Sydney-based journalist who has reviewed the importance of power and authority in the success of managers.[4]

In making his comments, Walsh largely refers to the work of Jeffrey Pfeffer.[5] Pfeffer has identified the characteristics for successfully acquiring and wielding power. These are:

< energy, endurance and physical stamina
< the ability to focus one's energy and to avoid wasted effort
< sensitivity, which makes it possible to read and understand others
< flexibility, particularly with respect to selecting various means in order to achieve one's goals
< the willingness to engage when necessary in conflict or in confrontation or, in other words, a certain degree of personal toughness
< the ability to submerge one's ego, at least temporarily, and to play the good subordinate or team player to enlist the help and support of others.

Walsh makes the comment that most of these skills are not taught in management or in education courses.

Pfeffer explores not only how people acquire power, but how they use it and how they lose it. With respect to the loss of power, he writes: 'Power is lost because changed circumstances render previous skills or networks obsolete'. Max Walsh has the final word when he indicates that in writing about politics, economics and business for over thirty years in key world centres, he has realised that beyond the superficial differences between these activities there are powerful parallels in any organisation. But then, of course, Machiavelli knew this five centuries ago!

Managing people

The management of people is perhaps the single most important role of the manager. Some have difficulty with this role; for others it is a pleasurable, rewarding activity. Unfortunately terms such as 'human resource management' and the 'human resource function' have become fashionable. The aim of these terms is presumably to create a specialisation in this field and to add credibility to those who practise it. But all managers have to manage people—all managers have to learn to be 'a boss'. These comments should not simply refer to the need to examine an organisation's staffing policies, or the need to examine the categories or education of staff; far from it. We argue that managers have an imperative to become involved with people as superiors, peers and subordinates. They create work conditions that enhance productivity and engender commitment. They achieve results through people by selecting the right people, designing meaningful jobs, developing their staff skills and career prospects, setting standards, rewarding good performance, and offering ongoing support and encouragement.

Selecting staff members

The first priority with respect to managing people is to recruit 'the right person for the right job'. Regardless of the prerogative for managers to hire and fire, it is an abject managerial failure when removal of staff becomes necessary.

In the health service field, there are few issues and difficulties involved in defining the job. This is because health services have such well-defined professional specialisations (over 130) and the job specifications and the formal credentials are very well established. For example, the need for a surgeon in a hospital is obvious; so are the credentials—namely, a basic medical qualification plus formal education and experience leading to membership of a professional organisation such as the Royal Australasian College of Surgeons. In some circumstances, because of an adequate supply, the selection will be from many excellent candidates. It is a situation most commercial enterprises would envy. In other situations, such as the provision of family physicians in rural areas, it is necessary to improvise and create special incentives to attract the right doctors.

Recruiting managers in the health services may also prove difficult in many settings. Experienced management talent is often in short supply, the educational requirements are far from clear and the personal attributes and interests of effective managers become much more of an issue. In recent times major efforts have been extended to encourage participation of clinicians in management. The concept of clinical governance has evolved to signify the special role clinicians may play in determining the most appropriate clinical pathways based on evidence of best practices. Clinician manager contribution is also essential in setting priorities, rationing services and allocating scarce resources. Senior managers need to consider the appropriate mix of skills and to find ways to integrate the efforts of managers from different disciplines.

The role of the prospective manager should, as far as practicable, be defined and recorded. This process of role definition will require careful negotiation, as the new manager will be sharing power, authority and territory with other members of the organisation.

Selection should be based on past performance in managerial roles. This will require personal approaches to past superiors, peers and colleagues, each of whom may offer a different perspective. This is a difficult process, as the candidate may wish to keep his or her candidature confidential. The issue of confidentiality and the need to know the past performance of candidates is often a compelling reason to appoint managers who are well-known to the organisation.

Interviews are of little help in this process and can be seriously misleading. The controversial psychologist, Eysenck, has correctly commented that 'many job selection interviews are merely opportunities to appoint images of ourselves'.[6]

In these days of the facsimile and photocopier, written references are also of limited value. Few are willing to put on paper remarks other than glowing comments; few will give an honest adverse assessment. What has been left out of a reference can become more important than what has been included. Also, the writing skills of the author may have a major and misleading impact on the selection process.

Encouragement

Carlopio and O'Donnell have provided a useful checklist for managers to follow when they manage colleagues.[7] The following suggestions are included.

‹ Be positive, rewarding and responsive.
‹ Value and recognise your staff's skills and contribution.
‹ Explain, provide reasons and involve your staff.
‹ Set agreed goals, encourage innovation and provide tangible awards.
‹ Offer appropriate discretion and avoid unnecessary proliferation of roles and procedures.

This checklist has strong underlying values and reflects the gradual change away from authoritarian, central-managerial control towards a much more group-oriented, participatory management style.

Education

The pace of change has become so great in technical fields such as health that the need to 'keep up to date' is paramount. Accordingly, a planned allocation of time and money should be directed to continuing education of all staff, but particularly of staff in management roles. Appropriate induction of staff to new responsibilities, changes in work procedures or technology will usually yield dividends by reducing the uncertainty and anxiety associated with change. Increasingly, the benefit of continuous, on-the-job learning is recognised as an essential component of people management. Learning organisations are characterised as places where people continue to develop and adapt in response to rapidly changing circumstances and challenges.

Managing resources

Managers of health services are responsible for many millions of dollars worth of buildings, equipment, vehicles and land, as well as the immense staff resources and the drugs and equipment they need to do their work. Regrettably, managing resources has been something of a Cinderella in the health services, mainly because of the dominance of urgent clinical issues—that is, until serious trouble arises, such as the collapse of power systems or the breakdown of refrigerators and sterilisers.

Asset assessment

It is of concern that too few public and private health sector managers have any detailed knowledge of ownership of land and buildings, and no knowledge of the range and quality of equipment.

'Asset assessment' is a rather good term for a procedure that aims to overcome these problems. This concept is simple: prepare a list of all the assets of the organisation, their date of requisition or construction, and an assessment of their current quality. This information can be analysed, and plans developed and implemented to:

‹ sell or remove surplus or obsolete assets
‹ update or replace assets
‹ set in place a system of renovation
‹ develop a process of maintenance.

This has unexpected benefits. The most important is that it highlights the need to create finance for maintenance of physical assets. The public sector health system rarely has such a financial system in place (pathology services are an important exception) and impossible needs for replacement and refurbishment have occurred.

Thinking strategically

The word 'strategic' has ominous meanings to some because of its military associations. However, in the health services, the term implies a need to think and plan for the long term—say, five to ten years into the future. Underpinning the notion of strategic thinking is the recognition of the many factors that impinge on the performance of the organisation or a particular service. Most management experts recommend that we continuously review the *Strengths* and *Weaknesses* unique to our organisation in relation to the *Opportunities* and *Threats* it is facing (SWOT analysis). We need to understand these forces, anticipate what might happen, make appropriate provisions and position ourselves for different eventualities. The notion of positioning is common in many areas. For example, a good tennis player anticipates where the ball might fall and seeks to be in a position from which to return the ball with most accuracy, strength and surprise. This way of thinking is also referred to as 'system thinking' in recognition of the dynamic interdependence among the many parts of the complex system we need to take into consideration.

Henry Mintzberg, the famed managerial analyst, argued that strategic planning has limited value, primarily because the future is so unpredictable.[8] We do not share his views. The future may be unpredictable but, if we have a map to help us navigate, when we choose a different path we know what we are deviating from and what we are deviating to. We further observe that, notwithstanding great uncertainty, some trends can be predicted with confidence. In the health service field, some trends are highly likely to continue. We have previously referred to them: continued rise in costs, continued increase in demand for health services, continued (for at least twenty-five years) ageing of the population, continued technological innovation. It may not be easy to predict the impact of these changes on a particular hospital or clinic but it is helpful to recognise major influences that may affect our future. As an example, a small non-government hospital in eastern Sydney, the Scottish Hospital, found its clientele diminishing. Clearly, the hospital was offering services that were no longer sought after. The management and board thought strategically, predicted future trends and needs, changed the role of the hospital and became very successful.

More difficult to predict are political changes. But often it is the rhetoric that changes and not the reality.

There is also value in developing a range of options that might be adopted according to a variety of changing circumstances. While it may never be necessary to implement any of the theoretical options, the exercise will educate staff to recognise that change has been, and will continue to be, a fact of life in the health service field.

EXAMPLE

A good example of the development of strategic options comes from a non-government organisation, the Crippled Children's Society of New South Wales. This organisation had developed a hospital for the care of poliomyelitis victims in the 1930s. When poliomyelitis was conquered by the development of the Salk vaccine, the role of the hospital changed to that of caring for children with asthma and a range of physical handicaps. By the 1970s, the need for hospital care of such children was rapidly declining and the management began to develop a range of strategic options that included entering the geriatric field, taking care of disabled adults and maintaining the status quo. This process prepared the organisation to make an even more radical change; namely, to sell the hospital for housing development and to use the financial resources for home-based care of disabled children.

Anticipating and responding to problems and opportunities

At present, there are adequate numbers of staff in most areas of the health services in New South Wales. But staffing is cyclical in terms of numbers, mix of skill and distribution; there have been shortages before and there will be shortages again. This is a good example of anticipating and responding to problems and opportunities. Staff require educating, nurturing, developing and belonging, and such activities should be promoted at all times, not just during periods of shortage.

Good managers also need to become opportunists. If objectives are clear, it is just a matter of waiting for the best time and opportunity. It is good to grasp the opportunity for widespread reform during a period of change, such as occupying new premises; for example, during the commissioning of the new Royal Children's Hospital in Melbourne in 1964 it was possible to introduce a wide range of reforms: open-hour visiting, improved medical records and links between specialist units. The changed premises prompted changes in the psychology and attitudes of staff, who began to initiate their own improvements.

More recently, in the 1990s, good managers in the health services have responded to the decline in Australia's economic fortunes by reforming workplace practice. These changes include multiskilling of staff in professional areas, such as laboratory technicians, and in support services, such as caterers, cleaners and porters. Multiskilling enables staff to do a wide range of tasks and has resulted in improved productivity. This would not have been possible in buoyant economic times because of opposition from staff.

Similarly, difficult economic climates have allowed opportunistic managers to close redundant hospitals and services and to redirect the resources to new fields of need. During the 1990s, literally hundreds of hospitals or departments in Australia were closed or their roles radically changed. Few of these activities would have been possible in earlier times.

Making decisions

There is a natural reluctance to make decisions, for to do so carries responsibility for the outcomes. However, the risks can be reduced by 'doing the homework'. The key preparation is the collection and analysis of relevant information, without being overwhelmed by minute details and conflicting advice. In the health service field there are three essential sources of information:

1 published biomedical and managerial literature, which can readily be obtained by computer searches
2 demographic and health status data published by government statistical organisations
3 data generated by individual hospitals and health services, which can be analysed and compared with data from similar services.

Because so many decisions have to be made in a brief time—regarding staffing levels, financial allocations, supplies—it is practical to confine the review of information to a level that will give a reasonable probability of making the correct decision. It is too slow and too expensive to collect exhaustive information on every issue. If the decision turns out to be wrong, change it. Do not procrastinate, as to do so is only making another negative decision. Having made the decision, it is reasonable to monitor and evaluate the outcome.

An essential part of modern decision making in Western countries is the process of involvement and participation by relevant staff and communities. Historically this was not so, and in some countries decisions remain the province of those in power. While such involvement inevitably slows the process of decision making, ultimately it is a beneficial process as the chance of attaining acceptance of decisions and willingness to implement them is greatly enhanced.

Such involvement must be sincere if the credibility of managers is to be preserved. Similarly, consultation should not necessarily imply acceptance of views by managers, who must ultimately bear responsibility.

Allocating resources

The allocation of resources is a major and important managerial responsibility. It is a more subtle and difficult process in the health service context than in many other fields, such as education, because clinicians—more so than managers—are required to make a great many decisions about individual patients, many of which will generate expenditure of finance. It is suggested that each clinician generates up to ten times his or her own income in diagnostic tests involving, for instance, X-rays, biochemistry and pathology, and further expense on treatments with medications and surgery. Virtually all these costs are outside the control of management, except in a very particular way—namely, the management decision to allocate resources to allow the employment of the clinicians. These decisions will determine not only future costs, but also the role and direction of the organisation; that is, towards surgery or obstetrics or paediatrics.

A current and important issue is the allocation of resources towards treatment services or prevention and health promotion. In our opinion, there are good arguments for seeking to allocate additional resources towards prevention and health promotion activities. Whether this should be by transferring to these other activities resources currently allocated to treatment or by expanding total expenditure beyond 8.5 per cent of GDP is a major issue. We argue for the transfer approach, however painful that may be. The reason is that other sectors of the economy, in addition to the health sector, have a major influence on health.

These sectors include education, policing, housing and transport—all of which need additional resources. Arguably, to add expenditure to health at the expense of these sectors could actually reduce the health status of the community.

In hospital settings, reallocation of resources can be a very painful process because all services have obvious value to both patients and staff (unlike public health, where the value of a health initiative, such as the adoption of a particular diet, may not be at all obvious). Comparisons between treatment services tend to come down to degrees of effectiveness; for example, the use of radiotherapy as compared with chemotherapy for cancer patients. As a result, the reallocation of resources between radiotherapy and chemotherapy departments is extraordinarily difficult.

Less dramatic reallocation of resources is involved in issues such as acute versus chronic care; for example, repair of fractured hips as compared with home-based geriatric programs. Reallocation of resources between medical services and allied health services may be necessary but has obvious difficulty given the power of one group of staff compared with others. Unless there are financial imperatives, it is difficult to transfer resources from clinical to non-clinical areas; for example, the medical record department has always been something of a Cinderella in hospitals—usually starved of staff and situated in the basement. It has had a major resurgence more recently because of payment to hospitals by DRGs, which are totally dependent on the medical records.

Teamwork

Teamwork does not just 'happen'; it requires much effort and goodwill. Teamwork implies interdependence. Teamwork occurs when people work together towards a common goal and are prepared to accept responsibility for the overall progress that is made. Teamwork may take different forms. The members may possess different skills and assume different responsibilities. Membership in the team may include various professions. The team members may be regarded as equal, or may assume different positions in a hierarchy. Whatever form or shape the team may adopt, the accent remains on the sharing of responsibility and expertise aimed at bringing the parts together in a combined effort.

Attainment of goals requires clear direction, proper distribution of labour, appropriate procedures and other organisational arrangements. Maintenance of teams often demands strenuous efforts to resolve conflicts and promote harmony.[9] It is apparent that effective teamwork is dependent on a predictable and common set of issues with which all teams must deal.[10] These issues stem from the reason for having the team in the first place—task interdependence.

As health services have become more technically based, and this has been followed by specialisation, it has become necessary for groups of up to ten or more from separate professional backgrounds to become involved in the care of an individual patient. This is particularly so with advanced and complicated surgery, but can also be the case with respect to chronically ill patients suffering from mental illness or the degenerative diseases associated with old age. In addition, teams of workers are required for the full range of clinical services needed in a hospital ward, as well as for the back-up services such as catering, cleaning and engineering. Accordingly, team building and organisation has become a key requirement in the health services.

Success is dependent on creating a climate of collaboration. This involves recruiting staff who by personality are 'team players' and are reasonably willing to reduce their own needs on behalf of the team. One of the key characteristics of successful team building is the development of relatively clearly defined roles for each member of the team. The best examples of this are the quite specific roles allocated to individual players in team games, where coaches have long learned the lesson that a champion team will always beat a team of champions.

How to improve team performance

In resolving team problems, it is important to proceed in a sequential order. Interpersonal problems (for example, 'We just can't get along') are more often than not symptoms of unresolved problems in one of the job-related issues (goals, roles and procedures). Teams very quickly see the logic of addressing the question: 'Who should be doing what?' (a role-type question) only after they have first come to an agreement on the question of 'what' (a goal-type question).

The procedural issues are contingent on the nature of the tasks and the participants. People tend to feel better about each other once they learn how to manage the issues that caused their interpersonal difficulties in the first place.

We observe how meetings often fail to address the agenda due to clashes and skirmishes among members. One may conclude wrongly that these people have inherent dislike for each other or that they carry personal 'baggage' that prevents them from cooperating. Our experience as team leaders has shown that the most common reason for communication failure is not personal relations but lack of understanding and acceptance of common goals and agreed roles and procedures. In other words, we argue because we talk at cross purposes, stepping on each other's toes and becoming frustrated about lack of progress. Difficulties in personal relations are most commonly the symptom rather than the cause of ineffective meetings.

How to focus your team energy

Goals are formulated with reference to needs and resources. This process, far from being objective, is political in nature. Perception of needs is sifted through the net of unique values, ideologies, orientations, norms, standards and vested interests. Team members often see what they expect or want to see.

In helping the team to formulate common goals, it is necessary to clarify the values and perceptions that underlie the choice of direction. It is necessary to review needs from different perspectives, to understand how they are interpreted by different team members. An opportunity must exist for members to define the needs and state the goals as they see them.

Involving team members in goal setting is likely to engender ownership and commitment. It is important, however, to set clear boundaries and to identify the discretion they may have. Certain goals may already have been determined at the higher echelon; policies and budgets may have been confirmed; external constraints and requirements may have been identified. The team members need to understand the situation and the rules of the game before they can fully contribute. Inviting them to make choices about things that have already been determined may cause them to feel that they are being manipulated. If they lose their trust in management the exercise of involvement may backfire and cause more damage than good.

How to define roles

Role conflict and confusion are common. To perform effectively, team members need to complement and support each other. It is not possible for all members to lead at the same time; for example, to complement the member who is providing information, there is a need for members who are willing to listen. If a discussion is heated, there is a need for somebody to contribute by relieving tension. Team members need to be sensitive to each other's expectations and flexible in the type of role they play.

What procedures does your team need?

Too little structure and too few procedures result in sloppiness and disorganisation, yet too many rules, regulations and standing orders block effective discussion and creative problem solving.

Since most of our cooperative work takes place in meetings, we shall concentrate on this aspect of teamwork. A universal problem with meetings is that they are often too lengthy, with little result to show for the effort spent. This phenomenon is usually due to lack of adequate planning. In setting the agenda, it is necessary to determine the topics and the outcomes (actions or decisions) that are expected to result.

In preparation for a meeting, it may be useful to distribute to members a planning slip requesting them to:

❮ list the topics they want to revise or discuss (or rank in order of priority a pre-circulated list of issues)
❮ specify the action or outcome they require (inform, consult, act)
❮ state the time they suggest should be allocated to each item.

A draft agenda is then distributed and agreement is sought on the priority of items and the desired action.

How do your team members relate to each other?

The focus of this section is on resolving interpersonal issues. Difficulties with interpersonal relations are often caused by unclear goals, ill-defined roles or inadequate procedures. At times, however, conflicts are caused by incompatibility among people. To explore such conflicts, it is necessary to pinpoint the specific behaviours that cause or contribute to negative feelings. Because the presence of tension makes it difficult for the people involved to explore their differences calmly, the help of a third party is often useful. A facilitator—a person independent of the group—may create conditions conducive to conflict resolution. Some of the important conditions are as follows:

❮ Both parties must be willing to admit that they may be part of the problem.
❮ Both parties must have an opportunity to ventilate or blame the other. This is a necessary release (catharsis) before people can discuss and resolve problems calmly.

‹ There must be a common definition and understanding of the problem.
‹ Both parties should feel confident that there is some binding quality to whatever agreement they reach.
‹ Both parties must receive something from the conflict resolution. This must be a quid pro quo.
‹ Both parties, with the help of the facilitator, should exhibit:
  – good listening
  – low defensiveness
  – ability to focus on the problems.

To help conflict resolution, the facilitator can invite both sides to identify the problem experienced, with particular attention to their contributions to the problem. Each should then state what he or she wants or needs from the other in order to feel more positive. It is helpful if each individual can suggest what first step he or she can take to solve the problem.

Having clarified the issues through active listening, there is a good chance that the 'tension' will be lessened and the parties will find common ground to permit a common problem-solving approach.

As in any other aspect of teamwork, there are no miracles. Some problems will be resolved only over time. Yet common sense, genuine effort and a lot of patience go a long way towards resolving most difficulties in human relations.

While teams and teamwork are of obvious value in response to continually increasing specialisation, this value must be balanced against the risk of diluting the acceptance of responsibility. In the less complex past, a single senior doctor accepted responsibility for the care of seriously ill as well as 'ordinary' patients. As teams of health professionals—such as the 'hypertensive' or the 'cancer' team—have come to care for patients, particularly those who are seriously ill in hospital, loss of responsibility and continuity has become a problem.

Negotiating

Negotiating is an intimate part of the professional manager's life. As shown in the section on what managers actually do (Chapter 4), senior managers may spend nearly all day every day conducting formal and informal negotiations. Obviously, it follows that to be a successful manager it is very helpful to be a successful negotiator.

There are many values inherent in negotiation. Our assumption is that the negotiators are honourable, trustworthy personalities who are seeking to do their best for their organisations and communities.

There are some simple guidelines. The main principle is that all parties to any negotiation believe in and have received a 'fair go', that there are no losers and that there are benefits for all. When there are losers, we prefer not to use the term negotiation, but to consider it domination by one interest group or person over another.

The most rewarding negotiations that health service managers may become involved with concern the development of health services for people and

case study when statistics become personal

Let us illustrate the second point. I [JSL] led a team that documented a high rate of severe lacerations occurring among children in northern Sydney as a consequence of falling or being accidentally pushed through glass doors or windows. We unsuccessfully negotiated for changes in the building codes directed at installing safety glass in high-risk areas.

Despite the most detailed statistics, progress was stalled on the quite reasonable grounds of cost until a government minister's 8-year-old child suffered horrific injuries after falling through a glass door at school. Within a matter of months, the building regulations were changed throughout Australia.

communities. These negotiations mainly concern the allocation of resources from governments and other sources of finance. In these circumstances, there are two basic necessities for the negotiator:

1 the availability of relevant information, particularly that which shows the comparative disadvantage of the negotiator's current resources
2 a good emotional case history to illustrate the situation—that is, a combination of statistics plus colourful examples that add meaning and that others can identify with.

A much more difficult negotiating area is in the field of industrial relations. The same guidelines apply; namely, the collection of information plus case histories. However, in addition to the issues at stake in a particular situation, industrial relations is very much about power. Great patience is required, as both sides are not acting for themselves but have a constituency that must be served. Again, sharing of information, courtesy and 'a fair go' all apply. From a manager's point of view, it is the long term that matters. Unions and professional association officials may well be aware that their case is unreasonable, but they cannot say so. If management's position is correct, then it may well be in the interests of both parties for management to hold firm and not to compromise. On the other hand, if there has been an unfair dismissal or an inappropriate use of authority, managers need to take the long view and seek face-saving compromises.

Very often the use of an independent facilitator (or arbitrator) can be very useful. There are guidelines and experiences that can be helpful to such facilitated negotiations. The first step is to outline the agreed-upon facts and information, as very often it is the information that is disputed.

The second step is to identify the points of agreement. Very often this will be a majority of them. The third and final step is to seek compromises or resolutions to the outstanding issues. If these cannot be resolved, then seek agreement to disagree at a later date. Above all, keep communicating!

Communicating

When staff in any organisation are asked what is their most immediate and important problem, they will nearly always say 'communication'. Why is it so difficult to achieve good communication in organisations?

One of the basic problems of communication in hospitals and health services is the continual change of staff. Such activity leads to great difficulty in maintaining adequate communication, particularly when the service is required to be provided on a 24-hour basis and therefore demands the use of shift methods of organisation. When there are such unstable and transient staffing patterns, the need for communication becomes even greater than it is in stable organisations.

The means of achieving reasonable communication in these circumstances inevitably relies on establishing a system that is standardised, so that changing staff will always use the same system. This means that staff have prepared protocols for their duties and that when their shift ends formal hand-overs are completed, both verbally and in written form. There is a strong and long tradition among nursing staff in this regard. Regrettably, this is not the case with many medical practitioners and other health professionals. Another means of communicating is to have group meetings at which affairs are discussed on a regular basis. These meetings demand time and energy, but are an essential part of the communication process in any organisation.

Hospitals and health services have a great deal to learn from other organisations, such as airlines and petrol companies, which have recognised the necessity of maintaining good information systems with the use of modern technology, particularly with computers. This means that, despite changing staff, information is always available at the press of a button.

Barriers to communication

Information bestows power and authority on the holder. Therefore, many of us confine information to ourselves or to a select group, in order to maintain control. This is seen in its most extreme form with respect to the development of new industrial technology, where the processes of manufacturing and the uses of technology are kept tightly secret for commercial purposes. While this has not been a tradition in any way in the health services, there are historical precedents in which treatments have been confined to individual families for generations, as was the case with respect to obstetric forceps. The altruistic philosophy of health services has been of major benefit to mankind, as openness and the sharing of new information has become a powerful tradition.

Another basic hindrance to communication is lack of trust among individuals. This translates into staff members not admitting to mistakes and therefore hiding information for fear of retribution. Hence, the need for the development of trust and good leadership so that staff can get on with their work, confident that inevitable errors of both chance and omission will be recognised and corrected, rather than remaining hidden.

Hepatitis B has become an important infection in Australian hospitals. An effective, inexpensive vaccine has been developed that prevents the development of the disease. Accordingly, a memo was sent from the state health department advising all hospital staff to have the vaccine. Despite the risk of infection, few staff members acted on the advice.

Why? There are several reasons.

First, the memo came from a distant bureaucracy. Second, the memo was merely one among many that were issued daily, and the detail was not read. Third, the memo was sent only to hospital chief executives, many of whom never passed on the information. Fourth, there was no education (apart from the memo) of staff about the issue. Fifth, there is an understandable fear about having injections. Sixth, there was no plan of action. Seventh, there was no follow-up, evaluation or monitoring.

For the desired action—namely, universal vaccination of hospital staff for hepatitis B—a mere memo was hopeless as a means of communication. An information campaign was necessary.

Conducting meetings

Meetings are commonly conducted in every organisation. In organisations as complex as hospitals and health services, managers will spend a good deal of their lives participating in and conducting them. Therefore, an essential skill is to be able to use the forum of a meeting to best advantage for both the manager and the organisation as well as for other participants.

Meetings are group processes. These processes can vary from the most formal meeting—such as the annual hospital meeting, which must by statute be carried out—to the many informal meetings held to discuss problems affecting patients and health services. There are a few simple messages about meetings we consider worth sharing.

‹ Keep them brief.
‹ Challenge their necessity.
‹ Keep a record of the outcomes of any decisions or resolutions that are made.
‹ Give everybody a fair go or in future they will not come and participate.
‹ Have a reasonably clear idea of the anticipated outcome of the meeting.
‹ Develop responsibility for follow-up action by way of negotiation at the meeting and by keeping a public record of allocated tasks, plus a delivery date.

Finally, take great care in choosing the chair of the meeting and the membership of any committee. Both the chair and membership confer power that can be very influential, particularly when resources are being allocated. There is said to be only one thing worse than being a member of a committee and that is not to be a member. Think about it!

All of this constitutes an art form that can be improved with experience.

When I [JSL] was a young hospital manager I took a week-long skiing holiday 200 kilometres from the hospital. However, some compulsion made me return midweek for the hospital board meeting. The agenda for the meeting has long been forgotten, but not the 400 kilometre return journey. Committees are where key decisions are made, or at least confirmed. Not to be a member or not to attend is to relinquish the major opportunity to influence events affecting the organisation.

Dealing with problems and conflict

To some degree, conflict is a normal part of human behaviour. Conflict usually arises because people perceive their needs as being different.

In an organisation with some thousands of personnel, it is inevitable that interpersonal conflict will arise on a regular basis. Indeed, interpersonal conflict can be one of the most difficult problems in any organisation, but there is a range of actions that can be taken to resolve it.

The first and the most important is prevention; that is, if possible avoid employing people who have strong records of being individualists rather than team players and who seem to thrive on conflict. If they are already employed, where practicable shift them to where they will do the least harm.

Modest levels of conflict are best overcome by seeking to improve communications, as very often conflicts are due to misunderstandings about certain information or about having no information at all. This is particularly the case when change is occurring. 'Integrative problem solving' is a term that has developed with respect to problems. It means that, if conflict arises, the participants work together in an open fashion to identify the problem and then work out a means of solving it.

This is tending to be regarded as preferable to solving problems by compromise. However, it does require an organisation in which there is a high degree of openness and trust.

Delegating

It is common practice for successful managers to delegate authority, responsibility and action to others. While such delegation may be good in theory and seemingly ideal in practice, there are problems with it; for example, there have to be competent people to whom work can be delegated, and this is far from always the case in difficult economic times. In addition, there have been many examples of inappropriate delegation to junior staff because of loss of incentives and loyalty to the organisation. A good and current example is in those countries where the senior medical staff have become estranged from their organisations because of

case study unresolved conflict

Mental health services are difficult both to develop and to manage. At one of four new community-based clinics in northern Sydney, an extreme conflict developed between the psychiatrist who had management responsibility for the clinic and a psychologist who had a heavy clinical load. The basic issue was the independence or otherwise of the psychologist vis-a-vis the psychiatrist. No amount of counselling, threatening or cajoling had any effect at all. The only solution was to separate them. We sent the psychologist to another clinic, with much loss of face. We chose to remove the psychologist rather than the psychiatrist on pragmatic grounds, because we had difficulty in recruiting psychiatrists, but not psychologists.

Managing strong personalities is not easy.

industrial disputes: with respect to patients who are classified as being public as distinct from private, fee-paying patients, they have delegated surgery and other major responsibilities to quite junior staff.

On a grander scale, there is no doubt that major organisations are slow to react if they are over-centralised: action is much quicker and more flexible at a local level. This is a common experience with respect to government-based activities which, in most circumstances, constitute modern health services. It is for this reason that there have been increasing efforts to reorganise health services so that authority is delegated to the lowest practical level. The most common form of such delegation has been the development of district or area health services for populations of 300 000 to 500 000 persons, in contrast to centralised bureaucracies that are responsible for populations running into many millions.

There is an amusing argument in favour of appointing lazy people as health service managers, for the very good reason that they delight in delegating the work to others. This is not so silly. Some of the most effective managers we know (no names) have been very responsible but lazy managers.

Some managers, unlike President Reagan (see page 92), have great difficulty in delegating. There are several reasons for this; the most common is insecurity, whereby managers lack confidence in both themselves and their staff and are worried that they may be blamed for any mistakes. Others do not delegate for fear of loss of power and authority. These problems can be very frustrating for those in subordinate positions who need to have greater responsibility in order to retain interest in their work and to develop their potential.

In current times, a very practical problem has resulted from the deletion of many middle-management positions: there is nobody left to whom the senior manager can delegate. An amusing outcome is the attendance of senior managers at typing classes because the cutback in staff, together with the availability of computers, has meant that even the trivial delegation of typing letters has had to be abandoned!

President Ronald Reagan was such a good delegator that some suggested he delegated the presidency itself. But this is not so. He set the parameters, he created the milieu, he defined levels of action beyond which it was not possible to move.

Delegation of authority in the health services has not been as dramatic, but over the years medical graduates have gradually delegated their roles. For example, my [JSL] doctor grandfather used to mix medications himself and conduct all his own tests.

Virtually no doctor on earth would do so now. As interns, we used to take and develop all X-rays ourselves. This has long been delegated to radiographers. We used to examine urine specimens, culture pus and examine cerebrospinal fluid, and make momentous decisions based on our findings. All this has long since been delegated to laboratory technicians.

Supervising

Supervision is a difficult task, but is it really necessary?

In an ideal modern world, groups of health service workers would begin their tasks early, cooperate with one another, care earnestly for their patients and stay on well after knock-off time. Experience indicates that about one-third of the health workforce not only do not require supervision, they work better independently. However, the balance—that is, the majority—without monitoring and supervision may be tempted to arrive late, do a modest day's work and leave early, and still believe they are doing a fair day's work. They do not perform for a variety of reasons that include changing attitudes towards work and work ethics and increased acceptance of the '9 to 5' mentality. Less than satisfactory performance may also relate to lack of job satisfaction. Family responsibilities are also a factor, particularly for women (who now account for a significant proportion of the workforce) for whom paid work is but one of a range of jobs for which they are responsible (including those of homemaker, wife, cleaner, child minder, cook and family accountant).

Hence the need for monitoring and supervision. The most ideal form of supervision is that provided by a supervisor who is really a mentor and teacher; this role is now common in the health services, where so many young health professionals model their careers and behaviour on superiors who may be doctors, nurses or pathology technicians. The monitoring role requires the supervisor to develop a range of specific goals and job specifications with the staff member. These specifications should include measures of output and performance. This is less important for professional staff than for members of the 'hotel' staff, but nevertheless applies to all members of the workforce. We recall a very well-known Melbourne surgeon who, as the paid surgeon to an accident clinic, talked for three hours about affairs of the world and reviewed precisely two patients. If only he had had a supervisor—and his output had been monitored!

Motivation

A commitment to success is obviously crucial to the manager. However, while humans are biologically similar, there may be substantial differences in their personalities and cultural backgrounds that determine levels of motivation as managers of organisations.

The commitment to success and to the organisation is legendary among the Germans, the Japanese and the Americans. However, even within these three cultures, individual managers vary enormously in levels of commitment and motivation

Attitude to work is affected by both intrinsic motives (such as self-satisfaction) and extrinsic motives (such as material rewards) and these may have different effects on different people at different times. As managers of people we need to understand what motivates our staff in different situations. Our managerial actions depend on our basic assumptions. If we assume that people are inclined to avoid hard work and responsibility, we may consider how to simplify and streamline their jobs and strengthen the supervision and control. If, on the other hand, we believe that people seek to contribute and extend themselves, our task as managers is to create conditions that releases untapped human energy and creativity (this dichotomy is known as Theory X and Theory Y).

From experience we know that, for a variety of reasons, 'work' has different meanings for different people. Our colleague, Anna Whelan, relates the story of the three stone masons who were asked to describe what they do. The first said he was paid to cut stones. The second replied that he used special techniques to shape stones in an exceptional way. The third smiled and said: I build cathedrals.

When we ask people to tell us about the meaning of work, some may tell us that work is a matter of survival; they work primarily to make a living wage and care for their family. Others may tell us that work allows them to relate to society, interact and develop relations with others, and provide opportunities to help others. Some may talk about developing self-respect, a sense of achievement, personal identity and status. Others may tell us that work helps them structure their time and even distracts them from worries, fears or depression.

How can we account for these differences between people and situations? And how will it affect our role in motivating others?

Three US theorists have provided the seminal work on understanding motivation based around levels of need; they are Maslow, writing in 1954,[11] Hertzberg in 1959,[12] and McLelland in 1961.[13] Each identified different levels of need. The first level is the need for survival; for a person to have sufficient food, drink and shelter, to participate in family life and to be protected from harm. The second level is the need to be approved, loved and appreciated by others, and the third level is the need to develop as a person and to obtain increasing satisfaction out of life. Levels two and three are heavily associated with the concept of self-esteem.

These levels were first defined by Maslow and subsequently expanded by Hertzberg, who labelled the basic level as 'maintenance'—relating to pay, job security and related factors—and the second level as 'motivation'—linked with the status of the job and the way employees feel about the work that they are doing. McLelland extended these theories of human motivation and developed the view that people have needs that to some extent involve affiliation with others, influence over others and achievement. Those with high affiliation needs work for the establishment of close, caring relationships with others; those who have high influence needs desire to have authority and power over others; and those people who are achievement-oriented seek job satisfaction from the results of their efforts. These theories of McLelland are particularly useful, because a good manager can seek to identify the prime needs of staff and to satisfy their needs.

Experience in the hospital and health care field strongly indicates that once basic needs of income and job security are met there is a high degree of satisfaction gained by staff at all levels, including management, by their affiliations and friendships with other colleagues. Equally important is the status offered by various jobs within the health services and the recognition given by the community for altruistic work. This recognition is a crucial motivating factor, particularly when the tasks needing to be done are frequently unpleasant. Accordingly, the enhancement of the organisation itself by managers becomes an important motivational factor for all staff who make up the organisation, because this becomes reflected in their professional pride and standing in the community. To this needs to be added identification or ownership of the organisation by those who work within it. Such identification leads to loyalty and trust, plus continuing incentives over a long period to do well. These old virtues are powerful motivating factors.

In recent times, as economic circumstances have become more difficult, survival of the organisation and the welfare of its workforce have both become top priorities. Hard-won experience has shown that ruthless and rational actions to reduce the workforce, reorganise and otherwise improve efficiency have a major adverse effect on loyalty and pride that can take years to remedy.

One of the recurring themes of management is: 'How do I motivate my staff?' It is helpful to begin by analysing the question. Firstly, there is a problem with the words 'I' and 'my'. No members of a modern organisation would accept such proprietorial language. They would expect terms such as 'we' instead of 'I' and 'our' or 'us' instead of 'my'. Modern organisations, particularly those with a high proportion of professional staff, are collegiate organisations to which all members of staff belong. If there is a need to motivate staff, it presumably means there is a major problem with respect to the culture and goals of the organisation, as professional staff by definition should be self-motivated (although in the real world that may not be so).

The need for health service organisations to have highly motivated staff is obvious. The problem is that the motivation of individual staff members will vary not only according to profession or job, but over time and at different stages of a person's life. For example, it is common for the priorities and motivation of both men and—especially—women to change when they become parents and accept the responsibilities of a family.

Furthermore, the personalities of individual staff members will often determine their enthusiasm and motivation. It is commonplace for some people to be vastly more ambitious, conscientious and motivated than others. Given these normal variations, can managers influence the motivation of health service staff? The brief answer is 'Yes'. The first step is to understand the motivational process and to learn to use it.

The motivational process

Motivation can be defined as the drive that moves a person towards achieving goals. Therefore, the manager needs to understand the basic need of staff. At the other end of the spectrum of need is the desire for recognition by others and for self-fulfilment.

Some examples illustrate these concepts well. During the 1970s, general medical practitioners in Canberra were paid in two separate ways: either with a fee for each service or by salary. While there was no apparent difference in quality of care, the doctors paid by fee for each service cared for approximately double the number of patients cared for by the salaried GPs. The motivation was clearly different.

Nurses have passed the first level of needs and currently complain that physicians do not accept them as full members of the health care team. They have clearly moved to higher levels of need. At a Perth hospital the chief executive officer was continually frustrated by his governing body, which could not allow him to make any significant operational decisions. Finally, he resigned. An analysis using Maslow's concepts suggests that it would have been ineffective to keep him in his job by offering a rise in salary; he had already passed through the physical needs level and wished to progress through the stage of self-fulfilment.

There is a range of motivation-related theories in addition to these of Maslow. They include Alderfer's theory, which suggests that there may be a range of needs operating at the same time.[14] McGregor's theory suggests that workers are motivated not only by the hierarchy of needs, as per Maslow, but also by identifying with the goals of the organisation.[15] Dewe has evolved a motivational theory based on equity.[16] He argues that individuals are motivated by their desire to be treated equitably with other individuals and with other groups. Further hypotheses include the expectancy theory, which links effort, performance and outcomes (most often rewards).[17] Finally, there is the goal-setting theory, which postulates that specific goals lead to higher performance than general goals and that difficult goals lead to higher performance than easy goals.

Arguably, all these theories have validity. It seems that they all contain motivating factors that operate either singly or in combination, at different times and in different circumstances.

The problem remains, however: how do managers motivate staff?

1   Working conditions and job security

The physical working conditions need to be as good as is practicable—clean, quiet and safe. The job needs long-term security. Despite opinions to the contrary, job insecurity does not lead to greater productivity; it leads to lack of loyalty. Combined with job security, there is a need for promotional possibilities—that is, for the development of a career.

2   Job specifications

Expectations and goals need to be defined. Rewards should follow the attainment of these goals, mainly in the form of recognition by peers and superiors.

3 Removal of constraints

There may be situational constraints that inhibit motivation and performance. For example, rotating shifts are a problem and cannot encourage the commitment gained from the continuity of regular timetables.

4 Recognition, praise, rewards

Recognition, as already stated, is an important motivator. To some extent, it has to be tailored to the needs of individuals. Some may respond to simple praise, others may need more formal recognition, such as in ceremonies and displays.

Rewards need to be tangible—money, promotion or increased responsibility. There are practical limits, but rewards have to be meaningful.

These approaches are commonplace in the hospitality industry, where photographs of the 'employee of the month' are displayed for all to see in the hotel lobby or the in-house magazine. Such simple and low-cost forms of recognition are very powerful sources of motivation.

Our experience in health service development in resource-poor countries convinced us of the importance of the formulation of goals, roles and procedures for staff morale and motivation. We found again and again that even if, and possibly particularly if, management cannot offer additional resources, people respond well when they have clarity about where they are going (goals and directions), what they and others are expected to do (roles), and how they get there (procedures). We came to believe that investment in a process of team planning that clarifies these issues is the most effective and lasting contribution we can make to staff morale. Most importantly, this process does not require additional resources and scarce extrinsic rewards—only respect, trust and mutual support.

Managing change

Change has become a continuing fact of life in the health service field. Managers have no choice but to give priority to the skills and stamina required to manage change successfully.

It is said by John Adams: 'All changes are irksome to the human mind, especially those which are attended with great dangers and uncertain effects'.[18]

Why are there so many changes in the hospital and health service field and why do people so often resist change?

The changes in the health service field are due to two powerful influences: changes in the national and local economy, and technological development on a worldwide scale but with major local impact.

Health services are totally dependent on the resources provided by general economic activity. Almost without exception, the amount of resources spent on health parallels an individual country's wealth; when national wealth increases or decreases, there is a direct impact on the health sector. In Australia, after a prolonged period of economic growth during the postwar period, expenditure on health rapidly increased. Circumstances changed in the late 1970s, and since that time the economic adjustments in the general economy have been reflected in the health services. This has brought about very painful change.

case study the motivated accountant

The demand for health services virtually always outstrips the availability of resources. This imbalance was particularly acute in the outer suburbs of Sydney in the 1970s, many of which had a 10 per cent annual population growth. One health service manager available was the obvious choice to tackle such a problem—an ex-accountant, Stan Billson.

Together we assessed the needs, which amounted to $130 million worth of new facilities, then we left him to it. Stan was amazing. Within three years he had mobilised 1200 volunteers, arranged to transfer money from one department to another, successfully lobbied for public funds, taken over unused school buildings, sold and bought real estate and magnificently achieved the objectives.

What motivates a person like Stan Billson? We discussed this with him on his day of retirement. He simply does not know. Perhaps he was unrecognised by his parents or school peers, perhaps his religious beliefs motivated him, perhaps building things gave him satisfaction. Yet he has a modest, quiet personality and does not seem to need memorials. Whatever the reasons, clearly his drive for achievement is unusual.

The changes brought about by developments in technology have been previously explained. The impact of such change is well understood and accepted in the health field.

Studies of change

The motives of people who plan change are very much like the motives of people who resist change. Where a person stands in relation to change is strongly influenced by where he or she sits.[19] Resistance arises when an individual or group perceives a change as a threat to the security of personal advantages associated with the status quo.

Conversely, resistance may also arise as a result of the anticipated disadvantages that accompany change.[20] Resistance to change is a natural phenomenon experienced by all employees who, to varying degrees, will resist the loss of what is familiar and dependable.[21]

Countless sources of resistance to change have been identified by numerous authors. They largely fall into two categories: one arising from a lack of knowledge, information, skills and managerial capacity and the other deriving from the reactions, perceptions and assumptions of individuals or groups in the organisation. Typical sources of resistance include:

〈 lack of information—people resist because they do not comprehend the need for change, the substance and details of the change or the consequences of the change
〈 a fear of loss of power, status and pay
〈 low-trust organisational climate and poor relationships between employees and managers

‹ lack of core skills and expertise
‹ poorly managed projects—staff will resist a change when they feel that the project is disorganised, poorly thought out and flawed
‹ an existing organisational culture and tradition that supports the status quo
‹ lack of leadership and direction, which promotes the level of uncertainty already inherent in the change process
‹ management's disregard of employee concerns, opinions and inputs
‹ inadequate resources allocated to the change process, including both funds and people.

Successfully managing the implementation of change will involve the identification and recognition of resistance-type behaviours and the sources from which they arise. This will allow the development of appropriate strategies to minimise the barriers to change. The program's success will also depend upon the relationships established in an organisation over time; trust and open and frank communication are products of long-term commitment to those ideals and cannot be manufactured overnight.

The question of trust is a crucial one. This was confirmed by our own studies of managers. Trust was one of the virtues held without exception by all successful public sector managers.[22]

Given a situation in which change is inevitable, requiring a reduction in staff without a reduction in workload, good morale or staff relationships, what approaches to change should be adopted?

The first step is to seek to share as much information as possible and to keep on sharing over the long term. It may not be possible to share all information, because local management is forbidden to do so by others—usually the head office—for commercial or political reasons. If this is the situation, staff should be informed that some information is confidential and that there are good reasons for this to be so.

The second step is to keep talking and to keep communicating. Such communication has been found to be essential. People are much more worried by the unknown than by even quite bad news.

The third step is to seek to act in the interests of staff by actively pursuing other jobs for them and by resisting any attempts to make them redundant. Staff are the essential resource in any hospital or health care system, and to lose them is a long-term disaster.

The fourth step is to seek to involve staff in the process of change; to seek to have them review future plans and be involved in implementing any change in direction. Remember that people do not resist change; they resist being changed, having change imposed on them.

The fifth step is to provide people with the opportunity to retrain themselves to acquire the new skills that may be needed as a consequence of the change.

Finally, good leadership is required, along with the age-old virtues of truth, trust, stamina and lack of self-interest.

The Eastern Sydney Area Health Service has a great many hospitals serving a declining population. The quite reasonable policy is to transfer resources from this health service to areas of greater need. The change in resources is dramatic and involves approximately 25 per cent of total running costs. It has required closure of hospitals, reduction of staff and consolidation of services—all extremely difficult and painful. However, these changes have been achieved without strikes, without a major public outcry and with an increase in the number of patients treated!

The management, led by an experienced health executive, Bill Lawrence, have implemented these changes according to all of the principles outlined in this chapter. The management have kept the staff and the community fully informed; their actions have been rational and reasonable; and, above all, they have created a climate of trust. No staff have been dismissed, jobs have been found for those made redundant and all major productivity gains have been achieved to such a degree that the Eastern Sydney Area Health Service was awarded the gold medal for achievement by the International Hospital Federation in 1994.

The success of change will inevitably reflect the soundness of interpersonal relations within a particular hospital or other health service setting. Trust is a major issue. If managers are trusted by staff, change can usually be dealt with positively. If managers are not trusted, change can ruin the organisation. For example, during the early 1980s in an Australian health department the management leadership dealt with change by simply transferring staff away; there was no regard for past service or for the skills staff had to offer. The surviving staff learnt not to trust the leadership. The leadership never recovered and, in turn, was also transferred elsewhere.

Team approach to change and development

A team approach to change and development includes the following:

‹ *Wholistic approaches.* Because the health system is complex, piecemeal approaches to development which focus on isolated factors, important as they may be, fail to produce results.

‹ *Integrating development.* It is ineffective to separate the development of people from the development of the systems they operate. Such separation is a major cause of irrelevance, difficulties in transfer, lack of ownership and insensitivity to constraints.

‹ *Need for guidance.* The people who operate a system have a practical understanding of how it works and how it can be developed. They need to be guided through a systematic process which enables them to clarify and negotiate directions, roles and procedures.

‹ *Learning by doing.* The participants in this process benefit from the opportunity to reflect on their experiences at work. They learn best by doing, and while in a supportive environment which permits self-direction and involvement.

‹ *Problem solving.* Given the opportunity and the encouragement, participants are able to examine real problems, in the context in which they arise, with the people on whose cooperation they depend for successful implementation of change.

‹ *Involvement.* It is important that the participants identify what needs to be changed and how the change can be made. What they decide at a particular time is an indication of what they understand, accept and are capable of doing.

‹ *Analytical skills.* Through participation in such activities, the participants identify deficiencies and design procedures to meet the unique needs of their health system. Through this process they develop skills which can be applied to other areas.

‹ *Team development.* By participating in this process with others, they create better working teams with mutual goals, clear roles and supportive interpersonal relations. These relations enable them, in turn, to maintain a momentum for improving related aspects of their work.

Acting as a politician

Readers will have noted the emphasis we have put on the political processes involved in management—the use of power, the need to manage conflict, the securing of resources, the need for committee skills. Indeed, it can be argued that unless managers can develop these skills, they are doomed to be ineffectual.

Many students ask us how you can learn political skills. The simple answer is—not out of a book! It seems that political skills need to be developed from first-hand experience. No doubt reading will help, and certainly observation of skilled practitioners is of advantage, but nothing takes the place of actually doing it!

Political experience needs to be incremental. The first experiences may well be as a participant in committees, as the manager of a staff roster or the person responsible for hospital admissions. Each of these seemingly simple roles is in fact bristling with politics as participants in the committees, the staff roster or the admissions process strive for position and advantage. Political errors at this level, while unpleasant, are not of great importance; however, they are an invaluable part of the process of accepting greater responsibility and developing keener political skills.

At each level of responsibility it is worth reviewing your own performance, identifying your successes and failures, and learning from the experience.

Industrial relations

Industrial relations have become a major concern for hospital and health service managers. The principles involved are no different from those previously discussed, but it is important to keep in mind several key (but often overlooked) points.

1 Industrial unions, professional associations and any group of staff have representatives who conduct negotiations. These representatives are not free agents; they must be constantly aware of the views and feelings of their constituencies. There may well be occasions when it suits them to have negative outcomes from a negotiation—they know the claims are outrageous, but dare not share their personal opinions with the membership.

2 In most situations, problems are caused by both parties to a dispute (this is no different from problems in marriage). By both parties, we mean management as well as staff. For example, management may have failed to provide adequate understandable information; in turn, staff may have failed to read or listen to the information provided.

3 Senior management, not the personnel manager, should take an active part in industrial relations. The issue of managing staff is too important to delegate to others.

4 In the hospital and health service field, staff are by far the most important factor in the provision of good services. Hence, industrial relations and management of staff are of the highest priority.

The importance of industrial relations and the need to give staff support and a real sense of 'belonging' has been realised since the 1983 doctors' strike in New South Wales. A decade later, considerable bitterness and alienation remain between some medical staff and the public hospital system, and there is experience that suggests these attitudes have adversely affected the care of patients.

For managers, the central question is: 'How can good, sound industrial relations be established and maintained?'

The answer is through involving staff in decisions that are relevant to them, recognising the value and contribution of staff members and, above all, giving staff a feeling of pride and ownership in the organisation. These requirements cannot be created overnight. They need long-term nurturing and commitment by both management and staff.

From time to time staff will seek improvements in pay and conditions. Such claims may well lead to conflict. If good relationships have been established between staff and management, such conflicts can be tolerated; however, if there are bad relationships, any major conflict can be disastrous.

Objectives, aims and goals

Management by objectives (MBO) became fashionable as a style of management in the 1960s. Military forces have managed for centuries by using quite specific objectives. There is some difficulty with the word 'objective', however, because over the years the military has also used words such as 'targets', 'aims' and 'goals', all of which can be regarded as meaning the same thing.

Although books and learned papers have debated the advantages and disadvantages of managing by objectives, in our view the process has stood a very long test of time. Managing by objectives needs to be practised with common sense; setting unattainable objectives is of little value. However, the setting of realistic objectives has major advantages; it clarifies the role of both organisations and individuals and allows the development of priorities for the achievement of those objectives.

Surprisingly, many managers have difficulty in clarifying their objectives. Yet if objectives tend to be obscure, there is little chance of them being achieved.

With respect to hospitals and health services, it is best to develop a range of objectives so that advances can occur on a reasonably broad front. This is because

We were in trouble. The personalities among the senior echelons of the state health service were pursuing their own survival while we were battling to maintain services to the public. We sought the help of Peter Davenport of the international management firm, PA Management. He rapidly helped us to clarify our objectives and develop plans to achieve them; they were (a) put the public interest first; (b) cover our backs by ensuring every cent of public money is accounted for; (c) balance the budget.

Why could Davenport be so helpful and be paid a hefty consultant's fee for offering such seemingly simple advice? Again the reason is simple. He was not emotionally involved; he could think ahead with clarity. We were threatened with loss of our jobs and prestige, and looming bank mortgages, and had difficulty thinking and acting clearly.

so many tasks in the health field take years to achieve; if objectives are taken one at a time, then progress across many important matters is far too slow. On the other hand, the number of objectives must be achievable.

It is very pleasing that, after a lapse, health departments around Australia are again developing specific goals and targets related to the improvement in the health status of the community. The Australian government's 'goals and targets' policies outline an enormous range of diseases and current problems—such as heart disease, cancers and accidents—and offer specific means of reducing their incidence and introducing more effective treatments.

The New South Wales Department of Health has developed similar policies, referred to as 'outcomes'. In addition to the national goals and targets, 'outcomes' policies include improvements to clinical practice, such as reducing surgical interventions when other options may be preferable. These programs are essentially aimed at increasing awareness and activity in the fields of evaluation and effectiveness.

Survival tips for health service managers

We finish this chapter by offering some tips on how to survive as a health service manager. They are based on hard-won experience rather than the usual mandatory, scientifically controlled trial; nevertheless, we believe they are helpful.

Collect and analyse as much information as you can

We believe it is a basic requirement for all successful managers to collect and analyse all the information they can about an issue before commenting or making any commitment. This is relevant advice regardless of the issue. It is particularly important when selecting new staff.

By way of an example, we recall a disastrous appointment that was the direct result of poor homework. A new planning officer was needed and the advertisement attracted many good applicants; however, we chose a young man with an academic background because of personal recommendations from his superiors. What his superiors did not tell us was that he lacked judgment and knowledge, and that he was lazy and financially bankrupt. He sat on a government salary for five years and finally left because of boredom.

Always be polite, courteous and kind

It is imperative to be polite, courteous and kind to your friends, your enemies and, above all, to those people whose influence you may perceive as negligible. While these are sound principles of civilised behaviour in any community, they are underpinned by a strong element of long-term self-interest. Friends, enemies and the uninfluential can all become influential as time goes by and circumstances alter. A colleague of ours was always kind and helpful to his subordinates—which was just as well, because his deputy ran for parliament, was elected, was appointed minister and so became his rather tyrannical boss. In contrast is the story of the head of the United Nations' Headquarters Division, who heaped derision on one of the divisional leaders. This person was subsequently appointed boss of the whole organisation. The divisional head lasted just ten days.

Never go over your boss's head

Even if it is a matter of life and death, do not go over your boss's head. Human nature has evolved over millennia. We are a group species, and groups need leaders. To challenge your boss means you are challenging basic biological instincts! When you approach a higher authority without involving your immediate superior, you are challenging his or her authority. You are inviting that superior to strike back—perhaps not today, but certainly tomorrow. I [JSL] made that mistake just once. I was very angry about some long-forgotten issue and wrote a letter of complaint to a superior authority, sending a copy to my immediate boss. The adverse consequences of that hasty action took years to resolve.

People who are apparently mature go over their bosses' heads all the time because they perceive immediate rewards as preferable to long-term gains. They have little insight into the power of the boss, who can quietly subvert a subsequent career in a host of ways; for example, by making adverse comments in selection committee meetings about an applicant's lack of commitment to the organisation, by offering faint praise with respect to a research application, or simply by failing to inform someone of career opportunities.

Always arrive for work early and leave late

Although there is no substitute for substance, impressions are crucial. Managers should lead by example. If you arrive for work early and leave late, inevitably you will be perceived as a person committed to the cause—even if you spend the middle of the day in the library and the legitimacy of that activity is not so obvious.

We have an accountant friend from Thailand who was dismayed to be reprimanded for laziness, as judged by his persistent late arrival at work. What the boss did not know was that Cliff Thai would spend nights working on a client's financial audits. Despite explanations, the adverse perception remained.

Suggesting that managers should arrive early and leave late is a way of illustrating the need to 'lead by example'. Credibility is an important managerial attribute and to be successful, managers need to demonstrate that they are hard workers, that they are competent and that they place the needs of the organisation and its staff before their own needs.

Set goals and objectives

Seek to develop objectives for yourself, the organisation and the community. Personal goals and objectives can be very helpful, particularly if they are divided into short-term and long-term issues. Despite the fact that external circumstances, such as job availability, will have a major effect on your career, it is amazing how often people with clear goals achieve them regardless of whether or not opportunities are available. Similarly, if simple goals can be identified for the organisation, most often they can be realised. The development of goals for the community may seem obscure and outside your field of influence; however, both you and your organisation are part of the community and can have some influence on its future direction.

As newly appointed leaders of health and education services in Australia, we found it possible to develop quite specific objectives with respect to health and education outcomes for the community that included reducing heart disease and lung cancer as well as implementing a range of health services, such as geriatric and mental health, and health promotion services. Over a period of five years all these objectives were achieved, primarily because of the setting of goals and targets. This is in contrast to many other health services, where no such goals were developed and after twenty years there are few effective basic services.

Take time

Remember, Rome was not built in a day. It normally takes about five years to achieve substantial change. Think about it: it takes about one year to become trusted, a second year to develop plans and achieve agreement, two further years to implement the changes and a final year of consolidation. We refer here to organisational changes, which require alterations to people's jobs and ways of working, including their attitudes to themselves and their work. It obviously takes much less time to introduce new technology, such as computerisation or laboratory machinery.

Therefore, be patient; be prepared for a key player to be conservative. You may have to wait for his or her retirement or death before progress can be made. Here are two examples.

‹ The chairperson of a major teaching hospital saw the hospital as a personal memorial. He obstructed all efforts towards coordination and cooperation with other services. He only dealt with the health minister himself—in his terms, he was highly influential because he owned a string of radio stations. He severely restricted progress, then suddenly died of a heart attack. Progress was immediate thereafter.

‹ Professor Vernon Collins, a revered Australian paediatrician and director of Melbourne's Children's Hospital, had a finely developed long-term view of events. The hospital had become greatly concerned about the lack of a specialist neurologist. After failing to make progress, Professor Collins was consulted. We learned that, years before, he had encouraged a young paediatrician to specialise in neurology in the United States and to ultimately return to Australia and meet the needs of the hospital. Within a year, this long-term goal had been achieved.

Be committed

Being a successful manager is most certainly not a 9 to 5 job. Success requires commitment 24 hours a day. The 'normal' office hours have to be spent encouraging and consulting colleagues, participating in meetings, conducting field visits, reviewing, receiving reports and negotiating with other organisations. The end of other people's ordinary day is the time to undertake written work, reading and telephoning peers who are too busy to be contacted during the day.

This need for commitment is well illustrated by John Paterson, a reformer appointed to improve the performance of a water supply authority. It took him the full five years already indicated to achieve his objectives, but when compared with the 200-year history of the authority, this was a relatively short period. He spent the days talking, educating and negotiating. He spent the nights preparing documentation. The outcome was a 50 per cent fall in costs produced by a system of 'user pays' that achieved full recovery of costs, plus extension of reticulated water and sewerage to the whole community.

Treat committees seriously

To be a good manager, skill in committee work is essential. All democratic communities are ultimately run by committees. Resource allocation is largely determined by a committee.

The first message is to become a member of the most important committees. If you are not a member, it is very difficult to influence events. The second message is to try to become the chairperson, as chairpersons are much more influential than mere members—this is because the chairperson controls the agenda and often achieves a quasi-executive role. The third message is to learn and develop 'committee skills', which include the following considerations:

‹ *Timing*. Speak only occasionally, towards the end of a discussion, in formal, important-sounding language with appropriate *gravitas*.
‹ *Facts*. Objective data, simply presented, constitutes by far the most influential factor in determining the outcome of committee meetings.

However, be wary about presenting threatening data at meetings. If the information is important, share it with other committee members well before the meeting to allow participants to become accustomed to any difficult implications.

‹ *Deferral.* Be prepared to defer decisions until later meetings. Again, this will allow participants to consult others and to assimilate the need for change.

‹ *Popularity and respect.* Never be guilty of 'putting down' a committee colleague, particularly in public. If you differ profoundly, seek deferment and subsequent consultation. Seek to support your committee colleagues on less substantial matters so that they will support you when needed. Remember, however, that what is substantial to you is often not substantial to them.

‹ *Records.* Most committee members will forget the outcome of meetings; therefore, keep a record. In the long term, the written word has much greater influence than the most elegant spoken word.

‹ *Homework.* If the issues are important, consult and lobby committee members well before the meeting. Few of us will make major decisions without ample warning, consultation and deliberation. Such consultation also provides intelligence; for example, who supports and who is against a particular course of action. Retreat, live to fight another day, if the numbers and support are not there.

‹ *Follow-up.*

Always be honest

We do not mean honest in the sense of not guilty of theft, but in the trustworthy sense. Experience has shown that, if managers are two-faced, overanxious, not willing to share information, unfair, or offer favours to some but not others, they will ultimately fail because their colleagues simply will not trust them.

Honesty and trustworthy behaviour are most often based on familial and childhood experiences and are difficult to acquire in adulthood. It is worth being aware of the issue, however. The need to be honest does not mean that all information has to be shared. Clearly, information about candidates for appointments cannot be shared. Equally, sharing the whole truth about a colleague's personal traits may be positively harmful. I [JSL] am reminded of my 94-year-old mother who, to the best of my knowledge, has never spoken a hurtful word throughout the twentieth century (she was born in 1899). She can always find something nice to say about everybody, including a complimentary comment about the lovely, shining hair of the most unpleasant woman I have ever met! Mother does not tell the whole truth, but she certainly helps maintain the harmony.

Remember the 'F' management guidelines

Try to keep the organisation of your hospital and health service:

‹ flexible (responsive to change)
‹ focused (with clear objectives)

- ‹ friendly (with good staff relations)
- ‹ fun (with staff who like going to work)
- ‹ flat (with no management hierarchy)
- ‹ forward-thinking.

Employ the loose and tight management approach

Loosen the management structure of your organisation so as to encourage local decisions, to improve its quality and to reduce costs.

Tighten up accountability. Do not delegate management of financial resources. The concept of clinical managers is a fine one, but clinical managers have divided loyalties and must lobby on behalf of their clinical divisions. They cannot be expected to cut their own budgets to please the hospital board—they may as well cut their own throats (in managerial terms!).

Loosening the management structure and tightening accountability go hand in hand. The challenge is to achieve the right balance.

Reflections for the reader

There is no difficulty in outlining the basic requirements for successful managers. However, management does not consist of a list of isolated skills. Managers are people who are complex and whose attributes change over time. Success does not require the complete set of attributes—indeed, highly successful managers can be readily identified who have characteristics that may well be opposite to those on the list! It just goes to show that management is a complex matter.

The question for readers is: 'How do I gain these skills?'

The first step is to reflect on yourself—do you have these skills? If not, can you gain them? Do not be disappointed if some of them are unattainable. The ability to cover missing skills—by delegation, by enthusiasm or whatever—can be acquired or cultivated.

The second step is to observe managers who use these skills successfully.

The third step is to try to use the skills in the workplace. By a process of trial and error, you can develop most skills to a reasonable level.

There is no better teacher than experience. Try to continue reading, reflecting and gaining experience. It takes time to become accustomed to the exercise of authority, to have to take unpopular decisions, to balance the interests of the organisation with those of the patients and clients. Becoming a successful manager is a gradual process.

6

Quality of care

The provision of safe, high-quality health care has precedence over all other health care issues and is by far the most important single management responsibility for clinicians and health service managers.

Historically, communities have simply assumed that health care is safe and of the highest possible quality. This view has been reinforced by the repeated rhetoric of our parliamentary leaders that 'we have the best health care in the world'. Recently, these assumptions have been rudely shattered by reports of many deaths due to 'adverse' events in Australian hospitals and clinics.[1] The incredible number of such deaths—allegedly 3900 per year in New South Wales alone, has led to much scepticism about the validity of these numbers. We have reviewed the published data relating to these incidents and conclude that, while the estimated numbers of adverse incidents is exaggerated, there is cause for serious concern. The apparent exaggeration appears to be due to the inclusion of adverse events where the patients would probably have died regardless of the quality of care and where high risk interventions were performed in a last hope of achieving survival.

An 'adverse' event can be defined as an event where the quality of care was less than expected. Our review confirms that such adverse events occur on a regular basis in Australian hospitals and clinics. On the other hand there is evidence which suggests that the quality of care for the vast majority of patients is extremely high. For example, the death rates from anaesthesia have halved every decade since 1960 and the deaths associated with childbirth have been virtually eliminated.

These general statements need to be given meaning by way of examples.

The question that arises from these case studies is: 'Why are exemplary standards of clinical practice achieved in some cases and appalling disasters in others?' There are no simple answers. However we know what does and does not work in some clinical areas.

high-quality care for a woman with a serious back injury

This 36-year-old mother of two boys experienced excruciating pain extending down the right sciatic nerve. The pain was so severe she could not get out of her car and had to be examined in the shopping centre car park. Magnetic resonance imaging demonstrated the likely cause of the problem was a large fragment of an intervertebral disc situated on the sciatic nerve. Immediate surgery allowed the removal of a 2-centimetre long fragment. She made an immediate dramatic recovery. There were no complications due to infection, haemorrhage or skeletal damage. The assessment and care of this patient exploited modern technology backed up by sound communications and skilful care by experienced, careful clinicians.

accurate diagnosis and skilful surgery following a serious eye injury

A 26-year-old police officer fell from a 10-metre diving board while skylarking at a city swimming pool after the annual police ball. Some weeks later he experienced double vision and collapse of the tissues surrounding the left eyeball. A diagnosis could not be established until he was assessed by an opthalmologist who had substantial experience in emergency departments in the United States. The police officer had fractured the left inferior orbit with damage to the associated nerves. After carefully explaining the risks of remedial surgery the opthalmologist repaired the damage and achieved a perfect outcome.

a tragic outcome for a young woman with uterine fibroids

A 44-year-old woman underwent a hysterectomy for fibroids and menorrhagia. On the seventh postoperative day she suffered a small but significant pulmonary embolism. Intravenous heparin was commenced. She haemorrhaged from the operative site. This problem was not recognised and she died of blood loss.

It later became apparent that the haemorrhage was an unfortunate consequence of an excessive dose of heparin. This adverse event occurred during the night, when the care was given by a nurse who had no training or experience in the use of a heparin infusion pump. The nurse was unaware of the consequences of administering excessive heparin. This nurse, who has been badly affected by this event, was not at fault. This tragic adverse outcome was due to a complicated range of factors associated with the organisation of the hospital, difficulties in recruiting experienced staff for unattractive night shifts, lack of awareness by senior medical and nursing staff of the dangers associated with such treatment—all compounded by financial restraints.

A 70-year-old woman developed a small carcinoma of the left kidney. This was a skilful and accurate diagnosis. On behalf of the patient the surgeon prepared the consent for surgery form. Unfortunately he erroneously wrote (R) instead of (L). The wrong kidney was removed. The patient did well postoperatively and survived for three years before dying of her renal cancer.

Surgery on the wrong side is the ultimate medical disaster. In this case the surgeon must accept responsibility, but there is little value in simply attibuting all the blame to him. Evaluation of this case revealed a range of systematic problems (problems with the organisation and circumstances in which the surgeon operated).

Successful experiences which enhance quality of health care

There are two ways in which the quality of health care can be improved.

1   *Sound education of health care professionals.* Nearly 100 years ago, Abraham Flexner reviewed the quality of medical education in the United States. He demonstrated that unregulated medical schools produced graduates of disturbing variability in quality. As a consequence, medical schools throughout the world have been independently regulating the quality of their teaching and graduates. In addition, virtually all types of health care professionals must be licensed to practise. In other words, it has become illegal to offer services to the community as a doctor, nurse or pharmacist without a licence attesting to graduation from an independently assessed educational institution.

    This regulation and policing of standards has been beneficial, however there is a major gap—namely, there is little meaningful mandatory continuing education of health professionals. In most Australian jurisdictions medical practitioners are required to provide evidence of continued education in their field of clinical practice. However this falls far short of the demanding continuous monitoring of, for example, airline pilots and yet the responsibilities are equally onerous.

2   *Regular auditing of poor outcomes.* During the past fifty years every maternal death in Australia has been audited. Where poor outcomes are judged to be a consequence of poor quality care, those responsible have been counselled. Independent observers agree that this approach has been extremely effective. Similar approaches have been adopted in the field of infant care, anaesthesia, coronary surgery and transplant surgery, with similar positive outcomes. However, these approaches have not been adopted in many other fields of clinical practice.

Unsuccessful experiences of quality enhancement

A range of very well-intentioned activities which are embraced by the term 'quality assurance' has been instituted. These activities range from inspections by government agencies of the general hygiene of hospitals to random audits of clinical records. While these activities have probably had a positive influence, their success is overshadowed by some stunning failures.

The most notorious failure became known as the Chelmsford affair. Chelmsford was a small private hospital in suburban Sydney where a group of like-minded psychiatrists practised what was known as 'sleep therapy'. This treatment involved sedating patients to a level of unconsciousness for periods of up to four weeks. The practice of sleep therapy had little scientific validity. Inevitably, some (possibly twenty-nine) of the patients died over a period of eight to ten years from sedation-induced respiratory problems. These practices continued, despite the deaths, until medical and nursing colleagues 'blew the whistle'.

Also in suburban Sydney, a public hospital was awarded 'high approval' by a quality assurance program. Two weeks later the senior managers were dismissed from office because of a series of patient deaths associated with preventable adverse events.

The main reason for the failure of quality assurance programs such as that one is that they have been imposed by outside agencies and as such are regarded with suspicion by medical and other health professionals. This has led to active avoidance of accountability to these agencies by the key participants in health care.

The catastrophes just outlined are quite unacceptable. Unfortunately, there are many additional catastrophes which are known to occur regularly in the Australian health care system (there is substantial anecdotal evidence in support of the published data relating to the incidence of adverse events in health care). An initial step forward is to give consideration to some of the factors which influence the quality of care. These include:

‹ avoidable and unavoidable inequalities in the provision of health care in differing geographic locations
‹ the different standards of care in central teaching hospitals as compared to some suburban hospitals
‹ the value placed on experience and skill among health professionals
‹ the application or otherwise of evidence based medicine.

There are unavoidable inequalities in health care in any community. The obvious Australian example is the impossibility of providing care in the outback as rapidly as in a central urban situation. Much less obvious is the differing standard of care between a major and a suburban centre. This latter problem occurs largely as a consequence of the democratic system of government which we enjoy, but it should be added that substantial differences in quality of health care exist in totalitarian countries! In the fight for voter support, our parliamentary representatives promise and deliver hospitals and clinics despite the advice that such facilities will be impossible to staff. A good example of this phenomenon is in the Central Coast to the north of Sydney, where the government of the day insisted that a new hospital should be provided 15 kilometres away from an existing good hospital facility. The purpose was to gain voter support in a swinging electorate. Despite advice that it would be impossible to attract professional staff, the project went ahead and has been a continuing problem with respect to the low quality of its services.

The serious nature of this disparity in quality of care between a central and a suburban hospital is illustrated by the two case studies opposite.

While youth has its advantages there is real value in clinical experience as demonstrated in the following case history.

For those interested in the value of a second opinion in serious circumstances we suggest you read Lance Armstrong's book.[2] Armstrong, the multiple winner of the cycling classic the Tour de France, developed testicular carcinoma with metastases to the lung and brain. He was offered several treatment options but demanded and received additional advice which literally resulted in not only resolution of the cancer but also retention of his physical prowess.

New ways forward

New and very exciting concepts and practices aimed at enhancing the quality of health care have evolved during the past decade. These concepts have in part evolved from experiences in the air transport field. The terms may be different but the principles are the same for both air transport and health care.

Institutional responsibility and accountability

As members of independent professions, health care practitioners such as doctors, nurses, pharmacists and laboratory scientists have traditionally regarded their particular professions as being the custodians of quality of care. Given the evidence that health care is extremely variable in quality, this tradition of unaccountable (to the community) professional independence is no longer tenable. Accordingly governments, area and district health boards, hospital governing authorities, senior managers and above all clinicians of all types must be required to ensure that safe, high-quality care is being provided. This development has become known as 'clinical governance'. The definition of 'clinical governance' is an evolving one, but is essentially concerned with issues of quality of clinical care.

This change has come from a deeper understanding of human factors and of systems approaches to quality. In the past, the quality of health care delivered to patients was 'doctors' and nurses' business'. It is becoming appreciated that it is also the responsibility of boards of directors to govern for safety and quality. Boards must set the strategic direction, allocate sufficient resources, monitor quality of care and make hard decisions to ensure safe care is actually occurring in their facilities.

The term 'clinical governance' emerged in the United Kingdom because of concern about the quality of care being offered to patients in National Health Service

case studies

sound care in a central facility

A 65-year-old man from the eastern suburbs of Sydney developed crushing chest pain. He presented to the emergency department of a central teaching hospital. Despite the absence of classic indicators of coronary artery disease an experienced physician was able to diagnose severe cardiac ischaemia. A stent was immediately inserted into his obstructed coronary artery and he made an uneventful recovery.

poor care in a suburban facility

A 55-year-old man from outer suburban Sydney experienced severe chest pain. He was assessed by a junior medical officer at the local suburban hospital (there was difficulty in recruiting experienced physicians to cover the roster). As the cardiac investigations were negative the patient was sent home with a letter to his general medical practitioner. Two weeks later the patient presented to the same hospital because of worsening crushing chest pain. Cardiac investigations on this occasion indicated a myocardial infarct. It was recognised that the patient would benefit from an intra-arterial stent but there was great difficulty arranging transfer to an inner city hospital where this procedure could be carried out. After a prolonged and hazardous delay the stent was inserted, by which time he had suffered irreparable damage to his myocardium.

An 81-year-old man with severe spinal canal stenosis, multiple sclerosis and cardiac arrhythmia developed difficulty passing urine. Rectal examination revealed an enlarged prostate. He was referred to a young urologist who immediately arranged to carry out a transurethral resection of the prostate, despite the extreme risks in such a patient. The family sought a second opinion. The patient was commenced on medical treatment of his prostatism after which he passed urine satisfactorily and did not ever require surgery.

(NHS) hospitals. The most widely used definition of clinical governance is:

> A framework through which NHS organisations are accountable for continually improving the quality of their services and safeguarding high standards of care by creating an environment in which excellence in clinical care will flourish.

The essential features of clinical governance are as follows:

❬ A duty to ensure delivery of quality care is placed on the governing authorities of health care services.
❬ Patient-centred care is at the heart of every health organisation. This means that patients are kept well informed and are given the oppourtunity to participate in their care.

‹ Good information about the quality of services is available to those providing the services as well as to patients and the public.

‹ Doctors, nurses and other health professionals work in teams to a consistently high standard and identify ways to provide safer and even better care for their patients.

‹ Risks and hazards to patients are reduced to as low a level as possible, creating a safety culture throughout health care services.

‹ Good practice and research evidence is systematically adopted.

The importance of the philosophy—patient-centred, safety conscious, multidisciplinary in delivery—is emphasised along with the methods to be used, such as continuous improvement at a number of organisational levels, tackling variation and using evidence.

The challenge of implementation

The concepts of quality and clinical governance have been widely accepted but the problem of implementation remains.

Implementing clinical governance requires the transformation of culture and ways of working, of attitudes and of systems in local hospitals and health care organisations. It must become a way of working and a way of thinking. Clinical governance is about changing the way people work, demonstrating that leadership, teamwork and communication are as important to high-quality care as risk management and clinical effectiveness.

Understanding error and human factors

Fallibility is part of the human condition and, although we cannot change the human condition, we can change the systems in which people work. This concept requires moving away from the blame culture to an understanding of the human factors and system cause of error.

'Human factors' are defined as the study of the interrelationship between humans, the tools they use and the environment in which they live and work. The work of the psychologist James Reason has been particularly important in the study of human factors. Reason developed the concept of the 'Swiss cheese' approach to incidents. He proposed that in any system there are a series of barriers to harm, but within these there are gaps. When the gaps are remote from the actual coalface they have been defined as 'latent errors'—in other words, hidden or waiting to happen. When an operator makes an error this is known as an 'active error', which exposes the latent errors and allows a disaster to happen. In any system errors are occurring all the time, but disasters do not occur because of all of the defences built up to protect the system. A disaster occurs when gaps in the defences against harm all line up.

It is helpful to return to the case of the wrong-sided kidney surgery to illustrate these concepts. A series of mishaps collectively led to the disaster.

The patient did not speak English and could not communicate without an interpreter. At the end of a long day and the previous night without sleep, the surgeon erroneously wrote (R) instead of (L) on the consent form. The patient could not read the consent form, the English-speaking relatives did not understand the abbreviations (R) and (L) for right and left. When the patient was admitted to hospital, the incorrect side was entered into the patient's file from the consent form. The hospital was chronically understaffed and no medical or nursing clerking and checking occurred on the ward. When the patient was checked into theatre, no family member attended and there could be no communication with the non-English-speaking patient. The theatre nurse could not, as is usual practice, confirm the side of the procedure. The operating theatre was running over schedule. The operation started after 6 pm when the private radiology (where the X-rays were performed) was closed and there was no way of chasing up the pathology and X-rays which were missing from the patient's file. The active error was the surgeon removing the wrong kidney, but a chain of latent errors lined up to allow the disaster to occur. Almost certainly surgeons write the incorrect side for operations from time to time, but wrong-sided surgery is comparatively rare because of all the other checks and balances. Punishing the surgeon will not prevent this from happening again. Fixing up all the system errors will (including training the surgeon to write out the full side, not just a symbol).

A change in culture

The turn of the twentieth century saw the rise of the great individual clinician, as exemplified by Sir William Osler. At the same time the practice of registration of doctors was instituted. This meant that rigorous training and examination was required before a person was allowed to practise medicine.

The concept of individual excellence and accountability has served us well over the last century. However with the sophistication of treatment regimes such as those used in cancer, trauma, cardiology, mental health and intensive care it is becoming increasingly apparent that multidisciplinary teams perform much more safely and effectively than individuals, no matter how brilliant. So the culture in hospitals has changed from individuals working on their craft to groups of professionals working together as a team.

Evidence-based medicine

'Evidence-based medicine' can be described as clinical practice that is based on sound evidence. Over the last ten to fifteen years it has been realised that much of what is taught and practised in medicine is not based on sound evidence, but passed on from generation to generation. So there has been a determined push to insert intellectual rigor into the evidence for therapeutic regimes. This in turn has led to determined efforts to convert evidence into practice through the implementation of evidence-based guidelines into clinical practice.

The active participation of consumers

The consumer has been recognised as the centre of all clinical activity. Systems and practices are being built around the need of the patient rather than the convenience of the clinicians—with dramatic improvement in efficiency and patient satisfaction.

Consumers are now represented on all major quality initiatives.

Implementing the big picture for quality

The development of a comprehensive plan to improve safety and quality rests around the following key elements:

❬ standards and guidelines
❬ inspection/clinical audits/monitoring to ensure that standards are being met.

Standards

Standards should include the following elements:

❬ staffing
  – ratios
  – competencies
  – supervision
  – training
  – role delineation and development
❬ leadership structures and performance
❬ equipment requirements
❬ processes such as daily ward rounds, handover.

Best practice guidelines

There should be regularly updated guidelines on how to manage common conditions such as breast cancer, lung cancer, melanoma, prostatism, depression and so on.

The following sources should be used:

❬ Guidelines Clearing House
❬ Cochrane Foundation
❬ National Health and Medical Research Council
❬ Cancer Council.

Inspection/clinical audits/monitoring

There should be a rigorous process of inspection of hospitals to ensure that standards of quality and clinical governance are met. In particular, there needs to be rigorous inspections for standards of patient safety. Such inspections could be based around the following:

- mortality for common, high-risk situations
- surgery-associated infections
- the occurrence of skin pressure ulcers
- the incidence of thromboembolism.

Safety improvement programs

The prime purpose of a safety improvement program is to make health care safer by constantly correcting system vulnerabilities. Until recently, it was common for incidents arising in health care to be blamed on the individual. However, this response is changing to a recognition that people do not come to work to do a bad job or make a mistake, but certain circumstances and the work environment combine to result in unwanted outcomes. Health care workers do not work in isolation. The cause of problems leading to incidents is usually found in the design of the system that permitted the event in the first place.

Root cause analysis has the following characteristics:

1 It focuses primarily on systems and processes, not individual performance.
2 It repeatedly digs deeper by asking 'Why?'
3 It identifies changes that could be made in systems and processes—through either redesign or development of new systems or processes.
4 Its focus is not punitive.
5 It digs into existing systems to find new ways to do things.

There are occasions, however, when a root cause analysis is not appropriate. These include:

- when there has been a criminal act
- when there has been an intentionally unsafe act
- when the act was related to alcohol or substance abuse of an impaired provider or staff member
- when the event involved alleged or suspected patient or staff abuse of any kind.

Action following an adverse event

The following actions might be taken when an adverse event or near-miss occurs:

- *Immediate action.* When an adverse event or near-miss occurs immediate action may need to be taken—such as removing a piece of faulty equipment from use.
- *Notification.* The adverse event should be notified to the patient manager.
- *Authorisation and involvement by senior management.* When an adverse event or near-miss occurs it should be confidentially notified to senior management. The senior manager should authorise and assist with the appointment of a small group of appropriate experts. The objective for the expert group is to develop actions that will prevent the adverse event from recurring. Recommendations should be made which will eliminate, control or accept the risks involved. The group should not include the individuals involved in the event, but should include staff as close to the 'action' as

possible so that the process and the solution is owned by them and does not come from 'big brother'. The group should then present the outcome of their investigation to the senior management for consideration and implementation.

Reflections for the reader

> Have you ever been involved in an 'adverse event'?
> What effect did it have on you?
> What effect did it have on your patient's welfare? What was the 'root cause' of the adverse event?
> Were any changes made as a consequence of that adverse event; and if so, what were they?

> Were any individuals blamed for the adverse event?
> Now that you have read this chapter, would you have handled the adverse event in a different way?

Further reading

The following publications provide further insights into the issues explored in this chapter:

< LT Kohn, JM Corrigan & MS Donaldson (eds), *To Err is Human: Building a Safer Health System*, Institute of Medicine National Academy Press, Washington DC, 1999.

< J Bagian, L Caryl, J Gosbee et al., 'Developing and deploying a patient safety program in a large health care system: you can't fix what you don't know about', *Joint Commission Journal of Quality Improvement*, vol. 27, 2001, pp. 522–32.

< J Bagian, L Caryl, G John et al., 'The Veterans Affairs root cause analysis system in action', *Joint Commission Journal of Quality Improvement*, vol. 28, 2002, pp. 531–45.

< C Vincent, S Taylor-Adams, J Chapman et al., 'How to investigate and analyse clinical incidents: clinical risk unit and association of litigation and risk management protocol', *British Medical Journal*, vol. 320, 2000, pp. 777–81.

< J Birkmeyer, T Stukel, A Siewers et al., 'Surgeon volume and operative mortality in the United States', *New England Journal of Medicine*, vol. 349, no. 22, 2003, pp. 2117–27.

Health service finance

Financial matters concerning health have dominated the attention of governments and health service managers for the past two decades to the detriment of issues concerning health status.

The cost of health service provision is a problem so complex and great that it is helpful to consider these matters under three key headings:

1 Why are hospitals and health services so expensive?
2 What can be done about the cost of health services?
3 Managing the money

Why are hospitals and health services so expensive?

There are three basic reasons:

1 the labour-intensive nature of health services
2 the impact of health care technology
3 the increasing expectations of citizens for even better health care.

The cost of labour

In economically developed countries with high labour costs, there have been modest improvements in productivity with respect to the hotel and financial components of the hospital and health services. For example, the development of mechanical washing machines has substantially reduced the cost of laundry. In addition, the use of disposable surgical packs and disposable plates and eating utensils, and the computerisation of patients' records, in particular their accounts, have all reduced labour costs.

On the other hand, despite advances in technology, the basic requirements for support from health service staff for individual patients remain necessarily high and increasingly expensive. For example, if a doctor is paid $150 per hour, the actual costs for discussion and assessment of a patient for an hour will include not only the doctor's income, but also all the back-up services for the doctor. This may include his or her component of the personnel service, office overheads, medical indemnity insurance and other costs, all of which can add an additional 50 per cent or more to the hourly rate.

It is equally alarming to consider the case of the nurse who receives, say, $25 per hour. For that nurse to provide counselling to a patient and his or her family, when overhead costs are considered, will cost $8 for every 15 minutes of attention.

These costs of labour have been exacerbated by changes in medical technology. Most, though not all, changes bring about an increase in costs. For example, the development of a new biochemistry test to measure the hormone levels of an infertile person is an additional cost; new ceramic joints are innovative but expensive; diagnostic technologies that provide images of parts of the body, such as computerised X-ray scanners, the electromagnetic wave and other highly sophisticated scanners, are magnificent technological advances but come at a colossal cost.

Unfortunately, this sophisticated new technology also has considerable overtones of prestige. Therefore, just as every nation feels it must have an airline as part of its national image, so every country seeks to have at least some share of the new medical technology. Hence, the situation arises that in quite poor countries, such as China, some of the major cities have more CAT scanners than are in New York.

During the past decade, however, a number of new technologies have evolved that have replaced expensive inpatient surgery, thereby allowing substantially reduced costs.

Of particular relevance is the development of keyhole surgery—using micro-surgical techniques and conducting the operation through tubes—that allows quite sophisticated joint, abdominal and brain surgery to be undertaken on a day-only basis. Similarly, other technologies have enabled the dissolution of gall-bladder stones, the shattering of stones in the kidney by ultrasound and the removal of the prostate gland by laser technology, all of which have removed or reduced the need for surgical intervention and hospital admission. Many of these new technologies can be done on a 'day surgery' basis which increases the number of patients that can be treated in the same facility—thereby reducing the per patient cost of each operation. However, while these new techniques replace former more expensive technologies, at the same time they have led to an increase in the range and types of procedures that can be performed, which in turn increases costs.

Incentives to spend

Almost all health services, regardless of the particular financial arrangements, offer substantial incentives for ever-increasing expenditures. Even in health care systems that are totally government-dominated, such as those seen in the former communist countries and to a similar extent in the United Kingdom and New Zealand, there are substantial incentives to spend. First, individual doctors and nurses have been brought up in the entirely appropriate ethos of doing everything possible for an individual patient. However, as the range of health services that can be offered to each patient expands, there is an accompanying increase in expenditure. In addition, politicians and administrators, whether socialists or capitalists, fall prey to the temptation of developing memorials for themselves, seeking community support or just seeking to do good. This leads to unwise decisions to build hospitals where they are not needed and clinics where there are few people to use them, and also encourages hard lobbying for medical technologies that are inappropriate.

Another factor concerns the relative ease with which community leaders are able to raise funds for health services from the community. Health services proposed on behalf of patients with cancer or of mothers and babies are emotionally appealing, and funds can readily be raised to buy new equipment, construct a building or provide a new vehicle. Rarely do these fundraisers consider that the real cost will not be in the capital expenditure, but in the continuing running cost. The running cost of a modern hospital for a single year currently approximates the capital costs of construction.

SOME EXAMPLES

The Launceston General Hospital (LGH) in the southern Australian state of Tasmania was refurbished and renovated to a very high standard at considerable expense. Because the LGH serves a politically sensitive area, a political decision was made to construct a completely new hospital—in addition to the old one! This was despite the fact that the area at the time had the highest hospital bed-to-population ratio in Australia.

In Newcastle, New South Wales, the local community raised funds for a new radiotherapy unit. The fundraising was so successful that there was enough finance for two sophisticated radiotherapy machines, which were immediately purchased despite the lack of need.

Fear of litigation has become a major incentive to spend. Although in comparison with the US experience the number of successful cases claiming medical negligence is low in Australia, there is widespread fear on the part of doctors and other health care professionals that they will be sued. The problem is not so much the amount of litigation payout, but the potential and actual stress and loss of credibility likely to be incurred. Accordingly, health professionals in general, and medical practitioners in particular, seek to cover all risks by ordering a range of tests and offering treatment such as antibiotics that, although justifiable, may not be necessary and can be very expensive. We recently surveyed all practising obstetricians in New South Wales regarding their attitudes to litigation. All except one respondent, an academic obstetrician, indicated that they were concerned at the prospect of litigation and that their practices and procedures were correspondingly affected. This is the practice of 'defensive medicine'.

The problems surrounding medical indemnity insurance in Australia were highlighted when United Medical Protection Ltd was placed in provisional liquidation with unfunded liabilities estimated to be around $400 million. As part of a federal government-funded rescue package there will be a financial levy on doctors in addition to their huge (in excess of $110 000 for some specialist medical practitioners) medical indemnity insurance premiums. Obstetricians, orthopaedic surgeons, neurosurgeons and procedural GPs—those who deliver babies and conduct minor operations—will be hit the hardest. Inevitably, these costs will be passed on to patients.

It is often believed that in a government or semi-government health service the managers have no incentive to spend. This is not the case. Very often the salaries of managers are linked to the size of their establishments and their prestige among peers is determined by the responsibilities they carry with respect to the quality of health services and the range and complexity of the services offered. Accordingly, there is considerable pressure for managers of government health services to gain as much money as possible from the government, and at least more than their colleagues in other areas or departments.

Modern pathology services have become increasingly technical. Whenever a newly developed analyser, microscope or blood cell counter becomes available, there is an almost instant demand from all hospitals in all countries to have one. Most hospital managers respond. As a memorial to this collective folly, there are literally thousands of machines sitting on laboratory benches either unpacked or with dust covers undisturbed because there was no need for the new machine, or the staff could not make the machine work, or the hospital could not afford the chemical reagents. We have personally observed this phenomenon in countries and laboratories as diverse as the Royal Melbourne Hospital, the Canton Central Health Laboratories in China and the Western Samoan Central Hospital in Apia!

'Open-ended finance'

In nearly all countries, the costs of health care are met by a so-called third party. This means that neither the provider (for example, a doctor) nor the patient actually pays the full cost of the service. The money is paid either by governments or by some form of insurer. If the provider is paid on a fee-for-service basis, there is an enormous incentive to keep busy. The inevitable consequence is that, overall, health systems that are funded on this fee-for-service basis are extremely expensive. The classic examples of such a system are those of the United States, Canada and Australia.

In a fee-for-service system, the costs can be kept under control if there are relatively few providers. The providers become so busy and financially successful that they have no more time for additional work and therefore do not increase the overall costs of service provision. However, when the number of providers exceeds a certain level, the tendency is for the work to expand to fill the available time and, given the nature of clinical practice, it is possible to legitimately generate more work. The same circumstance applies to diagnostic services and the various therapies. This is not necessarily an argument against the fee-for-service system, but the experience of the United States is salutary—20 per cent of all health expenditure goes into administrative overheads, primarily because of the handling of literally billions of individual accounts.[1] This is in marked contrast to the Canadian system, immediately to the north, where administrative costs are less than 5 per cent. In Australia, the experience has been similar to that of Canada. The cost of Medicare—a central government insurance agency—in place of the previous fragmented system of health insurance, plus firm budgetary controls, has stabilised expenditure on health services.

These adverse comments about payment of providers for individual services do not mean that there are no good features of such systems.

Clearly, the link between money and service can be an intimate one, leading to continuity of care between the patient and the provider. Fees for services rendered can provide a major incentive to provide 24-hour care by the one person, a service rarely achieved in salaried and other similarly funded health services. Studies in Norway have shown that the satisfaction level of patients is seven times greater when continuity of care is provided by a single doctor, as opposed to a succession of doctors.[2] This study confirms the personal experiences and wishes of many patients. In addition, the fee-for-service system is efficient where there is pay for actual work done, as distinct from effectively paying a retainer when there is no workload.

Another more subtle problem with salary-based systems is that many providers weary of handling other people's problems and, to a lesser or greater extent, seek to escape into quasi-managerial roles. Such roles can be pleasant, of high status and very non-productive. We recall a senior salaried anaesthetist who naturally tired over the years. He gradually gave up clinical work and created a nice teaching and managerial role for himself on full senior specialist pay. Other staff had to be employed to do his clinical work.

What can be done about the cost of health services?

The cost of health care systems, as exemplified by the United States, has become so great that in theory, if trends continue, health care service costs will ultimately consume a nation's total economy. While clearly this is impossible, it has been argued that expenditure on health care in the United States is so vast that it diverts money from the nation's other welfare priorities. To this must be added the problem of achieving equity for all, since fully 30 per cent of US citizens have some form of disadvantage in accessing good-quality health care.[3]

The available evidence from comparative international studies strongly suggests that the best way to control health care costs is through various forms of global budgeting.[4] By the term 'budget' is meant the allocation of a fixed sum of money for the provision of a defined hospital or health service. In this way, the managers and health care professionals providing those services are forced by the economics of their situation to determine priorities for all their activities with respect to numbers and types of patients seen, services provided, numbers of tests ordered and variety of treatments offered.

Among the OECD countries, this approach has been reasonably effective in controlling health care costs in the United Kingdom, Canada, Australia and New Zealand. In these four countries, the quality and range of health services provided matches that of other OECD countries, but it has been achieved at half to two-thirds of the expenditure of the United States. This is despite the introduction of payments by governments in the United States to certain sectors of the population (the aged and indigent) to allow a fixed sum to be offered to a provider for a defined service. While this US system, based on diagnostic related groups (DRGs), has proved to be very helpful, it is still open-ended; hospitals are free to generate services they decide are desirable, even though they know they will be receiving a predetermined sum of money for each service. This is in contrast to other parts of the US health care system—in particular, the health maintenance organisations, which have very effectively controlled costs, primarily through systems of budgeting.[5] In other words, a fixed allocation of a sum of money for a range of services appears to give the best result, whether or not that budget is determined by government or non-government organisations.

In our view, perhaps the ideal form of funding is that which has been adopted in the government sector of the health services in New South Wales, Australia.[6] In this state, with a population of approximately 6 million persons, 80 per cent of hospital beds are quasi-government-owned and virtually all services for the seriously mentally ill, as well as a wide range of community-based services, are also government-owned and government-funded. Most medical practitioner services and pharmacies in the community are financially supported, on a fee-for-service basis, through a universal health insurance scheme with a single national insurance agency. For government services, budgets are allocated on a population basis. Weightings are made with respect to these budgets according to historical patterns of expenditure; patient flows; the age, range and structure of the population; and levels of mortality and morbidity for the given populations. These budgets are then allocated to individual hospitals and other health services, taking into account a range of factors including historical funding, but also indications of activity as measured by diagnostic related groups.

This is a fairly simplistic summary of the funding mechanism, which has had the enormous advantage of keeping health expenditure under control over the past decade. At the same time it has allowed for the redistribution of income for the state as a whole, to take account of the growth and changing age structure of the population, while at the same time achieving very substantial improvements in productivity and redistribution of resources.

In direct contrast is the fee-for-service sector of the health services in New South Wales. These services are predominantly provided by private medical practitioners, where approximately three-quarters of the cost is reimbursed to the patient or direct-billed by the doctor to the national insurance fund. The cost of these services has escalated by approximately 5–10 per cent each year in the last ten years on a per capita basis, and is a cause of great concern.[7] Similarly, there has been growth in the open-ended provision of private diagnostic services, in particular pathology and radiology services. Again, the growth in these services on a per capita basis has been great. In an effort to address these problems various pilot activities are under way, nearly all of which have elements of a budgeting process in mind.

This Australian experience is very similar to that of Canada and the United Kingdom and to other English-speaking countries (apart from the United States), where expenditure on health overall has been maintained at a relatively constant level for the last ten years. The essential element in both of these services is the use of budgets, as distinct from open-ended fees for service or payment for individual items of work.

On the other hand 'mixed' systems of funding offer considerable promise. The best current example is in Victoria, Australia, where 40 per cent of funding to hospitals is offered by governments by way of payment for each patient treated. The level of payment is calculated by diagnostic related groups. The balance of the hospital's budget (60 per cent) is a block grant paid as a 'contract' for a range of services. This system provides incentives, and efficiency has been improved by 15–20 per cent in the first year of operation. The major issue with respect to payment systems based on DRGs is that priority and prestige may be offered to curative services that are of short-term duration and serious, long-term conditions may be downgraded.

National economics versus health economics

Health and other welfare services are paid for by economic activities elsewhere in the economy. As such, although health is a prime requisite for human wellbeing, it is dependent on the success or otherwise of the general economy. This raises the question as to how much a country should allocate to health expenditure. During the past decade, many of the OECD countries have stabilised their national expenditure on health at a level around 8 per cent of GDP. There are two major exceptions: the United Kingdom at a much lower level, 6 per cent, and the United States at a much higher level, around 14 per cent. However, the use of international comparisons based on health expenditure as a proportion of GDP needs care. There is considerable overlap between the health and welfare sectors, and the allocation of expenditure to either sector differs between countries. In addition, if the overall economy is expanding the proportion spent on health will appear low, as expanded expenditure on health takes years to achieve—entailing, for example, the building of additional hospitals and the training of health professionals.

There cannot be an exact level of expenditure on health services that is correct for any particular country because there are so many historical, cultural and financial factors involved.[8] In OECD countries, the major growth in the proportion of GDP spent on health occurred during the 1960s and 1970s, when the proportion nearly doubled from 4 to 8 per cent. This was quite extraordinary, because during the two decades of the 1960s and 1970s the mortality experience of the OECD countries had not improved, meaning that a doubling of expenditure had brought about no gain in health status.[9] The health status gains that then took place in the second half of the 1970s and throughout the 1980s were almost certainly brought about by a range of factors that were of limited relevance to the provision of health services. These factors were predominantly changes in health-related lifestyle behaviours such as the reduction in tobacco smoking, the reduced intake of saturated fats, the increase in exercise and the reduction in the number of traffic accidents. Perhaps the greatest assistance given by health services was in the more universal control of hypertension by medication, and by the continued development of vaccines for the prevention of communicable diseases.

The figure of 8 per cent of GDP therefore evolved predominantly because of the capacity of OECD countries to spend that amount of money on health services. Health expenditure expanded during the 1960s and 1970s basically in response to the demand for increased hospitals and health services, as distinct from a measured need. If health services are rigorously examined and a need is assessed according to a specific reduction in mortality or morbidity, then it is possible to reduce health expenditure from the 8 per cent mark to somewhere near 5 per cent. However, this requires the elimination of such services as the use of ambulances for patient transport, as distinct from lifesaving emergencies; and the use of radiotherapy for palliation, as distinct from lifesaving reasons. It also requires strict control over the use of antibiotics and other medicaments according to scientifically-based clinical guidelines, and the restriction of hotel services in hospitals to basic necessities.

High-quality health services, including a range of supporting welfare services, could be financially supported for all the community at around the level of 8.5 per cent of GDP in OECD countries in 2001. This is patently true, as it had already been achieved in most of Western Europe, Australasia and Canada.

A new look

Few health service managers will have the opportunity to directly influence national health care expenditures. However, as informed citizens they can and should seek to influence the priorities for financial allocation and to ensure efficient and effective expenditure.

Accordingly, health service managers need to have a sound knowledge of public health issues in general and the effectiveness of health care services in particular. A simple but very useful message is for the manager to imagine two unlikely situations: first, that there are no existing health services and second, that the current health service budget can be allocated accordingly to his or her wishes.

This is the concept of 'zero-base budgeting'. It is amazing how differently individual managers in this hypothetical situation allocate resources in comparison with historically-based allocations. Most often, such managers seek to achieve a good balance between preventive and health promoting services, hospital and community-based services and long-term care services. However, in the real world few health managers will offer to transfer finance from health to other sections of the economy, despite the better health outcomes that may be achieved. For example, it is probably more effective to transfer all funds allocated for lung cancer surgery to school-based anti-smoking education programs.

Our colleague, Dr Chris Scarfe, who was regional director responsible for health services in Sydney's vast western suburbs, often commented that he could develop top-class health services for his region well within existing financial

case studies the use of comparisons to cut costs

While in government-dominated systems major changes to funding of health services will be determined centrally, it is possible to improve productivity and reduce costs at a local level. The key is the concept of comparisons.

Example 1

We compared the cost of food at a large public teaching hospital in Sydney with that at a private hospital. The public hospital costs were exactly double and the quality no better, despite the use of the same food system. The reasons—excess staffing due to union power, excess costs of food transportation, excess waste. Improvements were achieved by managerial intervention, but the private costs could not be matched.

Example 2

We compared staffing levels between hospitals of similar size and with similar patients in Sydney. The difference was up to 30 per cent for a similar quality service. Staffing reductions were achieved following protracted negotiations (plus the use of power by the central funding authority).

Example 3

The costs of anti-cancer medications in several Sydney hospitals were doubling in each successive year. This experience was not shared by comparable hospitals and was beyond the funding authorities' capacity to pay. The cancer specialists were asked to examine their current prescribing patterns, to develop guidelines for treatment and to move towards some form of priority-setting based on potential benefit to patients. This simple request had a dramatic effect, with costs reduced by half with no apparent deleterious effect on patients.

resources if only he could have a free hand at allocating the finance and there was no commitment to historical patterns of expenditure.

Even though it will never be possible to have such a free hand, the concept of zero-base budgeting is extremely useful. Priorities can be clearly developed, and policies aimed at achieving a balanced health service can be created and implemented over time. Experience suggests that about 1 per cent of a global health or hospital budget can be reallocated each year to different priorities without causing too much pain. The 1 per cent does not seem much, but over the years implies a very substantial shift in resource allocation.

These principles, while most appropriate to area-wide health services involving over one million citizens, can also be applied to local circumstances such as a laboratory or a simple hospital ward or clinic.

The public/private mix—the issue of privatisation

In countries where hospital and health service provision has been dominated by governments, attempts have been made to reduce expenditure from the public purse by increasing the private sector involvement. This almost universal phenomenon has occurred in such disparate countries as China and Vietnam, as well as in OECD countries such as Australia and the United Kingdom. By implication, it has not occurred in countries such as the United States because of the predominance of non-government involvement in the provision of health services. In summary, the issue has been economically driven.

The term 'privatisation' in this context was initially used to describe the transfer of ownership and management of publicly owned assets or businesses to the private sector; for example, electricity and water supplies and, more lately, communications and aviation. In quite recent times privatisation has been considered for public health and welfare services.

It is helpful to distinguish between privatisation, involving transfer of ownership from the public to the private sector, and commercialisation, which involves the purchase of goods and services from the private sector for use in the public sector. Commercialisation—or outsourcing—has been a feature of public health services for over a century. Typically, this has involved hospitals purchasing from the private sector such basic hotel supplies as food, as well as surgical instruments and a range of other equipment. A relatively recent development has been the purchasing by the public health sector of services such as cleaning and catering. Even more radical have been the attempts to sell public hospitals to the private sector and to get private entrepreneurs to build private hospitals on publicly owned land adjacent to existing public hospitals.

There appears to be no criticism of commercialisation. We have only to look at Eastern versus Western Europe to see the advantages of competitive market economies. Market processes appear to have particular advantages for the supply and purchase of goods, but of services to a lesser extent. The commercialisation of services has introduced an element of competition into the public hospital sector, but this element has diminished since it has become evident that existing public hospital services can compete very effectively with the private sector. A further point is that monopoly situations may readily evolve in relation to services such as cleaning and catering, introducing all the adverse consequences implicit in monopolies.

The limited experience of privatisation involving public hospitals and clinics provides a powerful argument for caution. This view is based on a series of economic experiences in other sectors of the economy. For example, studies by Domberger and Piggot have clearly demonstrated that, while competition between enterprises does improve efficiency, ownership is not a major factor in efficiency.[10] In other words, it does not matter whether the enterprise or organisation is publicly or privately owned; provided there is competition, it will become more efficient.

There are some other relevant points to the privatisation debate. These include the fact that market forces rarely operate in the health service field. This is not only because health services developed in a regulated manner with respect to the various professions involved and the methods of payment, but also because hospitals and health service clinics receive a variety of financial subsidies. This situation exists because hospitals and health services have traditionally been recognised as being for the public good rather than as purely commercial enterprises. The US experience is a powerful argument against privatisation for its own sake. With at least two-thirds of its hospital and health services controlled by non-government agencies, the United States has a vastly more expensive hospital and health service system than any other country. This has led to the view that monopolistic health systems, whether publicly or privately owned and controlled, develop very expensive activities. In addition, and most importantly, privatisation rarely involves a measure of quality. It is relatively meaningless to consider the cost of the service without a formal measurement of quality.

There can be no ideal private and public mix. The proportion of public to private provision of health services must be a matter of evolution from a historical situation. There appears to be significant advantage in commercialising the provision of products used by hospital and health services, but this does not necessarily apply to the provision of services, such as catering and cleaning. Competition can be advantageous, particularly when it involves services and quality as distinct from cost. This type of healthy competition can occur between competing public institutions, all of which have an equivalent budget allocation of funds.

Whether or not medical and dental services should be privately or publicly provided is not clear. Inevitably, this will be a matter of historical evolution rather than a planned approach. China is currently an interesting example of a nation where privatisation of the provision of clinical and public health services has been attempted overnight and without detailed planning.[11] The result has been very mixed indeed. Extra income for the health services has been gained by allowing medical and other practitioners to operate privately, but the preventive services in many areas of China have collapsed or become ineffectual. It seems highly unlikely that population-wide services of a preventive nature can ever be privatised. Our own view with respect to medical and dental services is to encourage a range of options that include the continuing increase in employment of career specialists in hospitals and other health institutions but, where community-based general and specialist practitioners are concerned, an increasing use of budget allocations for the provision of specific services, particularly those that have a preventive element. This is an extension of the budgetary principle that appears to have been effective for the provision of hospital services.

In Australia, government policy in the late 1990s and early 2000s has been to encourage the growth of the private health sector. The numbers of private hospitals and inpatients are increasing (from 1.31 private hospital beds per 1000 population in 1997–98 to 1.40 per 1000 population in 2001–02). At the same time public hospital beds per 1000 population have fallen from 3.00 in 1997–98 to 2.63 in 2001–02.

The reasons for these trends are probably as follows:

‹ Governments have decreased the number of public hospital beds, mainly to save money. Also, many acute hospital beds have been redefined as long-stay beds, thereby altering the ratios.
‹ Changes in technology have reduced the length of hospital stay for specific conditions, such as fracture of the hip and torn knee cartilage. Medical treatment fashions have changed; for example, hospital stay for coronary artery disease has been reduced by over 50 per cent.
‹ The proportion of the population with private health insurance—and hence use of private hospitals—has increased because of government financial incentives and the introduction of lifetime cover.

Markets

It has been argued that health service provision should be market-based in order to improve efficiency and lower costs. These arguments have been advanced predominantly in the United Kingdom in the context of the collapse of the command economies of the Soviet Union and Eastern Europe.

However, there are equally sound arguments against reliance on markets in the health care field. The best contrary example is seen in the United States, where market-based health services have become vastly more costly than the centrally funded UK health service.

The basic problems with market-oriented health provision are the lack of knowledge by buyers (that is, patients), the monopolistic position of some providers, the difficulty of achieving equity and the ability of providers to create profitable but unnecessary services. These problems are compounded when third-party insurers or governments pay the bills.

A refinement of the market-oriented approach is a concept known as 'managed competition'. This concept has been developed by a US economist, Alain Enthoven, in response to the US situation of rising costs and low levels of government authority.[12] The concept implies a heavily regulated health care system with 'internal markets'. The best example is the UK purchaser–provider split. This concept divides the provider of a hospital or health service from the fund-raising and financing responsibility. Different hospitals can compete for contracts, with the finance coming from the central government sources. The purchaser–provider split is attractive for hospitals and has been a long-term feature of health services in several Australian states, including Victoria. However, the most effective control on costs appears to be the provision and financing of health services by a central government authority. In Australia, this is well demonstrated by a comparison of costs between the states. For many years Queensland has had the lowest costs and has had the most centrally funded and controlled health services. There is an argument, however, that many Queensland services—such as mental health—are seriously underfunded.

Rationing

Not since World War II has rationing of services been a serious consideration. However, the inability of advanced economies to pay for all demands for health services has led to some forms of rationing. The term 'rationing' is in fact rarely used, but is implied wherever finite budgets are set, waiting lists are created and priorities developed. Rationing and priority-setting are issues that will be a fact of life for health service managers into the foreseeable future.

There have been various attempts to develop rational approaches to rationing of health services. The Netherlands, New Zealand and various states in the United States (in particular Oregon) have attempted to identify priorities for health care in a formal way. No universally satisfactory approach has evolved. However, the current Australian approach at least has the virtue of being practical. This approach is to refuse to approve new procedures and medications for government financial

In response to increasing hospital costs, the state government of New South Wales introduced competitive tendering for hospital catering, laundry and cleaning services in each of its hospitals. Existing hospital-run services could compete with private tenderers. Despite union opposition, the initiative has been very successful mainly because the existing hospital services dramatically improved their efficiency and found they could compete very successfully.

support until there is a consensus regarding their benefits and affordability. Together with queuing (that is, waiting lists), this approach appears to be working.

Economic evaluation of health care

As so much money is spent on health care it is not surprising that governments have become increasingly interested in the efficiency of different treatments and interventions. As it is usually possible to treat the same patient in a number of different ways—and with different costs—is it important to know which treatment gives the best outcome for the least cost? One way of determining the efficiency of a particular treatment is to conduct an economic evaluation. There are three main types of economic evaluation:

1 *Cost–benefit analysis* (CBA) usually involves measuring all the costs and benefits of a particular health program in monetary terms. It sets out to discover whether the benefits of a particular program, project or policy intervention outweigh its costs. Cost–benefit analysis is helpful in attempting to answer the question: 'Is the treatment (or intervention) worthwhile or how much do we pursue a chosen objective?' As benefits and costs are all measured in dollar terms it is possible to compare radically different health care programs—such as the benefits from spending an extra $10 million on vaccinations to those from spending this money on additional aged-care services.

2 *Cost–effectiveness analysis* (CEA) is more often helpful in attempting to answer the question: 'What is the most efficient way to treat (or intervene), given that we have already chosen to meet a particular (treatment) objective?' CEA measures health benefits in units such as the number of lives saved, the number of people inoculated and educated in a preventive program or treated and restored to health or satisfactory bodily functioning. Cost–effectiveness analysis is in one sense less precise than CBA but is more readily applied to a wider range of problems, mainly because it concentrates on the costs of different ways of obtaining what is thought to be the same objective. For example, you could compare the costs of treating people in their own homes with admitting them to hospital—assuming that the same health outcome would be achieved in both cases.

3 *Cost–utility analysis* (CUA) is similar to CEA but measures health benefits in both a qualitative and quantitative manner using measures such as quality adjusted life years (QALYs). So cost–utility analysis explicitly recognises that it is not just the number of life years saved but the quality of life during those years that is important.

Unfortunately, in the health field most economic evaluations of particular courses of action offer confusing and difficult choices. This is because the outcomes may not be clear, the effectiveness of an intervention may not be proven and there may be considerable difficulties in accurately measuring the cost. In addition, there is always the question of equity—that is, who actually receives the benefits of the health care program? For example, you would expect that it would be more cost-effective to provide health care services to people in the city than in remote country areas as higher population densities and lower transport costs would result in the cost per patient in the city being lower than in the country. But on equity grounds you could not argue that health care programs should not be delivered in country areas.

Garry Egger of the University of Newcastle has reviewed the cost-effective aspect of prevention of disease and injury in Australia.[13] His work is an example of using cost–benefit techniques on a grand scale. He has shown that preventive activities in Australia have probably saved approximately 30 000 lives during the period 1960–1988 at an overall rate reduction in health costs of approximately $7–8 billion. His purpose in undertaking these studies was to advocate the value of preventive approaches in the health field.

The effectiveness of expenditure in the health service field has not traditionally attracted attention. However, as the need has increased for better expenditure of the 'health service dollar', attempts have been made to introduce cost–benefit analyses into the field.

A useful approach has been developed by Professor Alan Williams in the United Kingdom.[14] He developed the simple but important concept that a procedure that gives, say, an extra year of healthy life is of higher quality than a procedure that gives an extra year of unhealthy life (for example, partly disabled and in some distress). This has become known as a 'quality adjusted life year' (QALY). To this measure he has added a cost. The results are both useful and interesting. A heart transplant per QALY costs approximately $36 000 compared with a kidney transplant ($8000) and a hip replacement ($2000).

A model for cost–effectiveness analysis is that conducted by Weinstein and Stason in 1976 with respect to the treatment of hypertension.[15] They showed that treatment of a patient with hypertension by pharmaceuticals would cost approximately $40 000 per QALY saved. The cost would be much greater at current costs and due to the higher costs of more recently developed hypertensive agents. Susan Hurley of Melbourne has reviewed cost–effectiveness analyses.[16] Her tables, which are reproduced as Table 7.1 and Table 7.2 (see page 133), clearly illustrate the general value of these approaches and, in particular, the value of modifying health-related behaviour in populations as opposed to screening and treatment approaches.

Economic analyses have been extensively used as part of the debate about fluoridation of water supplies. The best known (and perhaps the most

Table 7.1
Cost–effectiveness analyses of strategies aimed at cardiovascular disease control

Strategy	Cost–effectiveness ($/life year saved)
Prevention	
Advice to quit smoking	1400
Exercise	15300*
Antihypertensives	39600*
Cholestyramine	95800
Treatment	
β-blockers after myocardial infarction	4200
Coronary artery bypass grafting	55000*
Coronary-care units	230200*

*$/QALY saved

Table 7.2
Cost–effectiveness analyses of strategies aimed at cancer control

Strategy	Cost–effectiveness ($/life year saved)
Prevention	
Advice to quit smoking	1400
Research, diet and breast cancer	15000
Elective hysterectomy	22800*
Screening	
Mammography	8300
Pap smears	47100
Treatment	
Chemotherapy—lung cancer	19000
Leukocyte transfusion (leukaemia)	40000

*$/QALY saved

influential) analysis was conducted by Fidler in the United Kingdom in 1977.[17] He demonstrated that, in purely economic terms and with no allowance made for relief of pain and disability, fluoridation was approximately four times more effective than were treatment approaches.

The prevention of tuberculosis provides an interesting example of these techniques. BCG (Bacilli Calmette-Guerin) vaccination is safe and inexpensive and provides effective protection against tuberculosis for over twenty years. However, because the incidence of tuberculosis has fallen to historically low levels and because this fall is primarily dependent on factors other than the vaccine (mainly rising living standards), it is no longer cost-effective to vaccinate whole populations with BCG.

The examples outlined in this section give the impression that economic analyses are simple and that solid conclusions can be made. In practice, this is not so. These analyses are merely one part of the decision making process in the health field, where values are put on life, disability and safety that cannot be measured in purely financial terms. For example, it can be argued that there is no cost benefit with respect to 'quit smoking' programs, despite the benefits showed in Table 7.1. This is because cancers of the lung that may occur because of tobacco smoking tend to cause deaths among people of retiring age—thereby avoiding costly pensions. However, when decisions have to be made, judgments based on competing values and priorities are inevitable and these analyses play a valuable part in complex decision making.

Because of these complexities and because of the considerable resources that have to be allocated to conducting economic analyses, they are not commonly used in everyday management. Therefore, a less complex and more practical approach known as 'marginal analysis' has evolved. This approach offers a rational and useful response when a health service manager receives instructions to cut the budget by 5 per cent—a common experience!

Marginal analysis is a variant of zero-based budgeting whereby budgets are based on a theoretical situation in which a health service is being developed for the first time, without regard for historical patterns of expenditure.

In summary, marginal analysis involves taking the existing patterns of expenditure as the starting point and rationally examining the effect of small changes to that pattern.[18] There are five basic principles involved.

1 Invaluable health benefit resources are scarce compared with needs and demands; therefore, choices have to be made.
2 Decisions about priorities should be made on specific criteria, such as efficiency, and not on emotional criteria, such as future pain and suffering.
3 The allocation of resources to one program means reducing the benefits that the resources may have achieved in another program; this is the economists' 'opportunity cost' concept.
4 The relation between benefits and costs depends on the amount of activity. For example, a screening program aimed at high-risk groups may show a low cost per patient detected, but as the program is expanded to low-risk groups, the cost per patient detected will rise. This is referred to as 'diminishing returns'.
5 Marginal analysis aims to show the effect of shifting resources between programs; as a result, it identifies where additional resources should be targeted, where reductions can be made or how resources can be relocated to achieve a gain in benefits with no overall change in expenditure.

These concepts are best understood by way of simple examples. When faced with expenditure costs of 5–10 per cent in overall budgets in the North Region health services, we applied the fifth principle outlined above—namely, an analysis of the benefits of shifting resources between programs. We analysed the work and benefits of the early childhood services, which provide preventive programs for mothers and their infants, as compared with those of administrative staff who managed the personnel section of the regional office. The analysis demonstrated that, while both activities were of importance, resources could and should be shifted from personnel to the early childhood services. Accordingly, the decision was made to maintain the clinical services but to reduce the services to staff.

However, there is obviously a limit to such reallocation of resources. Using the above example, this is demonstrated by the response two years later when a further reduction of 5 per cent in the annual budget was announced. Again the principles of marginal analysis were applied. The analyses showed that there was no possibility of reallocating resources and, therefore, that services had to be reduced—but which services? Analyses demonstrated that it was possible and preferable to close one whole hospital rather than to restrict services across many. The one chosen for closure was a convalescent hospital of some 120 beds. The work of that hospital was replaced with the expansion of a much less costly community care program.

Marginal analyses can and should be applied to all health service activities. It is a practical, readily understandable approach to the need to control costs.

Managing the money

'It does not matter if you find the cure for cancer; if you do not balance your budget, you will be sacked!'[19] This statement is sad, but true. Many very fine health service managers have foundered in recent years because they did not give sufficient attention to managing the money.

Information

The most important priority in order to manage the money is to have good information. What is the budget? What are the past spending patterns? What are the predicted spending patterns? What is the expected income? These are the key questions for the general manager. The answer to each one is totally dependent on the establishment of an adequate data and information system plus the ability to predict the future in both the short (four weeks) and long term (six months). Of course, this information is only useful if it is acted upon.

Cost centres

A knowledge of the global situation of the organisation, while useful, is not sufficient. More detail is required if actions to remedy a problem are going to be specific and are not to cause unnecessary harm throughout the organisation. Hence, the concept of cost centres. With respect to hospitals, the number of possible cost centres is immense; therefore, the development of some priorities is useful. The first priority is to identify centres and activities that can be readily and accurately costed. Examples include the costs of staff (which may account for over 80 per cent of total expenditure), food, power and pharmaceuticals. These costs should be predictable, and should be considered in parallel with data concerning patient activities.

More sophisticated cost centres can and should be developed. Examples include discrete departments such as physiotherapy, radiology, pathology, biochemistry and, finally and with more difficulty, the cost of operating theatres, inpatient services and even whole service programs, such as geriatrics, which have predominantly community-based components.

Costing by way of DRGs and the use of comparisons is also emerging. In the Australian context, the use of DRGs for costing purposes is proving valuable at an interhospital level. DRGs are increasingly being used to compare the costs of treating patients by individual surgeons and medical practitioners.

Cost and effectiveness (benefit) are complex issues, as discussed in the previous section.

Detail and frequency

Some guidelines with respect to the required level of detail of financial monitoring may be helpful. Traditionally, the financial accounts of Australian organisations, whether they be companies, hotels or hospitals, are given a public review at yearly intervals. In the current economic context, an annual review is inadequate. A simple hospital may be tens of millions of dollars in debt by the time of an annual review; accordingly, monthly or even weekly reviews of the financial situation have become the norm. In the private sector, where the need to 'balance the books' is paramount, financial monitoring is currently being undertaken on a monthly basis. Such reviews are undertaken in considerable detail and include a comparison of income and expenditure with target figures for all cost centres in a specific hospital. While this may present a seemingly overwhelming task, it has been accomplished without difficulty by senior managers responsible for over 200 hospitals in New South Wales by use of 'management by exception'. Management by exception simply means reviewing and examining only those cost centres that are significantly above or below the target figures.

Defalcation

Upon arrival in New South Wales as a health service manager, I [JSL] was warned to be careful of defalcation. I imagined defalcation to be a local disorder of the bowel: in fact it is sophisticated stealing—a breach of trust concerning money.

Believe it or not, people in high places in the health system steal money. The director of finance at a Sydney hospital got away with thousands of dollars; the manager of a Red Cross home for the elderly stole successfully for years; and the accountant at a large area health service channelled enormous sums through his private bank account. Some defalcation is less dramatic, like that of the hospital manager who let the hospital cleaning contracts to his wife, and the clinic cook who borrowed whole sheep to feed his relatives.

Quite recent examples that have been identified include purchasing officers who have entered into collusion with tenderers for hospital contracts, the theft of unclaimed salary cheques and the manipulation of computer salary data for personal financial gain.

The message for managers is—beware! Systems have to be put in place to prevent defalcation and to increase the likelihood of detection. Hard-won credibility of a health service organisation can be totally destroyed by a single significant, irresponsible financial act.

Profits are not cash flow

It is important to understand that profits are not the same as cash flow. In Australia the government sector now uses a system called 'accrual accounting' and this can cause some problems for managers with a clinical background. Under accrual accounting, revenues are recognised when they are 'earned'—not when the money is actually received. Expenses are recognised when they are 'incurred'—not when they are paid.

Let's look at an example of how accrual accounting works. Suppose that in a six-month period a hospital provided services worth $5 million. Patients are not required to pay when they receive these services but are given thirty days to pay. At the end of the six-month period, the hospital has actually collected $4.5 million from its patients and there is still $0.5 million outstanding.

Under accrual accounting the entire $5 million would be included as 'revenue' in the hospital's profit and loss statement (also known as an operating statement for non-profit organisations) as this revenue has been 'earned'—even though the hospital has only received $4.5 million in cash. The remaining $0.5 million will appear under the asset 'accounts receivable' in the hospital's balance sheet.

Similarly, suppose the hospital received a phone bill for $5000 but had not paid it yet. This $5000 would be included as an expense in the profit and loss statement as it had been 'incurred'. In the hospital's balance sheet there would be $5000 as a liability under the item 'accounts payable'.

The three main financial statements

The main types of financial statement produced by all organisations are:

1 *Balance sheet*—only contains assets, liabilities and owners' equity. This is sometimes called a Statement of Financial Position.
2 *Profit and loss statement*—only contains revenues and expenses. This is sometimes called an Income or Operating Statement or a Statement of Financial Performance.
3 *Cash flow statement*—measures actual cash inflow and outflow over a period of time.

The balance sheet is a financial statement that summarises, as at a particular time, the company's assets, liabilities and owners' equity. It is a financial snapshot of the company at a specified date. A balance sheet can be prepared on any day of the year but it is most commonly prepared on the last day of the financial year. In Australia this is 30 June.

The equation of the balance sheet is:

$$\text{Assets} = \text{liabilities} + \text{owners' equity}$$

The balance sheet must be 'in balance'—that is, assets must equal liabilities plus owners' equity. The difference between assets and liabilities is known as 'net assets' or 'net worth'. In theory, this measures how much would be left over if all the hospital's assets were sold and all its liabilities repaid.

It is important to note that the dollar amounts recorded for assets in a balance sheet do not necessarily show the amounts that would be received today if these assets were sold. Rather they show the historical cost of the assets on the date they were purchased. This is also called the 'book' value of the hospital's assets—that is, the value that appears in the hospital's accounting books. This can be vastly different from the market value of a particular asset.

The main assets that are affected by the difference between book value and market value are the hospital's land and buildings. If these assets were bought several years ago and the property market has risen sharply in the meantime, the book value of these assets could significantly understate their real value.

The profit and loss statement shows how profitable a business is by summarising its revenues and expenses over a period of time—usually either six or twelve months. The bottom line of this statement is the profit or loss for the period.

Note that only assets, liabilities and owners' equity appear in the balance sheet. Only revenues and expenses appear in the profit and loss statement.

If you want to know how much cash the hospital actually paid and collected you need to consult the cash flow statement.

A cash flow statement shows where cash inflow was derived during the year and how this money was spent. It also shows the changes that have taken place in the hospital's financial structure. For example, the cash flow statement might show that the hospital has gone further into debt.

Cash flow statements are generally divided into three sections:

1 *Cash flow from operating activities*—this is cash coming in and going out as a result of the hospital's normal activities, such as providing medical services. The main cash inflow items are revenues received for providing patient services, payments from private health insurance companies, government grants, donations and income from rent or other investments. The main cash outflows are payments to employees and to outside suppliers such as drug companies and power and telephone companies.
2 *Cash flow from investing activities*—'investing' here is a more general term meaning buying land and equipment that will be used to generate profits in the business. Cash inflow comes when you sell land, buildings and equipment. Cash outflow is where you buy land, buildings and equipment.
3 *Cash flow from financing activities*—summarises money raised and repaid to other financiers, such as the government for public hospitals and banks and shareholders for private hospitals. For private hospitals, cash inflow comes from new borrowings from banks or other lending institutions and injections of more capital by shareholders. Cash outflow comes from repayment of debt and payment of dividends to shareholders.

Systematic approaches to 'managing the money'

Nothing is so terrifying for clinicians accustomed to daily issues of life and death as to be given responsibility for the financial affairs of their hospital division. Therefore, it is useful to develop a simple, systematic approach to financial matters. The simplicity that follows may well offend professional accountants; the aim, however, is not to educate clinicians to be quasi-accountants, but to offer them and their hospitals and health services some security—and perhaps, in the longer term, improved efficiency. Using a hospital as an example, we offer an approach based on the following steps.

Steps in preparing a budget

1 *Collect data.* You need both financial and non-financial data—such as statistics on historical and anticipated casemix, number of inpatients and outpatients, average length of stay, day surgery numbers and categories of staff.

2 *Outline the assumptions on which the budget will be based.* Are you anticipating a change in casemix? More patients? Fewer patients? Changes to the way the service is delivered?

3 *Determine staffing requirements.* What staff will you need? What types of staff? How much will they cost to employ? Full-time or part-time? Can these be divided into fixed and variable expenses? (Fixed costs are those that do not change as patient numbers change—such as insurance and rent. Variable costs do change as patient numbers change—such as drugs, food and consumables.)

4 *Determine other costs incurred to provide the service.* Do you expect the prices of these items to change?

5 *Estimate capital expenditures.* Does equipment need to be replaced or new equipment bought?

6 *Seek approval.* After a draft budget is established at a departmental level there is usually negotiation on different aspects of the budget—particularly staffing levels. This highlights the political nature of the budgeting process— it is often the best negotiator who gets the best budget allocation.

Once adopted, budgets tend to become carved in stone. Higher levels of management quite naturally are suspicious that requests for budget adjustments may be attempts to evade budget goals or may be excuses for substandard performance. But there can be unexpected developments—events that were not foreseen at the time of making up the budget, such as a SARS outbreak. The budget should be adjusted for such developments.

Management control

Making good decisions with poor control can turn out just as disastrously as making bad decisions in the first place. Management control needs feedback on actual performance that is compared against goals, objectives, budgets and plans to detect any variances so that managers can take corrective action to bring performance back on track. It is essential for this feedback to be received quickly—information received too late can result in costly delays before problems are corrected. Not all problems come to the manager's attention through the accounting system. Some problems can be detected by keeping an eye on patient complaints, absenteeism and breakdowns in infection control.

In analysing a budget you are primarily concerned with such things as expenses being higher than planned, cash inflow being slower than planned, and patient numbers being higher or lower than expected. Even when things are going to plan, managers still need information to tell them this.

It's a good idea to identify a few success factors—such as staff costs or patient numbers—and keep a constant watch on them. By their nature management control reports are highly sensitive because they often discuss 'mistakes' and how decisions went wrong. Of course, some degree of uncertainty surrounds all business decisions—but management control reports often pass judgment on a manager's ability to make good decisions.

Usually management compares this month's performance with last month's performance, with the budgeted outcome and with the performance for the same time last year. This should be only part of the process. The danger of using this 'look back' approach is that you get into the habit of looking behind, not looking ahead. Accordingly, effective management control needs a system of forecasts, even though they may not be precise.

While the example that has been discussed is a hospital, the principles apply to all organisations—large and small. With experience, financial management is not so difficult. However, some additional tips may help.

‹ Once the organisation reaches a level of any size or complexity, the finances require a professional accountant (no explanation needed).

‹ Keep very careful records of all financial transactions, both expenditure and revenue.

‹ Have two signatures for all but the petty cash accounts. Not only do the nicest people steal money, but also the adverse consequences of a false accusation that you have stolen money can be devastating.

‹ Never borrow money from the petty cash for private purposes—even for a taxi fare home when the car breaks down. Malevolent colleagues may use such actions against you in times of trouble.

‹ Ensure that the financial affairs of the organisation are regularly audited, particularly if you are leaving for a new job. Again, propriety needs to be seen to exist.

Reflections for the reader

It is salutary for clinicians to estimate the costs of a range of treatments that they have implemented for patients; for example, the cost of medication for high blood pressure for one year. It may be possible for you to compare these costs with alternative approaches. For the patient with high blood pressure, the alternatives may be the use of less expensive medications or changes in the patient's health-related lifestyle.

In institutional settings, it may be possible for you to estimate both the cost and the value of caring for patients in different ways; for example, as day-only patients rather than as inpatients.

If you find that financial savings can be made without loss of benefit to the patient, how would you reallocate the savings?

With respect to financial management, there is no alternative to experience. Reading about budgets is no substitute for preparing one. Reading about audits is no substitute for receiving one.

Exceeding your budget can be regarded as a sin.

8

Health service management in different contexts

The difference in managing private and public hospitals

The principles of private and public hospital management are the same. The details and incentives are different.

Our colleague, Mary Foley, has experienced and studied the differences between the two sectors. One of her major points is that the private hospital sector is rapidly expanding in both size and complexity. Private hospitals have come to offer emergency services, open-heart surgery and radiotherapy as well as continuing to fulfil their traditional role in obstetrics, elective surgery and the care of chronically ill patients.

She has identified key differences between the public and private hospital sectors in Australia (see Table 8.1 on page 143), but in so doing makes no judgments about whether they are good or bad.

In recent times, many features of the private sector—such as improvements in efficiency and in managing labour—have been introduced into the public sector. The essential difference remains, however: the private sector has to give priority to financial survival. The financial survival imperative offers powerful incentives to manage in detail and on time; the best and most important example is the monitoring of staff requirements according to the workload.

Private hospital staffing hours closely parallel the number of patients. In the public sector, while adjustments are made, it is difficult to achieve such a match. Not only does a close match of staff and workload achieve lower costs, but it also results in an improvement in quality, as 'staff shortages' do not occur during peak workloads.

The private sector achieves this matching for several reasons.

Table 8.1
Key differences between the public and private hospital sectors in Australia

Private hospitals	Public hospitals
1 Seek to capture market share	Ration care (that is, while private hospitals try to fill beds, public hospitals try to empty beds)
2 Revenue driven, seek payment for services as they are offered	Have an annual global budget
3 Respond to demand by increasing services	Ration services
4 Actively seek new markets (provided these markets can generate finance)	Identify unmet needs, then seek public finance
5 Reduce costs by improving efficiency	Reduce costs by restricting services; for example, by shutting beds during Christmas period
6 Treat all costs as variable—in particular, manage labour	Treat labour as a fixed cost
7 Finance capital by recurrent revenue	With capital a rare but public good, have no planned replacement of buildings and equipment
8 Employ a 'balance sheet' discipline	Present as a command-and-control model
9 Present as a market model	Present as a command-and-control model

1 There is a financial incentive.
2 Workloads, staffing levels and finances are monitored on a daily basis, with weekly reviews of performance against budget.
3 Private hospitals are small by comparison with public teaching hospitals; therefore, staffing can be organised to accommodate the needs of individuals and casual workers are pleased to work on an intermittent basis.

There are other subtle differences. For example, in the private sector computers are simple but essential management tools; in the public sector they are complex and the data bank is huge, but rarely analysed and used. In addition, middle management positions have virtually disappeared in the private sector whereas, while there has been a reduction in such positions, in public hospitals many remain. Finally, considerable resources are allocated to management education in the private sector. While this was once the case in the public sector, management education has been drastically reduced as part of overall cost reductions.

Managing health services in international settings

The most remarkable feature of hospitals and health services is how similar they are in all countries.[1] Western medical teaching and traditions now dominate the globe. Traditional medicine remains in traditional societies, but very much as an adjunct to the technology of the West.

In addition, regardless of the level of economic development, trends in health service delivery are similar in virtually all countries. The authors have had the privilege of working in many different countries and participating in a range of international meetings at which health service managers from all five continents of the world have shared their experiences. The universal trends are:

1 difficulty in raising sufficient finance to satisfy the needs of the health service
2 rising costs
3 reductions in length of hospital stay
4 conflicts with professional staff, particularly medical staff
5 decentralisation of services
6 the introduction of some form of markets in public sector dominated health systems, such as those in the United Kingdom and New Zealand, and an increase in public sector involvement in privately dominated health systems, such as those in the United States, South Korea and Japan.

Health problems are becoming similar in countries that either are or are becoming economically developed, such as the United States, European countries, China, Japan and South Korea. These problems include chronic conditions associated with the ageing of the population, coronary heart disease, cancer and trauma. HIV/AIDS is of universal concern. Malaria, diarrhoeal diseases and tuberculosis remain as major problems in countries that are still developing, such as India, Bangladesh, Indonesia, the Philippines and the Solomons.

There are, however, significant differences in detail that require different ethical approaches and different managerial approaches to the provision and management of health services. For example, neonatal intensive care and in-vitro fertilisation programs are unethical in China, where population issues are so vital and dominating, whereas such programs are the pinnacle of scientific medicine in many Western countries.

In the field of public health, while the main causes of premature death may be similar, detailed examination reveals very different patterns of disease. These are shown in Figures 8.1 and 8.2 (see page 145) . The types of cancer causing death in Japan, South Korea, China and Hong Kong are quite different from the fatal cancers of Western countries; breast and prostate cancer are respectively twenty and ten times more common in the West than in the East. The problems of coronary artery disease show similar differences These epidemiological differences demand quite different allocation of resources and quite different approaches to public health.

Expectations of consumers (that is, patients) also differ. Privacy, short waiting times for consultation, comfort and detailed explanations are expected in

Figure 8.1
Death rates per 100 000 caused by breast cancer (age standardised)

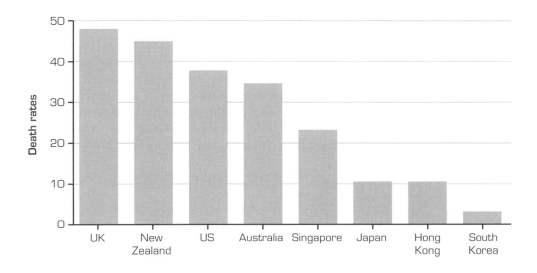

Figure 8.2
Death rates per 100 000 caused by coronary artery disease (age standardised)

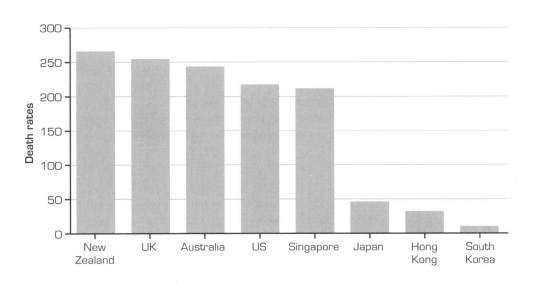

economically developed countries. While expectations in developing countries will rise, patients expect much less and are prepared to wait for days, if necessary, for a 5-minute consultation.

Developing countries can learn a great deal from the hard-won experience of developed countries. This experience leads to the following observations.

❮ It is necessary to avoid dominance of health service finance by hospitals at the expense of other important sectors of the health services.
❮ It is necessary to develop hospitals as part of health service networks.
❮ Public sector dominated health systems cost much less than privately dominated systems, although markets do have a place.
❮ Public health prevention approaches remain a high priority in terms of the health of the whole community. Tobacco consumption and HIV/AIDS remain the best examples of prevention having a major priority over care.

Managing public health services

The problem with addressing the issue of managing public health services is one of definition: what are public health services? There is no universally accepted definition. All we have is the statement that 'public health is concerned with the health of populations as distinct from the care of individuals'.[2]

It may be helpful to examine approaches to managing two major activities, both of which could be considered as being in the domain of public health; namely, anti-tobacco activities and management of maternal and child care preventive health activities.

The management of anti-tobacco activities

Some argue with validity that 'management' is an inappropriate term in the context of the anti-smoking movement. However, when these activities are listed, it is apparent that management is an essential element in their implementation.

1   Education of the public

Mass education requires mass media programs. Resources need to be created: advertising agencies must be hired, and activities and action developed to follow the media messages. There must be evaluation of the education programs, and education needs to be continuous over decades.

In addition, special education of schoolchildren is needed in this field. This means developing programs in collaboration with education authorities and organisations.

2   Legislation

Legal sanctions are needed against smoking in public places and selling tobacco to minors, and requiring 'danger' labels to be placed on advertising packs. Laws are needed to enable taxes to be levied on tobacco products.

3 Monitoring

Data must be collected and information prepared concerning rates of tobacco consumption among different segments of the population. The impact of anti-smoking programs needs to be measured.

The management of such programs ideally needs people with entrepreneurial tendencies—people who are willing to take risks and willing to speak out publicly, but who are also capable of negotiating with educational authorities, governments and lawmakers and interested in doing so. Such management needs to be patient, to operate over decades, and to exploit opportunities as they arise. The personalities and skills of managers in this field are very different from those of our other example—managing preventive health programs for mothers and children.

The management of maternal and child care preventive health programs

The essential feature of such programs is that they are structured, hierarchical and dominated by health professionals, particularly nurses. Particular features are antenatal clinics for pregnant women, early childhood centres for new babies and immunisation programs run by local governments, voluntary organisations and general practitioners.

The management requirements are the traditional ones: sound guidelines, good education for staff, careful monitoring of activities and performance, and regular evaluation of the outcomes. What is not needed is entrepreneurial, charismatic management.

Requirements for management

We have opposite requirements for management in these two vital areas of public health. It is really a question of 'horses for courses', illustrated by way of the following example.

Professor Simon Chapman has been an 'activist'—an anti-smoking leader (or manager)—for twenty years. He is totally flexible in his approach and fearless in attacking vested interests. His has been a very effective influence. By way of contrast, Dr Woodrow Hemphill has been responsible for maternal and child health services, also for twenty years. He is a quiet but equally effective person in ensuring delivery and continuity of these programs. These are two personality opposites, equally appropriate and effective in their different roles.

Managing long-term care organisations

As the population ages, the need to develop services for the chronically ill and disabled has grown. In terms of cost, by far the largest is in the nursing home sector.

The principles of management are constant and apply equally to nursing homes and to teaching and referral hospitals. However, there are some features special to the management of long-term care services, including the need to keep such services small and (therefore) intimate, the need to keep staff keen and interested, and the need to offer the patients or residents hope for a better future.

Small and intimate

The traditional, enormous mental hospitals and large, public geriatric institutions for men offer very good lessons on what to avoid. These organisations grew to house over 2000 patients on the one geographical site. Inevitably, they were difficult to manage, the resources were always inadequate and maintenance of the facilities was poor. The adverse consequences were personal loss of identity for patients, loss of credibility of these services within the community and, ultimately, extreme difficulty in attracting and retaining staff.

While there has to be some balance, experience strongly indicates there are substantial advantages for both staff and patients if long-term stay services are kept reasonably small.

Staff motivation

There is a need for staff of long-stay services to be given continual incentives to retain their interest. Apart from financial incentives (which are perfectly reasonable), the staff need to be closely involved in all aspects of the organisation, including participation in continuing education activities, pilot programs and rotation of duties.

Hope

The stark fact is that for many long-stay patients there is little hope for the future, particularly in the field of geriatrics. While managers and staff must be realistic, there is a need to encourage hope. This may not need to be hope for a longer life, but can certainly be hope for a better life in terms of both quality and spirit. Therefore, managers need to ensure that every effort is made to diagnose early and seek to redress failures of sight, sound and movement. For example, the horse-racing results may be a key to the contentment of a 98-year-old male nursing home resident and he has no time to wait for new glasses, a cataract operation or a hearing aid. In another instance, early repairs to failing dentition may allow better enjoyment of meals in the last months of life.

Managing community-based services
Medical and dental services

The need to consider management issues in the context of general medical and dental practitioners has not until quite recently been recognised. General practitioners and dentists have traditionally been small professional businesses and have suffered loss of prestige, income and even relevance in the face of the increasing dominance of specialisation. The professional isolation of these practitioners is recognised as a major difficulty. In addition, they have been largely unaccountable to the community with respect to the quality of their work. While market and other forces have led to the establishment of group practices and 24-hour clinics, there has been only modest progress with the issues of quality, accountability and productivity.

Initiatives to address these problems, including the creation of divisions of medical practice, have met with limited success.

There are no quick answers available within the current financial context of payment to doctors and dentists by fee for service. In the long term, alternative options for remuneration may mean that progress can be made in measuring quality and accountability.

Nursing services

Community-based nursing has a long and honoured place in the provision of health services. There are few problems of management, largely because these services are primarily in the public sector and therefore are an integral part of the overall health services.

There is a small issue with respect to specialisation. Some believe there is a case for having a more general role for community-based services; others are of the view that a substantial degree of specialisation is necessary to maintain standards.

Community-based nurses are gradually developing more professional independence, primarily as a consequence of improved educational programs. This trend is inevitable and will certainly lead to professional disputes with general practitioners as they compete for work.

Reflections for the reader

We must not assume that all is good in the private sector as opposed to the public sector. However, the sharing of experiences can only be of value. If payments to hospitals by diagnostic related groups become universal in both private and public sectors, many of the financial incentives will become the same. Accordingly, public sector managers would do well to prepare for this eventuality.

Readers from countries other than Australia might consider developing a list of health problems of importance in their home countries. It could be useful for such readers to consider how appropriate is the current provision of health services in their own countries. It may well be that changes in health priorities will require changes in health service provision.

In addition, such readers may have experiences that could be of benefit to Australia's health services.

How do you educate managers of public health services who have differing requirements? In our view, you offer similar basic skills, with the knowledge that their personal attributes will take them in different directions. This suits the culture and market economy of Australia. However, flexible managers in the style of Simon Chapman may have difficulties in countries with different cultures and command economies.

Health service management and the law

General role of law in facilitating the objectives of health service provision[1]

To what extent does the law facilitate—and to what extent does it inhibit—the organisation and delivery of health services? A key function of law may be to state objectives. In addition, legislation can provide a structure within which institutions and programs can be constituted and deliver services. It may also establish a framework of enforceable rights and duties.

Australia is a member of the World Health Organization (WHO). The WHO has proposed and adopted a general framework to facilitate the review and updating of health legislation in relation to national goals and objectives.[2] The WHO has also stressed the importance of ongoing monitoring and evaluation of laws to determine whether the objectives are being realised.[3]

Many nations, including Australia, have used legislation to protect public health. But there is a growing trend for nations also to use health legislation more deliberately and frequently to restructure their systems of health service organisation and management and the delivery of clinical services, and to promote healthier lifestyles and improved environmental health.[4] This higher level of activity throughout the world may have been inspired by the WHO's global strategy of 'Health for All by the Year 2000'.

A second trend is that many nations, including Australia, are responding to the guidance and the encouragement of the WHO to improve the quality of their health legislation and to share and compare their experience in implementing such legislation. Nations are attempting to be more systematic in assessing the effects of existing legislation and considering new proposals.

Thirdly, there has been a huge volume of legislation in Australia and throughout the world specifically seeking to prevent and control the spread of human immunodeficiency viral infection (HIV infection) and acquired immunodeficiency syndrome (AIDS). No other public health issue in world history has generated so much legislation and so quickly.[5] By 1990 (less than a decade after HIV and AIDS were first diagnosed), sixty-eight nations,[6] including Australia,[7] had enacted specific HIV/AIDS legislation. The WHO has recommended some general guiding principles for health service legislation.

1. The object of the proposed legal measure should be defined with precision.

2. It should be based on current scientific knowledge and current public health strategies.

3. It should be asked whether a legal solution is necessary or appropriate to achieve the object or whether non-legal measures (e.g. public education or proper professional practice) would be adequate; and

4. Any coercive provisions in legal measures should be restricted to the object as defined and care should be taken to avoid the overextension of the law.

11. If the proposed measure limits individual rights, the restriction should be:
    (a) either with the voluntary consent of the affected individual or clearly authorised by law;
    (b) shown to be necessarily required for a clearly established public purpose; and
    (c) limited and strictly proportional to the achievement of the defined object.

12. The implementation of the measure should:
    (a) ensure co-ordination with other relevant agencies (e.g. health administration, justice, education, employment, welfare, immigration, travel and tourism); and
    (b) ensure conformity with the defined objective.[8]

The report also recommended that the implementation of all laws should be monitored so that any such law can be revised if it is 'inappropriate or ineffective'.[9] Even if a law is investigated very carefully before it is promulgated, unforeseen factors may interfere with and frustrate its intended operation.[10] For example, laws enacted in a number of countries in the early stages of the AIDS pandemic have been revised in the light of experience.

Some of the older legislation also adopted coercive and discriminatory legal measures against individuals. It is more often recognised in newer legislation, however, that safeguards to protect confidentiality and guard [against] group discrimination can support public health strategies to reduce spread of the virus by encouraging individuals who suspect they may be infected to come forward for early diagnosis, counselling and management of these conditions.
    Comparison between the legislation of the 68 member countries of WHO shows that:

‹ Nearly all 68 deal with public health surveillance (notification, screening, testing); 49 of these deal with notification of AIDS, and some of these deal separately with notification also of HIV infection; 29 of the 68 countries have introduced laws for compulsory screening and protection of blood supply.

‹ About 25 have promulgated laws to reduce the social impact of HIV infection and AIDS on infected individuals, such as protection of confidentiality.

‹ Coercive legal measures are often ineffective or counterproductive. Coercive measures need to be limited very carefully.[11]

A WHO expert committee issued a report entitled *Strengthening Ministries of Health for Primary Health Care.*[12] After discussing the subject of health legislation,[13] they concluded:

1. Health legislation is important in strengthening ministries of health so that they can play the directing and coordinating role in national health systems. It serves to buttress the policies that have been developed by government authorities.
2. Health legislation may be particularly useful in decentralization of health care, intersectoral collaboration, community participation, and other strategies for achieving health for all.
3. Widespread consultation is necessary prior to the formulation and implementation of legislation. A statutory commission may sometimes prove useful in obtaining views and reaching a consensus on what legislation is needed.[14]

What is 'law'?[15]

Positivism

Probably the most common way of thinking about the idea of law in Western societies is that it is a *system of binding rules* constituting the formal basis of government and political organisation and establishing minimally acceptable standards of behaviour. Breaches of these standards, if detected and prosecuted, may lead to the imposition of sanctions ranging from extreme punishments and penalties, such as imprisonment, down to monetary impositions (for example, fines and orders to pay compensation) and a range of other creative coercions such as licence cancellations, deregistration and so on. This way of thinking about the law is also linked with an associated set of *socially accepted institutions and processes* (parliaments, courts, police, armed forces) for enforcing laws and changing laws (that is, altering norms and sanctions).

Models of legal thought in this vein are technically described as 'positivist' ones. This is an eighteenth-century English term that captures the suggestive image that the law in general, and specific laws in particular, are imposed or 'posited' on the community by high sovereign power to which most members of society owe both loyal allegiance and an enforceable obligation of obedience. The sovereign in a monarchy and the presidential head of state in a republic symbolise and personify the ultimate legitimate authority (social, political and governmental) whom the bulk of citizens habitually obey.

Legal practitioners and judges

Positivism is the professional orientation of practising solicitors or barristers who are formally asked to give legal advice or to represent clients in oral or written advocacy roles. Positivism is also the main professional orientation of judges and others who preside over courts and other official tribunals to apply the law to the resolution of disputes. The focus of judicial inquiry is usually to ascertain the precise meaning, scope and intent of relevant laws (a) laid down by parliament,

(b) laid down by other bodies or officials to which parliament has delegated authority, and/or (c) established by previous court decisions (known as judicial 'precedents'). The inquiry then concentrates on what should be done, according to the identified norms and standards, in the situation in dispute.

Hierarchical norms of authority

Positivists recognise that legal pronouncements, interpretations and utterances vary in their degree of authoritativeness. Legislation (enacted by parliament or by a delegate of the parliament) and cases (decided by courts) have more status than other sources. Courts give binding interpretations and rulings on matters in dispute. If relevant legislation exists (and it may not), courts will refer to it to ascertain the norms of behaviour and social values that should be used to resolve the dispute. Courts are also guided by previous court decisions, known as 'precedents' or 'case law', in which disputes similar to the current one have arisen for adjudication. These traditional methods of judicial reasoning are known as 'common law' and 'equity'. Common law and equity have developed slowly and incrementally over many centuries by means of case-by-case determinations, and much of the law applying to clinical practice has developed this way—for example, basic legal principles dealing with 'consent' to treatment and with the minimum 'reasonable' standard of acceptable care and treatment.

Legislative provisions that have been given authoritative judicial interpretation in the context of specific court cases are more meaningful than legislative provisions that have not yet been subjected to judicial interpretation. The interpretation of the latter remains more in the realm of speculation and conjecture.

Not all legislation is equally authoritative. For example, important constitutional documents that establish the political basis of the nation are more authoritative legal norms than is other legislation.

Nor do all courts have equal authority and status; they are institutionally arranged in a system of ascending superiority of power. In the most inferior position at the bottom of the judicial hierarchy are the magistrates' courts, also known in different states and territories as local courts or courts of petty sessions or police courts. The coroners' courts are part of the magistrates' court system. Above them are successive layers of other trial courts and appeal courts that resolve disputes and formulate binding rulings and interpretations through the operation of the doctrine of precedent. The High Court of Australia is now Australia's highest court, and appeals no longer are taken from Australia to the Privy Council in England.

Official versus unofficial rulings

Practising solicitors and barristers, and other persons trained in positivist techniques (for example, academic lawyers) are skilled in identifying, explaining and applying to particular situations the rules established by legislation and case law. But the pronouncements, opinions, advices and summaries of legal practitioners, academics and other legal advisers (such as government law officers) are not conclusive or authoritative 'official' pronouncements. A strict positivist would rather regard them as professional explanations of what has been determined or as informed predictions, guided by professional experience, of how a court would resolve the matter if it were litigated.

Ignorance of the law is no excuse

The positivist obligation on all citizens to give loyal allegiance and dutiful obedience is also reflected in the proposition (which is itself a rule of law and is consistently upheld by the courts) that 'ignorance of the law is no excuse'—that lack of knowledge of applicable legal rules is not and will not be accepted by courts as a valid defence to a charge or action brought against a person who has been prosecuted or sued for alleged breach of a specific law. A person who is ignorant of a law accordingly runs the risk of the consequences of breaking that law. In effect, positivism obliges any member of the community who wishes to avoid conviction to learn and know what the law requires, and to obey it.

In fairness, then, one might think that the law's requirements should be stated clearly and should be easily ascertained. However, this immediately highlights a paradox inherent in the positivist approach. On the one hand, positivist ideology (as embodied in existing legal norms and sanctions) insists that citizens should know their obligations. But, on the other hand, positivism also recognises (somewhat inconsistently) that the meaning of specific laws and their application to particular situations may be so unclear that a system of ascending judicial appeal courts exists for the very purpose of clarifying these puzzling cases! Furthermore, in practice it may be time-consuming and expensive to take legal advice and test laws in court.

Professional legal services are of variable quality. Governments, wealthy citizens and organisations with large resources may be more able than others in the community to seek experienced and skilled advice and representation and to litigate contentious judicial rulings at the trial level and through the appeal courts to seek a favourable outcome. Thus, although positivist ideology promotes the *ideal* that everyone is equally entitled to the protection of law, in *reality* there are great differences in the capacity of citizens to gain access to the law via legal processes.

Compliance with the law

Compliance with the law may be difficult and onerous in practice even if the requirements are clearly known. Many laws are very stringent and inflexible (for example, much of the so-called 'strict liability' legislation relating to the safety of food, equipment, premises, workplaces and industrial practices). In such instances, the difficulty or expense of compliance would *not* usually be accepted by a court as a valid defence to action or prosecution for breach. Those who carry out an activity must meet the specified requirements or cease the activity unless they are willing to run the risk of detection, prosecution and penalty. If penalties are too low, then it may be more economic for an offender to practise the activity anyway, and pay any fines incurred, than to meet the safety standards or cease the activity.

Other laws are more flexible, and may take more account of compliance difficulties. For example, in cases where one of the issues is whether the defendant's conduct at a particular time was 'reasonable' (see the section 'Negligence' later in this chapter), courts will usually balance a number of factors:

> ... the magnitude of the risk and the degree of probability of its occurrence, along with the expense difficulty and inconvenience of taking alleviating action and any other conflicting responsibilities the defendant may have. It is only when these matters are balanced out that the tribunal of fact can confidently assert what is the standard of response to be ascribed to the reasonable man placed in the defendant's position.[16]

The tension between the competing policies summarised in the preceding two paragraphs has been highlighted by one author as follows:

> The Supreme Court of Canada has held that if a business cannot be run reasonably safely and still be a positive economic proposition, the solution is not to run it unsafely, but to shut it down. The court was speaking of icecream vendor trucks in a case where a young child was seriously injured because of lack of supervision. Hospitals and icecream trucks are not of the same level of necessity in our society. The issue may well become: are we better off with a hospital with a level of staff or equipment that is unreasonable in terms of safety—that is, falls within the definition of a negligent system—or no hospital at all?[17]

Another author asks rhetorically: 'How will a jury respond when economic rather than medical considerations are offered as the reason for a diagnostic or treatment decision that has led to a malpractice claim?'[18] Later he continues:

> But why should a sick and anxious patient accept the doctor's economic calculation? What is the patient's interest in reducing the economic risk to the doctor or the aggregate cost of health care by forgoing a bed in the coronary care unit or a CAT scan? It is one thing to entrust your life and health in times of crisis to a physician who is committed to the practical ethics that involves a quest for excellence and who may err on the side of doing too much. It is quite another to entrust your life and health in times of crisis to a physician whose diagnostic and therapeutic interventions are limited by new regulatory constraints or incentives of competitive efficiency that 'place the provider at economic risk'.

Refer also, in this respect, to the case of *R. v. Cambridge Health Authority*, ex parte 'B' [1995] 2 All ER 129, where England's Court of Appeal refused to disturb a decision made by a health authority that it would not agree to a father's request that it should authorise expenditure of up to £75 000 for chemotherapy and bone-marrow transplants that had only a 10–20 per cent chance of saving the life of a 10½-year-old girl suffering from acute myeloid leukaemia. Without the treatment, the girl had only six to eight weeks to live. The court said that: 'Difficult and agonising judgments have to be made as to how a limited budget is best allocated to the maximum advantage of the maximum number of patients. That is not a judgment that the court can make.'

Of course, even where particular laws *are* clear and known, and compliance *is* both feasible and reasonable, it would still be necessary (in order not to break the law) that persons affected by the law should be *motivated and willing* to obey rather than disobey the requirements. Positivist ideology was developed in the eighteenth century in a relatively peaceful political environment, and drew comfort from empirical social observation that the bulk of citizens were 'habitually obedient'. Contemporary versions of positivist ideology are reflected, for example, in political 'law and order' campaigns, which stress the utilitarian virtue of civil obedience in maintaining an ordered, secure society. Positivism also tries to encourage and instil attitudes of social obedience by appealing to human nature and the supposed virtues of political democracy; that is, laws are 'good' because they have been made by democratic parliamentary procedures or by socially accepted judicial processes that bind everyone. Thus, society is ruled by the law and by laws (which is good) rather than by arbitrary despotic or capricious whims (which would be bad); the laws made in this way generally reflect the moral values of the community (which is good). However, positivists recognise that some persons may remain cynical or unconvinced by these noble ideals, and hence compliant obedience is also sought and coerced by having and publicising the existence of enforcement agencies (such as the police) whose role is to detect and prosecute breaches and infractions.

Limits of positivism

Despite all of these positivist exhortations particular laws, including the rules of professional liability, may—and, indeed, almost certainly will—be intentionally or unwittingly disregarded in practice on a small or large scale. Various reasons will be given, such as accident, misadventure, ignorance, inconvenience, expense, stubbornness, rebelliousness, perversity, stupidity, strong moral convictions, low risk of detection, small penalties that are not severe enough to discourage breach of the norm, or mass disobedience (for example, political demonstrations and industrial protests).

Other normative systems

Positivism as an ideology assumes, perhaps naively, that 'the law'—both as a pervasive social institution and in the form of particular laws—is more significant in influencing behaviour than are other normative systems. But most people belong to a diverse range of voluntary and involuntary groups and organisations, each of which may seek to impose distinct normative standards or codes of behaviour on its members. Families, professional associations, peers, colleagues, clubs, religious organisations and political parties all demand loyalties and allegiances that in some situations may be more powerful and immediate influences on the behaviour and attitudes of their members than more distant laws over which most citizens have little real influence.

Summary of legal positivism

Legal positivism is an influential social doctrine and underlies the main practical concerns that clinicians have regarding the impact of law on their professional activities. However, the successful implementation of legal positivism depends on a climate of loyalty, knowledge and obedience that can be quite unrealistic in practice. Positivism can also be socially and organisationally dysfunctional if it engenders a climate of fear among service providers, who then respond by practising so-called 'defensive medicine' in which practices are adopted primarily for the legal protection of the provider rather than for the clinical welfare of the patient. Positivist ideology may give too much emphasis to the 'good' of having and following established rules and procedures as ends in themselves, regardless of whether their strict observance actually promotes the overall goals of health service delivery. Strict positivists are more concerned with matters of procedure (that is, whether the rule was properly made by legitimate authority) and obedience (whether the rule is observed) than with issues of justice (whether the rule is fair and appropriate). While due regard to rules is necessary for the efficient organisation and delivery of service provision, there is a risk that the service will be unresponsive to patient needs and welfare unless its delivery is tempered flexibly in individual cases by humane concern for the wellbeing and autonomy of the patient.

Legal 'realism'

Legal realism designates philosophical approaches developed mainly in the United States and Scandinavia in the late nineteenth and early twentieth centuries, in reaction against positivism. Realism sceptically points to the discrepancy between the noble *ideals* of positivism and what, less nobly, happens in *practice* arising out of ignorance of the law, myths and misconceptions about the law, unequal access to the law, poor motivation to obey the law and so forth. During the past decade a modern realist movement known as 'critical legal theory' has become very active. The 'realist attitude' of mind is helpful in its constant reminder of the tension between theory and practice, and in the way it focuses attention on discrepancies between ideology/rhetoric and reality. Clinicians are practical people, concerned with action and outcomes, and need to know the likely practical impact of the law on their activities—not merely what the legal rules say in theory. Clinicians will usually benefit from seeking advice from legal practitioners possessing the skill, experience and sensitivity to combine positivist and realist perspectives in the advice given.

The realist movement has also helped to stimulate the carrying out of various empirical studies and surveys of the practical operation of the legal system, and studies of the effectiveness of laws in achieving intended objectives.

Much empirical work has been carried out, mainly in the United States and more recently in Australia, on whether litigation has *raised* the quality of services (by encouraging practitioners to be careful) or *lowered* the quality of services (by encouraging practitioners to engage in so-called 'defensive' clinical practices that are not indicated on clinical grounds but are done to guard against legal liability).[19] It does seem that Australia's practitioners are more fearful of being sued than they used to be, but it is not clear what impact that fear has had on quality of care and defensive medicine. An influential government study in the

United States drew attention to interpersonal problems in the clinician–patient relationship as a significant factor in stimulating litigation:

> The importance of human relations in the malpractice problem has been recognised by nearly everyone who has attempted to analyse the cause of malpractice litigation. In fact, there are those who believe the malpractice problem is essentially a human relations problem, and that greater attention to the human component is the only sure solution.[20]

We would offer the following overall 'preventive' guidance in general terms to clinical staff who are mindful of their legal position.

1 (a) Act in the best therapeutic interests of the patient.
  (b) But do not impose yourself and your views unduly on the patient; respect your patient's autonomy, which may mean that the patient chooses, after being appropriately informed, nevertheless to act against his or her best therapeutic interests as perceived by the clinician.
2 Do not knowingly harm your patient, and be careful not to do so inadvertently.
3 Keep your patient's confidences; do not gossip.
4 Consult an experienced colleague or independent expert on a discreet and tactful basis if you have doubts about what course of action to take.
5 Keep good records, but remember that all records may eventually become public in legal proceedings.
6 Above all, conduct yourself as a caring and independent professional.

Law, morality and ethical dilemmas

Institutions and people who administer and provide health services are often faced with dilemmas concerning treatment options that are morally or ethically controversial. Such conundrums perhaps arise most typically and obviously in life-or-death situations where decisions must be made between:

‹ trying to prolong human life of dubious quality (for example, operating to stem the spread of cancer temporarily in an irreversibly disease-riddled and pain-stricken patient)
‹ not interfering with or trying to halt biological processess that are already in train (such as a decline towards death) or
‹ actively terminating life or potential human life (as in abortion).

However, dilemmas on what is the 'right' course of action to follow can arise in every area of health service delivery—for example, requests for contraceptive agents made by adolescents without parental knowledge or consent; requests made by addicts for supplies of disposable syringes to be used to inject illegal drugs of addiction; requests made by patients for medical certificates on spurious clinical grounds; the carrying out of blood tests on patients in hospital without their knowledge and consent to check whether HIV (that is, AIDS) virus is present; and the use of new and relatively unevaluated methods of treatment on patients who are not informed and do not understand the nature of the innovation.

Morality or ethics (these terms are used interchangeably here) is concerned with the right action to take, and with the supporting reasons.

Personal or individual morality (for example, one's personal attitude to abortion) is a matter of conscience and is not binding or enforceable by external social sanctions. The ethical codes and codes of ethics of major professional associations, industry groups and government regulatory organisations differ from individual or personal ethics. A legal *realist* would observe that, in practice, in relation to those persons affected by them the former codes are often equivalent in their character, scope and coercive effect to binding laws. Non-compliance may attract sanctions with grave professional effect, such as expulsion from membership of an association or withdrawal of research funding or other privileges from both the infracting individual and his or her organisation.

Even a legal *positivist* would presumably concede that ethical codes have legal effect in at least two situations:

‹ *directly*, where parliaments expressly legislate or courts expressly adopt the code (for example, industrial safety legislation may expressly endorse industry codes of practice)
‹ *indirectly*, where courts or statutory tribunals exercising legal powers (such as disciplinary tribunals) take account of the ethical codes and standards recommended by professional organisations to help determine what constitutes acceptable or unacceptable conduct.

Natural law

Positivists contend that laws should be complied with even if they are immoral. *Realists* recognise that non-compliance may occur for a variety of practical reasons. *Natural law* is a philosophical tradition that contends that there is a moral duty to disobey 'unjust' laws in certain circumstances.

Natural law philosophy originated with the Greeks and found early expression in the writings of Aristotle and Cicero; it was most creatively developed in medieval Roman Catholic theology in the writings of Aquinas. In the eighteenth and nineteenth centuries this philosophy influenced important statements of human rights that evolved out of the French and American revolutions. During the twentieth century it inspired much of the international human rights movements, including the principles governing human experimentation articulated at the Nuremberg war crimes trials, and the United Nations Declaration on Human Rights.

There are many versions of natural law. Some are highly theological and religious; others are more humanistic. However, central to all natural law theorising are some key ideas:

‹ secular law is not a self-contained system of normative obligations
‹ the normative obligations reflected in and enforced by laws of the secular legal system must in turn be evaluated against paramount and overriding normative criteria that are established independently of the legal system (for example, biblical commandments, humanistic morality, custom, tradition)

⟨ ultimately law does not define paramount normative obligations, but proceeds from them

⟨ accordingly, laws may be unjust, immoral and wicked even if they have been promulgated after the adoption of all the usual political or judicial procedures

⟨ the immorality of particular secular laws (or even of the whole legal system) may be so great that the citizen's higher obligation is to disobey them.

However, natural law is not necessarily a doctrine subversive of the ruling order. More often it is used to reinforce the political system by leaders and demagogues who appeal to natural law ideals as a way of eliciting popular support or claiming legitimacy for controversial social programs.

Natural law is often characterised by reference to religious beliefs or to 'conscience' as the alleged reasons for disobeying or not complying with positivist laws in controversial issues such as abortion, euthanasia and contraception. Sometimes positivist laws will permit exceptions from compliance for these reasons.[21]

The world's legal systems
Classification

The world's legal systems can be classified into a number of related groups or families. The following outline is necessarily brief and does not classify every single system, but encompasses most of them.

The *common law* family includes Australia. The common law family encompasses legal systems based on the English legal system, most of which were formed by colonisation during the eighteenth and nineteenth centuries at the height of the British Empire. The legal systems of nations such as the United States retain the broad characteristics of this family even though they have severed their monarchical links with the United Kingdom. The term 'common law' is a reminder of the gradual emergence in England during the eleventh and twelfth centuries, under the Norman conquerors, of a body of law common to the whole of England in place of the many different Anglo-Saxon communal laws. Practising lawyers and judges also use the term in a narrower, technical sense to *distinguish* between judge-made law (common law) and legislation.

The *Romano-Germanic* or *civil law* family includes the legal systems of nations of Western Europe and the European Community that were formerly part of the extended Roman and French empires.

The *Eastern Socialist* family includes Russia and previous Eastern Bloc satellite countries that adopted Marxism as the foundation of their legal systems early in the twentieth century. More recently, a number of these countries have departed from their strict Marxism and restored at least partial capitalism.

The *Islamic* family encompasses those legal systems, mainly in the Middle East and Indonesia, that adopt a natural law approach of basing their secular laws on the higher inspiration of the Islamic religion.

The *Asian* family is distinguished by the influence of Eastern mystic philosophies such as Buddhism and Confucianism. In comparison with the

West, these traditions downplay the role of law as a technique of external and coercive social control and prefer instead to use other social controls (such as honour, shame, public criticism and community education), which reinforce individual restraint and control of self and have priority over external controls such as legislation. Even in countries (such as Japan) that have been subject to much Western influence there is a small number of lawyers per head of the population by Western standards, and disputes tend to be resolved without recourse to law.

The *decolonisation indigenous* family refers to the legal systems—mainly in India and Africa, but also in places such as Papua New Guinea and in the Pacific— in countries that regained independent, indigenous rule last century as part of widespread decolonisation by former imperialist powers. The legal systems in these countries are best described as evolving hybrids. The former colonial system (usually either common law reflecting English invasion or Romano-Germanic resulting from French, Dutch or Portuguese invasion) generally forms the basis of the existing order. However, ongoing modifications are under way to incorporate and give official recognition to customary tribal notions of personal and family relationships, ownership of property, criminal responsibility and other matters. Some countries have adopted Marxist models of law.

Some other terminology

Public international law refers to the law that regulates relationships between nations, such as the law of the United Nations and the World Health Organization and the law of diplomatic immunity. Some international law also deals with the role of individuals in relation to international dealings. Much international law is now established by international agreement in the form of documents known as treaties and conventions; these may be multilateral (having many participating countries) or bilateral (negotiated between two countries). However, not all international law derives from negotiated treaties; part of it still derives from customary rules that largely developed when the Romans, French and English were colonial powers. Legal realists are normally more comfortable than legal positivists in recognising that international law is in fact a form of 'law'. Strict positivists may have difficulty in giving these international arrangements the status and classification of law because of the absence of enforcement mechanisms to police breaches of international obligations. Positivists also find difficulty arising out of the absence of a defined 'sovereign' international body to which countries pay habitual obedience.

The Commonwealth Constitution and the *Australia Act 1986* (Cwlth and UK) vest most power over Australia's international relations in the Commonwealth of Australia and in the Commonwealth government. The states have little international role, except in trade matters.

Domestic, municipal or *internal law* refers to the laws that apply within the legal system of a nation such as Australia or within a specific state or territory, depending on the context. Internal law is in turn classified into major fields of study such as public and private law, criminal and civil law.

Private international law, otherwise known as *conflict of laws*, should not be confused with public international law. Whereas public international law deals mainly with relationships between countries, private international law is a branch of the internal law of a country, and each autonomous legal system has its own unique rules. Private international law comprises the rules used by a particular legal system to determine how much recognition shall be given to the laws of another legal system. For example, if a man from an Islamic country in which the laws recognise polygamy migrates with several of his wives to Australia with the intention to become a resident or citizen, will Australia recognise the validity of the polygamous relationships for the purposes of Australian law? Or will Australia recognise one only of the women as the man's lawful wife since Australian domestic law recognises monogamous rather than polygamous unions? Or will the man be prosecuted for the criminal offence in Australia of bigamy? How many dependent wives can be claimed by the husband in his taxation return? Can all the wives claim social security benefits? The internal rules used in Australia to resolve such conflicts form part of private international law or conflict of laws. Again, if a hospital were to import new equipment that turned out to be defective, then the hospital's possible remedies (if any) against the foreign manufacturer might be determined by considerations both of public international law (such as the existence of a relevant international treaty) and of private international law (for example, whether the warranty is based on a law of the Commonwealth of Australia or of a particular state or is based on law of the country of the manufacturer).

Private international law issues can also arise within Australia under our federal system. For example, in Australia the laws of defamation (that is, harm to reputation caused by publication of certain prejudicial information) are state and territory laws rather than national (Commonwealth) laws. Each state and territory has its own defamation laws and they differ in various ways. However, magazine or newspaper publications, radio broadcasts and telecasts frequently cross state and territory borders. If one or more legal actions were brought to recover damages for alleged defamation in respect of publications crossing borders, courts would have to decide, according to the principles of private international law, which set of defamation laws would govern the resolution of the dispute.

Development of the Australian legal system

The two major factors in the development of the Australian legal system have been its UK origin and the federal Constitution of 1900.

The English origin of the Australian legal system

When the various parts of Australia were first settled by UK colonists, the settlers brought with them the common law and statutes of England.

As to the question of what laws apply in a newly founded colony, the legal theory was (and, indeed, still is) that English colonists took with them only so much of the English law as was applicable to their own situation and to the conditions of the infant colony. The fact that Australian settlement began as a penal colony brought some obvious problems in this regard, but for New South Wales and Van Diemen's Land that problem was largely resolved by an Act of the UK parliament, in 1828, which provided that all laws and statutes in force in the realm of England on 25 July of that year applied in the colony so far as they could. In matters of doubt the governor, on advice of the Legislative Council, was to declare whether certain laws and statutes were deemed to extend to the colonies and be in force.

Not all of the Australian continent experienced the same penal-colony problems. Other colonies—free colonies—were founded: Western Australia was constituted a colony in June 1829 and South Australia was officially proclaimed on 28 December 1836. The former Port Phillip District of New South Wales was constituted the colony of Victoria in 1851, and the northern squatting districts of Moreton, Darling Downs, Burnett, Wide Bay, Maranoa, Leichhardt and Port Curtis were granted an independent administration and formed into a distinct colony under the name of Queensland by letters patent dated 6 June 1859.

By 1865, by the Colonial Laws Validity Act (UK), all colonies were vested with the legislative power to make laws for peace, order and good government.

When these local law-making bodies were established, the law so brought in was gradually modified and augmented by local legislation, but the imperial parliament in London also continued to legislate (to a lesser and lesser extent) in respect of Australia.

Federation

On 1 January 1901 all the colonies were federated under the name of 'The Commonwealth of Australia', the designation 'colonies' being at the same time changed to 'states'. This was effected legally by the Commonwealth of Australia Constitution Act 1900 (UK), also known as the federal Constitution.

The federal Constitution of 1900 limited the legislative power of state parliaments in some respects and created a federal legislature. With the passage of the *Australia Act 1986* (Cwlth and UK), the UK parliament gave up its remaining powers to legislate for Australia. The sources of Australian law of today are found, therefore, in Commonwealth and state legislation, in some imperial legislation (such as the Commonwealth Constitution itself) and in the judge-made common law.

Each state has its own Constitution, and the Commonwealth Constitution is contained in clause 9 of the Commonwealth of Australia Constitution Act 1900 (UK). The Northern Territory is not a state, even though it has a large measure of autonomy. However, the Commonwealth Constitution permits federal parliament to create new or additional states, and if that power were exercised the Northern Territory could become a state.

The Commonwealth Constitution allocates certain powers to the Commonwealth; the residual powers may be exercised by the states. So far as health services are concerned, the Commonwealth has the key powers to *raise taxation revenue and to fund health services and health insurance* and the states have the main powers to *implement the actual provision of health services*. (This is a broad summary; there are variations and exceptions.[22])

Separation of public powers for checks and balances

Constitutional law and administrative law are concerned with different but related aspects of public power. 'Public power' is the power to govern. The nature of the relationship has been expressed in various ways, but will be explained here in terms of the notion of 'separation of powers'.

Constitutional law as a field of study is concerned with the overall nature, types, classifications of and relationships between different kinds of public power, especially the power to make and change laws. *Administrative law* as a field of study focuses more specifically on the control and review of powers and discretions exercised by public agencies and officials and, to a smaller extent, the non-government sector, in particular administrative situations.

Separation of powers is intended to prevent overconcentration of power in any single individual or agency of government. It defines a system of checks and balances to prevent abuse of public power. Traditionally, three broad types of public power are distinguished: legislative, executive (or administrative) and judicial. The Constitution allocates these to different institutions, a procedure that is intended to constitute that system of checks and balances. Legislative power—that is, the power to enact and change laws—is entrusted to parliament. Judicial power, the power to interpret and declare laws and to adjudicate upon disputes, is entrusted to courts. Executive (or administrative) power, the power to manage and implement general or specific policies within a legally defined framework, is entrusted to ministers and other public officials, including the police and the public service.

Legislative power is usually concerned with laws of wide and general application. These powers are entrusted to Commonwealth and state parliaments (including the Crown). Parliaments often delegate certain legislative powers to other agencies (for example, government departments) and officials (such as ministers of the Crown). Some of the agencies that exercise delegated legislative power are described as 'quasi-legislative' bodies. (The word 'quasi' means 'resembling ... seemingly, but not actually'.[23]) For example, in recent years a number of anti-discrimination and human rights tribunals and boards have been established that are typically quasi-legislative bodies—they develop, publicise and seek to enforce a variety of human rights standards and charters. These bodies can usually impose fines or other penalties for breaches of the standards, and may be able to award compensation.

Judicial power to interpret and declare law is vested primarily in courts. The courts have a very limited role in making and changing laws through the establishment of 'precedents'; they also have an important role in interpreting the nature and limits of legislative, executive and judicial powers. Accordingly, the courts are vested with an important 'constitutional' role of so-called 'judicial review' in this respect. In recent years they have also played a larger role in reviewing actions and decisions of the executive branch of government.

Most executive powers, especially those of the Crown, derive from UK traditions and practices. Most such powers in Australia are conferred by written constitutions (for example, by the Commonwealth of Australia Constitution Act 1900 and by state

Constitutions) or by delegated legislative authority from parliament to governors, ministers, public service departments and officials, police, statutory authorities and others. Traditionally, parliaments (that is, the legislative branch of government) have exercised the primary and major source of control and review over executive action, since much executive action has been carried out under delegated legislative authority. For example, ministers are accountable to parliament for the administration of their portfolios. Parliaments have found it increasingly difficult, however, to monitor the burgeoning activities and discretions that have been delegated to the executive branch of government. Executive authority may be so intrusive and widespread that, in practice, an administrative scheme is nearly indistinguishable from a legislative one in terms of the number of citizens affected, the significance of decisions involved and so forth. This can make it hard to maintain the reality of the formal distinction between legislative and executive powers. Parliaments have also established various other mechanisms (for example, ombudsmen; special tribunals, such as the Commonwealth Administrative Appeals Tribunal; Freedom of Information legislation in certain jurisdictions) to increase the accountability of the executive branch.

The expression 'quasi-judicial' power is also encountered. For example, a disciplinary tribunal is usually required by law to proceed in an impartial and unbiased way and to give the accused person notice of the charges and an opportunity to study and challenge the evidence at a fair and properly constituted hearing. These safeguards are similar to ones routinely followed by all courts and are called 'quasi-judicial' proceedings when they are adopted by administrative bodies other than the courts. However, although there are lots of tribunals, they are not courts, but are part of the executive branch of government. A person dissatisfied with the decision of a tribunal usually has a right to appeal to a court.

Some terminology used in court proceedings

Litigants may have the choice of multiple courts in which the proceedings can commence—from magistrates' courts to the High Court itself in appropriate cases.

Civil and criminal proceedings

Civil proceedings are court actions in which the plaintiff (the person bringing the action) sues (that is, seeks damages or other remedies from) the defendant (the person being sued) either for having allegedly committed a wrong to the plaintiff or to prevent the defendant from wronging the plaintiff.

Criminal proceedings are court proceedings in which the prosecutor (that is, the Crown or a representative of the Crown, such as the attorney-general) or a person known as a complainant or informant (such as a policeman, a government inspector or a victim of a crime) prosecutes (that is, asks the court to impose a penalty, such as a fine or imprisonment) the accused/defendant/offender (the person charged with the offence) for having allegedly committed or attempted to commit a crime against the state.

Letter of demand

Before the commencement of legal proceedings, it is common for the claimant to contact the other party and inform him or her that unless the debt or damages are paid within a specified time, legal proceedings will be commenced to enforce payment. This approach may be made orally, but is usually done in writing by letter or formal notice to inform the debtor or other person of the action that will be taken if the debt (or claim) is not paid or an acceptable offer for payment is not made.

'Without prejudice' negotiations

Often correspondence between parties (or potential parties) to litigation—and, more particularly, between their legal representatives—is labelled 'without prejudice'. The reason for using this term is to place a confidential umbrella over negotiations, so that if those negotiations fail and the matter proceeds further in court anything said during the negotiations cannot later be used against the party who said it. However, there are some limits on the confidentiality. For example, after the whole dispute is resolved the court may look at what offers, if any, were made to settle it by negotiation, as this may affect the court's decision on which party should bear the legal costs of the proceedings.

Settling disputes 'out of court'

In all Australian jurisdictions, settlement out of court (that is, resolution of a dispute on an agreed rather than an imposed basis) is the most common conclusion to defended civil cases. In one sense, the terminology of settling 'out of court' is misleading. It simply means that the parties agree on the outcome, but usually the agreement is reduced to writing and approved by the court, so to that extent it is really 'in' rather than 'out of' court.

Subpoenas

During litigation, any of the parties may require access to relevant documentary evidence (such as confidential medical records) or may require relevant witnesses to attend and give evidence. The custodians of those documents and those witnesses may in the circumstances be reluctant to produce or to attend, or may be prevented by rules of confidentiality from releasing the information unless compelled by a court order, which overrules confidentiality. The rules of court therefore provide a procedure for compelling production or attendance; this involves the issuing of 'subpoenas' (literally, *sub poena* translates to 'under a penalty', indicating the force of the document that notes on its face that 'if you do not comply with this subpoena you may be arrested').

A subpoena for 'production' (or *subpoena duces tecum*) compels the person to whom it is directed to attend and produce the documents and things described in the schedule. If the subpoena requires confidential records to be produced, such as patient records, they must be sent *to the court directly*; they must *not* be given to the party who has asked for the documents, as the court must decide who is allowed to see them.

A subpoena to give 'evidence' (or *subpoena ad testificandum*) compels the person to whom it is directed to attend the court and give evidence.

Witnesses

There are two kinds of witness in court proceedings.

The *lay* witness is an ordinary citizen, without any special expertise, who has seen or heard something or who has other personal knowledge that will assist the court in its deliberations.

The *expert* witness, however, by virtue of special qualifications, training or experience, is able to assist the court in matters requiring expertise or opinion.

Medical practitioners who have treated a patient are commonly asked to provide medical reports on that patient and to give oral evidence in court in their capacity as expert witnesses. Other practitioners who have not actually treated the patient concerned may nevertheless be asked to examine the person before trial to enable them to qualify as experts who can assist the court in matters of contention.

The expert, although retained by one or other of the parties, must discharge his or her role impartially and frankly. The advice tendered to the party requesting the report is confidential and cannot be disclosed by the expert to anyone without the permission of the person requesting the report. If the party receiving the report does not like its contents because they are unfavourable to that party's case, then the legal representatives of that party are usually not obliged to use the report and are permitted to seek another independent opinion.

Persons who are asked to prepare expert reports should bear some practical precautions in mind. It is always important to set out very clearly the factual material or the assumptions upon which the expert relies and the basis of the expert's knowledge of those supposed facts. It may well be that what is relied on by the expert as a fact is merely an assumption or is derived from some secondary source that the expert has not been able to verify. While it may be necessary in the report to rely—at least in part—on unverified assertions, the expert should nevertheless be careful to qualify, as a protection, any conclusions that may depend on such unverified assumptions or hearsay material. It can be very embarrassing and, indeed, highly damaging to a party's case and to the expert's reputation if an expert makes an unequivocal statement that is later shown to be without a proper foundation in fact or assumption.

Similarly, the expert's report should draw as far as possible a clear distinction between matters of fact (or assumed fact) on the one hand and matters of comment or opinion on the other. The relationship between factual material (or the data) and expert comment or opinion should be made clear in the text of the report.

The expert should always remember that if the matter does proceed to a full hearing it is quite possible, and even likely, that he or she may be cross-examined on contentious matters by legal representatives of the opposing party. Accordingly, it is wise to be careful and cautious in the manner of expression used in the report.

Giving oral evidence in court

A person giving evidence is normally required to answer a series of questions. The person is not allowed to narrate an uninterrupted story.

On many occasions the person in the witness box may be interrupted by objecting lawyers if he or she tries to give evidence based on second-hand knowledge (called 'hearsay') rather than direct personal knowledge. For example, if the witness has observed someone knocked down by a car, he or she can testify about what was personally seen, heard, felt, tasted or smelt. However, if the witness's knowledge of the accident is only second-hand (because someone told him or her about it) then the knowledge as to whether an accident occurred is hearsay and proves only that the witness was told about an accident—it does not prove that an accident did occur.

Confidentiality and privilege

Courts have power to require parties to override ordinary confidentiality that outside of court would prevent them from disclosing information without their clients' consent.

The relationship between a *doctor* and a *patient* or a *hospital* and a *patient* is normally confidential, although there are exceptions,[24] but courts can often demand access to such records (see the previous section on subpoenas) and compel doctors to disclose what the patients said and what the doctors observed. However, there are some matters that are confidential even from courts, and those matters are termed 'privileged'; privilege entails a higher form of confidentiality than ordinary confidentiality. *Ordinary confidentiality can be overridden by a court, but the confidentiality of privileged communications cannot be overridden.*

Most aspects of doctor–patient relationships are confidential but not privileged; however, three jurisdictions do make certain of such communications privileged and not merely confidential. In the Northern Territory, Tasmania and Victoria doctors are not allowed to disclose—and cannot be made to disclose—information about patients in most types of civil proceedings without the patient's consent. The privilege has been created by evidence legislation. It belongs to the patient and can only be waived by the patient or by his or her personal representative. Moreover, the privilege and the power to waive it continue after the patient's death, being then vested in the patient's personal representative. However, it is confined to civil proceedings and does not extend to other legal proceedings such as criminal actions. In Victoria this privilege also extends to inquiries by a complaints investigator. The type of information it covers is '... any information which (the doctor) has acquired in attending the patient and which was necessary to enable him to prescribe or act for the patient'. In the Northern Territory and Tasmania it is more narrowly confined to '... any communication made to (the doctor) in his professional character by (such) patient and necessary to enable him to prescribe or act for (such) patient'.

This privilege is, however, subject to statutory exceptions, when information must be given to the court. No evidentiary privilege exists for these exceptions, and doctors can be forced by a court to give information without the patient's consent. However, a doctor should not volunteer such confidential information without being legally forced by the court; otherwise the patient could sue the doctor and/or the doctor could be charged with a disciplinary offence of professional misconduct.

No similar privilege applies in Australia to any other health professionals. However, most jurisdictions have enacted—or are intending to enact—evidence legislation that confers privilege in both civil and criminal proceedings with respect to confessions made by penitent persons to *religious advisers*.

Communications between *husband and wife* are usually privileged. Normally a wife cannot be compelled to give evidence against her husband, and vice versa, but in a number of judicatures there is an exception to privilege if a wife or a husband lays a complaint with the police that she or he has been the victim of domestic assault committed by the spouse. In such a case, the wife or husband laying the complaint can be compelled to give evidence in court.

The relationship between a *client* and a *lawyer* is normally privileged in all states and territories of Australia, and under federal law. That is to say, communications occurring between a registered lawyer and his or her client are usually privileged (and cannot be compelled by a court to be disclosed) provided that the communications were made for the *sole purpose* of giving or receiving legal advice, or were made with reference to litigation that was actually taking place or was in the reasonable contemplation of the client. In addition, if the lawyer communicates with a third party (such as a doctor or an expert witness) to enable the lawyer to advise the client, then the third-party communication is also protected by the same legal privilege from disclosure in court without the client's consent.

Medical confidentiality outside of court is further discussed in the section 'Civil liability of clinicians', subsection 'Confidentiality'.

Affidavits

An affidavit is a written statement voluntarily signed and sworn to, and it is the method by which written evidence is put before a court. The person making an affidavit is called the *deponent*.

The same rules apply to affidavit evidence as to oral evidence, so that statements in an affidavit must use the first person, 'I'; direct speech must be used, hearsay evidence is not usually permitted, opinion evidence is admissible on a limited number of occasions only and all the statements in the affidavit (that is, the evidence) must be relevant.

Affidavits are of great variety and may be used, for example, to verify documents or to tender exhibits.

An affidavit is sworn on the Bible or is affirmed before a Justice of the Peace or other similarly authorised functionary. It constitutes perjury to give false evidence by affidavit.

Due process of law

The procedures of the courts and statutory tribunals represent due process of law in operation, and three fundamental principles must always mark that operation.

Natural justice

The concept of natural justice as used in a court of law is narrower and more specific than the general philosophy of natural justice in a moral sense, referred to earlier in this chapter in the subsection 'Natural law'. As used in courts, natural justice mainly means two things: first, the proceedings must be conducted impartially and without bias, or even the appearance of bias; second, the hearing must be fair. In particular, each party must be given adequate notice of the case to be met, and each party must have adequate opportunity to present his or her case and to answer or challenge any prejudicial evidence. Natural justice also must be observed in disciplinary contexts, and by means of bodies or tribunals (for example, medical registration boards, professional associations and licensing authorities) that exercise statutory powers to affect the professional interests of persons subject to their jurisdiction. Natural justice is also called 'procedural fairness'.

Equality

There must be equality before the law, with privilege and unfairness excluded.

Public justice

The principle is always that not only must justice be done, it must be seen to be done.

Civil liability of clinicians
Defining the area

'Civil liability' defines the circumstances in which monetary damages are payable by a practitioner or institution to a patient arising out of the professional relationship with the patient. In some circumstances, legal remedies other than damages are appropriate—for example, an injunction to restrain a foreshadowed breach of confidence.

The positivist rules of civil liability in Australia are a combination of legislation and common law (judge-made law). Legislative bodies and courts may take account of ethical standards in certain situations. On the whole the rules are fairly settled, but some issues are in a state of development, such as the degree of information that should be disclosed to patients contemplating treatment, refusal of treatment by institutionalised patients, proxy consent by nominees or substituted consent by guardians on behalf of incapable patients. Some of these issues are considered in the following subsections.

Investigation

The lawyer will investigate the client's claim before recommending commencement of legal action, and will advise the client of the likelihood of success and failure in litigation.

Formulation of the case

If the client wishes to proceed, the lawyer will try to formulate the plaintiff's case so that it displays the allegations of recognised types of legal claim in the official documents to be filed in court and served on each of the defendants. Each type of claim has its own name, such as negligence, assault, battery, false imprisonment, breach of statutory duty or breach of contract. The lawyer will formulate the client's case in as many recognised ways as possible to optimise the chances of succeeding in the action. It is unethical and a disciplinary offence for a lawyer to allege a case in a way which he or she knows is not supported by any evidence or client instruction whatsoever. However, no offence is committed merely by alleging a case that is unlikely to succeed, provided that there appears to be at least *some* tenable evidence in support of the claim.

Normally, all the claims arising out of one incident may be alleged ('pleaded') in the one action for damages. However, the plaintiff will only get one lot of damages even if he or she can establish more than one of the recognised claims.

Limitation periods

Action must be commenced within certain time periods, known as 'limitation periods', set out in legislation. The periods vary according to the jurisdiction where the proceedings are commenced and the type of claim.

Persons and organisations to be sued as defendants

The lawyer will advise the client (patient) of which one or more human or corporate persons and organisations should be made defendants in the proceedings. The potential defendants cannot control this decision, and this is a major reason why professional indemnity insurance is a wise precaution. It is important to emphasise, however, that contrary to the widespread misconception of most doctors, membership of a medical defence organisation does *not* provide professional indemnity insurance, as the organisation retains complete *discretion* on whether to give assistance in each instance.[25]

Cost of litigation

Personal injury litigation is expensive, and in Australia would often cost each plaintiff and defendant in the vicinity of A$5000–8000 for each day of the trial, in addition to costs incurred before trial.

Unsuccessful parties usually must bear all their own costs, must reimburse a proportion of costs known as 'taxed costs' incurred by the successful party (usually in the vicinity of one-third to one-half of the costs actually incurred), and must also pay any damages that may have been awarded.

A *successful plaintiff* who gains an award of damages therefore remains liable for approximately one-half to two-thirds of his or her 'untaxable' costs, which cannot be claimed back directly from the unsuccessul defendants and will therefore reduce the net value of the damages awarded.

A *successful defendant* has the satisfaction of knowing that the action by the plaintiff has been dismissed without any damages being awarded. But the successful defendant will nevertheless be heavily out of pocket, as there is no award of damages that can help to defray the one-half to two-thirds of his or her 'untaxable' costs that cannot be claimed back directly from the unsuccessful plaintiff.

Thus, all plaintiffs without legal aid, and all uninsured defendants, are at considerable financial risk of incurring substantial costs regardless of whether they are successful or unsuccessful. Professional indemnity insurance meets the costs of defending the action and meets any verdict up to the limit of the policy.

Burden of proof

The plaintiff in a civil action for damages has the forensic 'burden of proving' or establishing that the defendant is guilty. This means that the plaintiff has the forensic onus or obligation of proving each of the key allegations, and that each defendant is presumed innocent and is entitled to a verdict of not guilty if such proof is not sustained. On some particular issues, such as alleged contributory negligence of the plaintiff, the defendant may have the burden of proof.

Degree or standard of proof

The required 'standard of proof' (that is, the degree or extent of proof required to discharge the burden) in a civil case is that the plaintiff must prove each and all of the essential allegations of his or her claims on the 'balance of probabilities', meaning that it is *more likely than not* that each of the essential allegations is true. The law of professional liability depends on the probability, rather than the certainty, of the events having occurred in the manner alleged. Rules of evidence and procedure regulate the manner in which it is permissible to prove or defend allegations in the litigation. (In a *criminal case*, a more rigorous standard of proof is required. The prosecution must prove its case not merely on the balance of probabilities, but *beyond all reasonable doubt*.)

Monetary damages

If liability can be demonstrated, then damages should normally be assessed at the amount that would compensate the plaintiff for the *reasonably foreseeable* loss and damage he or she has suffered because of the defendant's breach. The purpose of an award of damages is to compensate the plaintiff with the money equivalent of the injury and loss caused by the defendant. Only very rarely is the court permitted to add to the compensatory damages awarded to the plaintiff a further amount, known as exemplary or punitive damages, to punish the defendant for wrongful conduct.

Main grounds of liability

The main situations in which legislation and/or judge-made law gives patients the right to sue for damages are where patients:

- suffer injury or harm (physical, mental, property, financial) caused or materially contributed to by lack of reasonable care by an institution, practitioners or staff (civil negligence)
- are treated without consent while they are of sound mind (assault and battery)
- are physically restrained or detained against their will while they are of sound mind (false imprisonment)
- have confidential personal information disclosed without their consent or lawful authority (breach of confidence, breach of contract and/or breach of statutory duty)
- are not treated as required by a legislative obligation (breach of statutory duty)
- participate in sexual relationships with the medical practitioner
- have damaging assertions made publicly, impugning their reputation (defamation).

These situations are considered in the following sections.

Negligence

Civil and criminal negligence distinguished

Negligence in the *civil* sense differs from negligence in the criminal sense. In the civil sense it embodies the idea of a legal duty breached by conduct that is unreasonable when it is assessed against accepted standards.

In the *criminal* sense, however, negligence refers to conduct that is more seriously deficient in being grossly careless or recklessly indifferent to the likely risk of causing human injury or death, giving rise to liability for criminal prosecution by the state. In one such case, an anaesthetist was found by a jury to have been guilty of criminal negligence causing manslaughter when he failed for too long during an operation to detect lack of oxygen reaching the patient.[26]

Narrow and broad meanings of civil negligence

Negligence in the civil sense is often used in a narrow way to identify the defendant's alleged *unreasonable behaviour*, in terms of *specific breaches* of duty of care and skill. Negligence in this sense can occur by *conduct* (either by actions or by omissions to act) or by *words*. Practitioners must exercise *reasonable skill and care* in diagnosis, treatment and advice.

However, the legal action for civil negligence more broadly embraces *all* the allegations necessary to sustain an action for negligence, namely:

- the owing of a legal *duty* by the defendant to the plaintiff
- the *breach* or breaches of such duty by the defendant personally and/or by the defendant's servants and agents
- *injury* or damage to the plaintiff that is in fact *caused* or materially contributed to by such breach(es) and is also a reasonably foreseeable consequence of such breaches.

The concept of 'reasonable' conduct

The legal concept of reasonable care and skill has a special meaning. Reasonable care in the context of civil negligence is an *objective* (external) standard, not a subjective (purely individual) one. A practitioner must exercise the standard of care and skill of a reasonably competent and skilled practitioner in the relevant clinical field—for example, general medical practice, general dental practice, particular fields of specialist medical or dental practice, nursing practice, pharmaceutical practice and so forth. It is not necessary to exercise the skill of the most skilled practitioner in the relevant field, but neither would it be acceptable to exercise the skill of an incompetent practitioner. It is no defence to an allegation of negligent breach of duty that a practitioner did his or her best if an objectively reasonable standard of care and skill was not displayed.

The law does not require perfection or the highest possible skill, but provides remedy against fault (in the sense of objectively unreasonable conduct).

Most allegations of civil negligence appear to arise out of quick but careless conduct, but even considered decisions may be held negligent if the underlying clinical judgment is unreasonable.

Negligence is judged in relation to the particular incident that gave rise to damage. It is not a judgment of a whole career. It is irrelevant to a finding of negligence that a practitioner is usually careful.

A practitioner usually acts reasonably in adopting or choosing any practice or method that has a *responsible body* of expert support in the circumstances of its use, not necessarily majority or general support. The word 'practice' is used in various ways and might, depending on the context, mean any of the following: the practice recommended by a particular individual; the practice actually adopted by a particular individual; the practice usually adopted by a particular individual; the practice or school of thought recommended by a certain group of practitioners; the practice or school of thought actually adopted by a certain group of practitioners; the practice or school of thought usually adopted by a certain group of practitioners.

A practitioner usually acts unreasonably in adopting a practice that is really against the whole of informed professional opinion, unless there is a reasonable basis for the practitioner's rejection of that opinion or practice.

In some instances, however, judges have held accepted clinical practices to be unreasonable and have ruled that it was a breach of duty for the practitioner to have adopted such a practice even though the latter's conduct was supported by reputable peers, as illustrated in the discussion dealing with the obligation to disclose information about material risks.

Practitioners are not expected to cure patients, but are required to exercise reasonable skill and care in diagnosis, treatment, advice and management. A practitioner would be unwise to guarantee to cure the patient or achieve a successful outcome. Such a guarantee could expose the practitioner to action for damages for breach of contract even if all reasonable care had been exercised in the procedure.

An undesired outcome is not of itself reason enough to sue. Thus, the aphorism 'the operation was a success, but the patient died' reflects a legal truth that there is no breach of duty if everything that could reasonably be expected to be done was done, but the patient succumbed anyway owing to an inherent risk.

The law recognises the inherent uncertainties and unpredictabilities of clinical practice, and its progressive and evolving nature. The standard of care and skill that may reasonably be expected must be assessed in the light of what was reasonably known and the state of clinical practice when a decision was made. The required standard of care must not, at the time of the trial of the action, be assessed against new developments or knowledge that has been established since the date of treatment. Innovative techniques may be adopted if there are reasonable grounds for so doing and if the patient is adequately informed.

Australian law recognises that such compromises and balancing of goals and methods are inevitable in a practical world. The law usually insists, however, that whichever compromise is ultimately chosen must nevertheless be one that it is 'reasonable' to adopt in all the circumstances.[27] If so, the choice is legally protected in this regard, even if it is not the best or optimal choice and even if other equally reasonable or preferable choices were rejected in its favour. The 'reasonableness' principle limits the minimum standard of care that is legally acceptable to guard against civil negligence.

Role of expert evidence

The court will base its knowledge of technical and scientific aspects, and its knowledge of professional practices at the relevant times, by assessing evidence given in the action by one or more experts called by the parties as witnesses. The court relies on such evidence to inform itself, as an expert on factual matter, of what professional practice or practices were actually current and supported by responsible practitioners at the time of advising, diagnosing or treating the patient. In some cases, courts have accordingly reached divergent findings on what clinical practices of advice, diagnosis or treatment were current and/or appropriate at a particular time because different expert evidence was adduced in each litigation.

Usually they do accept the reasonableness of any practices having reputable professional support at the time of use, but there have been some notable Australian cases in which they have rejected the reasonableness of such common practices, and have held that it was a breach of the practitioner's legal duty to the patient to have adhered to them.[28]

In cases decided without a jury, it would appear that judges—without receiving evidence on the point—sometimes simply assert that certain clinical knowledge has percolated beyond the circle of experts and become part of the general information that ordinary citizens in the broad community would typically know; and that ordinary citizens and the plaintiff should therefore be *deemed* to be aware of such information regardless of whether citizens generally or the plaintiff actually knew about it. Bromberger has forcefully argued in a critique that such 'judicial notice' is unsatisfactory and may cause substantial injustice owing to unrealistic assumptions and presumptions. He submits that the parties to the litigation should first be permitted to present wide-ranging social evidence from which judges would then make relevant formal findings as to what it is reasonable to presume that a person in the situation of the plaintiff ought to know.[29]

The concept of 'causation'

Negligent conduct is not actionable unless damage is actually *caused* or *materially contributed to* by the breach. For example, if a patient were overdosed with a drug because the label had not been checked by the nurse, that would be a breach of duty, but if the patient did not become ill, then no action in negligence could be sustained. Likewise, even if it were a breach of duty in a particular situation not to diagnose a presenting condition, no action for negligence could be sustained if the plaintiff could not demonstrate that earlier correct diagnosis and appropriate treatment would, more probably than not, have led to an improved outcome.

Proving causation

Where there is evidence that a number of separate factors may have been operative in producing the plaintiff's injury or loss, and that some of the identified factors do not relate to any alleged breach of duty of the defendant, it can be difficult in practice for the plaintiff to discharge the burden of proving that it is more probable than not that the defendant's alleged breaches of duty caused or materially contributed to the injury or loss.

Liability for negligence extends to *reasonably foreseeable consequences* caused by a breach; it does not extend to consequences that are not reasonably foreseeable. The extent to which the consequences that actually ensued had been reasonably foreseeable *at the time of the advice or treatment* may be a difficult question that the court must resolve.

Members of clinical teams

Every member of a clinical team owes a legal duty of care to the patient. That duty of care will in some situations be more compelling than separate legal duties that the members of the team owe each other or their employing institutions.

For example, the express or implied terms of the contract of employment by a hospital of a nurse or a junior doctor may be such that the employee is normally expected to carry out the orders of the senior medical head of the team. But if the junior were given an instruction by a senior which a reasonably competent junior should realise was 'manifestly wrong' and would endanger the patient, then the junior's duty to the patient would, in law, have greater priority than the duty to carry out the instructions of the senior; it would not be a defence to an action for negligence that the junior had carried out such manifestly wrong orders or instructions, at least without having queried them at the time. In such a situation the senior could be held negligent for having given the instruction, the junior could be held negligent for carrying it out, and the hospital could also be held negligent vicariously for the conduct of the senior and junior personnel.[30] Similarly, a pharmacist has a duty to the patient to intercept a doctor's prescription that would be manifestly wrong to a reasonably competent pharmacist. Whether liability would be imposed on the person following instructions would depend on how obvious the error should have been. In marginal cases it might suffice to clarify instructions with the team head or someone else with appropriate expertise, and then add an entry in the patient records for added protection.

Team heads are, in the absence of contrary indications, entitled to assume that members of the team employed by the institution are competent to carry out tasks or functions that have reasonably been assigned and for which adequate orders or instructions have been given. The team head is not negligent merely on acccount of negligence by a member of the team—only if he or she fails to exercise adequate monitoring or supervision.

Of course, it is important that members of the team are adequately competent in terms of qualifications, training and skills to carry out assigned tasks; otherwise, the inexperienced or incompetent person, the team head and the employing institution might each and all be held liable for negligence if the patient suffered injury.

Consent to patient treatment and/or experimentation

Health professionals must normally obtain consent to treatment either from the patient or from a person, public official, tribunal or court with power to consent on behalf of the patient.

In various specific situations, legislation authorises particular kinds of treatment without patient consent or over the objections of the patient—for example, legislation for involuntary mental patients and public health legislation for compulsory detention and treatment of persons suffering infectious or communicable diseases.

If the patient is capable of understanding what is proposed, then he or she possesses the requisite legal capacity to consent to or to refuse the procedure. In relation to a minor, there is no absolute age below which he or she cannot consent. There is a presumption in New South Wales that a 14-year-old can consent,[31] but this is not an inflexible rule, and if there is conflict between parent (or guardian) and minor, courts can decide if necessary.[32] In an English case, which has been approved by the High Court of Australia,[33] the House of Lords endorsed the following propositions:

> ... the desirability of the doctor being entitled in some cases, in the girl's best interest, to give her contraceptive advice and treatment if necessary without the consent or even knowledge of her parents. The only practicable course is to entrust the doctor with a discretion to act in accordance with his view of what is best in the interests of the girl who is his patient. He should, of course, always seek to persuade her to tell her parents that she is seeking contraceptive advice, and the nature of the advice that she receives. But there may well be cases, and I think there will be some cases, where the girl refuses to tell the parents herself or to permit the doctor to do so and in such cases, the doctor will, in my opinion, be justified in proceeding without the parents' consent or even knowledge provided he is satisfied of the following matters: (1) that the girl (although under 16 years of age) will understand his advice; (2) that he cannot persuade her to inform her parents or to allow him to inform the parents that she is seeking contraceptive advice; (3) that she is very likely to begin or continue having sexual intercourse with or without contraceptive treatment; (4) that unless she receives contraceptive advice or treatment her physical or mental health or both are likely to suffer; (5) that her best interests require him to give her contraceptive advice, treatment or both without the parental consent.

> The result ought not to be regarded as a licence for doctors to disregard the wishes of parents on this matter whenever they find it convenient to do so. Any doctor who behaves in such a way would be failing to discharge his professional responsibilities, and I would expect would be disciplined by his own professional body accordingly. The medical profession have in modern times come to be entrusted with very wide discretionary powers going beyond the strict limits of clinical judgment and there is nothing strange about entrusting them with this further responsibility which they alone are in a position to discharge satisfactorily.[34]

Parents and guardians are empowered to consent to treatment in the best interests of those in their charge. Traditionally, it was expensive and cumbersome to apply to courts to appoint a guardian of a mentally infirm person, but many jurisdictions have established new guardianship boards and tribunals in recent years to simplify, speed up and reduce the expense of these applications. Parents and guardians must act in the best interests of their charges, and courts or tribunals can review disputed or controversial decisions; for example, whether a mentally handicapped girl should be sterilised during adolescence.

The judicial doctrine of 'necessity' allows health providers to give minimally necessary therapeutic emergency treatment to those who are in need of such treatment but whose mental state is temporarily or permanently impaired regarding decision making.[35] A number of jurisdictions now allow adults to plan for such situations by appointing someone in writing as their agent or proxy to make decisions on their behalf in the event of supervening incapacity.

Adult patients of sound mind who do not wish to be subjected to treatment in a hospital that they have voluntarily attended can refuse treatment and can discharge themselves from the institution if they wish, even if that course of action is clinically undesirable and injury or even death will ensue. This is discussed more fully in the section 'Some issues in criminal legal responsibility'.

Consent forms

Consent is a mental quality of understanding. It is well established that consent forms are only paper evidence of what was being consented to by the patient, and are not conclusive.[36] In any dispute, the court will also consider other sources of information that the patient relied on, such as conversations with the doctor or staff.

The substance of consent

The law distinguishes between consent to (a) the general nature of proposed procedures and (b) more detailed information, advice or warnings about proposed procedures (including the risks and the alternatives).

Consent to the general nature of the procedure

Unless a patient has first agreed in *broad general terms* to undergo the procedure, treatment is regarded as being performed with no consent at all, which gives rise to an action for one or more intentional legal wrongs collectively known as 'torts of trespass to the person' and specifically as 'assault', 'battery' or 'false imprisonment'.

If the patient's apparent consent to the broad nature of the procedure was procured by fraud or misrepresentation, this may invalidate the consent, in which case the treatment constitutes assault, battery and/or false imprisonment.

Civil *assault* occurs when a person (such as a practitioner) intentionally and directly creates in another person (such as a patient) a belief, which is reasonable in the circumstances, that imminent physical contact (such as medical treatment) is threatened. If the patient was unaware prior to the actual physical contact that treatment was imminent, then there would be no action for assault.

Battery is the actual application of physical force (such as the laying on of hands, forcible medication or injection, compelled X-rays). Thus, an assault *and* battery occurs when the patient is both aware of the imminent contact and then actually experiences such contact. If the patient apprehends imminent physical contact but the perpetrator desists before contact, then there is an assault but no battery. Conversely, if the patient is struck without prior warning there is a battery, but no assault.

False imprisonment occurs when the patient's liberty of physical movement is restrained; for example, if a door is locked or if crutches are removed.

Consent is the major defence to assault, battery and/or false imprisonment. Other defences include necessity (that is, the exercise of a *reasonable* degree of physical force to defend person or property against physical harm, or to administer necessary care to persons whose mental state does not permit them to apprehend what is proposed); ordinary social contact (such as tapping someone lightly to gain attention or to brush through a crowd); supervision of young children or of persons whose mental faculties have permanently or temporarily departed; and statutory authority (for example, legislation regarding involuntary mental patients).

Some legal guidance on physical restraint of patients

Delicate situations often arise in nursing care when, on the one hand, restraining a patient runs the risk of committing an intentional wrong of assault, battery and/or false imprisonment, but on the other hand failure to restrain that patient runs the risk of negligence if the patient injures himself or herself. In a publication commissioned by the Commonwealth and distributed to all nursing homes in Australia, co-authored by the present writer, the following guidance was given:

> Health professionals involved in giving nursing home services may find that, while they have a duty to ensure that no harm comes to a confused elderly person, they also have a duty to protect other residents and their possessions from those who are confused and aggressive. Failure to restrain residents where it would have been considered reasonable to do so by a reputable body of professional opinion could result in an action in negligence if the resident or someone else suffers injury as a result of not using restraints.
>
> The necessity for restraint is a matter for nursing or medical judgment. Under ordinary circumstances the decision to use restraints must be based on the outcome of assessment by a physician or registered nurse and not as a result of a decision taken by enrolled nurses or ancillary staff or anyone without nursing or medical expertise. Where physicians write a request for the application

of restraints by nurses, the request must reflect the documentation, by the physician, of the medical assessment that has been made of the resident and the circumstances which indicated that restraints should be used in each case.

It is unlawful to restrain residents merely for the convenience of staff or other residents. Restraint will be lawful only in order to guard against physical injury to the resident or to others who might be hurt by the resident, or to protect property which the resident is threatening. The method of restraint used must be the least restrictive alternative that would successfully ensure protection. Restraint must also be ceased when the resident's condition improves, or it becomes feasible for a less restrictive method of restraint to be used. The condition of a resident who is under restraint must be monitored regularly so that the degree of restraint is able to be altered appropriately. Adequate documentation should be kept to justify the method and duration of restraints used in each instance.

If nurses disagree with medical assessment of the need for restraint, then this is a matter for professional discussion. Until this is resolved it is wise to apply the restraints because a medical assessment would establish that the danger which could arise from not having the resident restrained had been foreseen. Alternatively, assessment by registered nurses that the need for restraint exists places the physician in a similar situation.

Where there are no statutory provisions which clarify a particular situation, such as mental health legislation, the defence to an accusation of unauthorised restraint and confinement must rely on the overriding need which existed in order to prevent harm to the resident or others.

If the matter is taken to court, the decision not to use restraints, or to use restraints of a particular type and for a particular length of time, would have to stand on its merits. The circumstances which would be examined by the court would include the availability and condition and types of restraints and the method of restraint used to control the resident's behaviour. The courts would also examine the appropriateness of the choice of restraint in the circumstances, the length of time during which the restraints were used and the extent of the indignity (if under trespass) which the resident was forced to endure or, if under negligence, the extent of any injury which occurred as a result of the lack of supervision given to the resident during that time. The value of clear and accurate records cannot be stressed too heavily![37]

However:

... it would be difficult to defend the routine restraint of certain residents on the basis that they might possibly come to minor harm. This robs these residents of the dignity associated with self-determination and liberty.[38]

Proving intentional wrongs

An action for the intentional wrongs of assault, battery or false imprisonment is easier to prove than an action for negligence, because supporting expert evidence of unreasonableness is not required in an action for an intentional wrong.

In such an action the central issues are first, whether the plaintiff was in fact treated and, second, whether treatment was without broad consent. It is immaterial whether the treatment was reasonably undertaken or performed by the defendant. If the patient did not consent in broad terms, damages can be awarded even if it was appropriate and competently administered.

Obligation to make a 'reasonable' disclosure of information and to give adequate information to patients about material risks

If a patient (or his or her guardian) has been informed of intended procedures in *broad terms*, then any claim for assault, battery or false imprisonment will fail.

However, a *concurrent* claim by the patient for *negligence* will *succeed* if the court determines that the level of disclosure to the patient was unreasonably small, that the patient should have been given more information, advice or warnings of inherent material risks and treatment options, and that if the patient had known more, he or she would have refused the procedure.

The issue of how much detail should 'reasonably' be disclosed to a patient is very controversial. The answer depends on where courts draw the line between the philosophies of paternalism (that is, the view that courts or tribunals or clinicians should determine the patient's best interests) and autonomy (the view that patients should be empowered to determine what treatments they wish to undergo or refuse, regardless of what may or may not be in their best interests). Courts may be influenced by up to four different sources of evidence:

1 the *judges' own views* independently of evidence—so-called 'judicial notice'
2 *expert evidence* by clinicians as to what disclosure they believe was desirable in the patient's best interest
3 what a *reasonable* patient in the plaintiff's situation would have wanted to know before undergoing the intervention, and/or
4 what the *particular* plaintiff would have wanted to know before undergoing the intervention, having regard to the individual idiosyncrasies and personality of that patient regardless of what a reasonable patient might have wished to know.

Unlike UK decisions, which have been heavily paternalistic and favour the health professional, Australian decisions in recent years have given more emphasis to the rights of patients to be informed,[39] as in Canada and the United States. This trend has now been confirmed and given the final imprimatur by the decision of the High Court of Australia in *Rogers v. Whitaker* (1992) 175 CLR 479.

The expression 'informed consent' was said to be 'apt to mislead' by the High Court of Australia in *Rogers* as it does not explain '... the balancing process that is involved in the determination of whether there has been a breach of the duty of disclosure' (p. 490, author's emphasis). The court said that:

> The law should recognize that a doctor has a duty to warn a patient of a material risk inherent in the proposed treatment; a risk is *material* if, in the circumstances of the particular case, a *reasonable person* in the patient's position, if warned of the risk, would be likely to attach significance to it or if the medical practitioner is or should be reasonably aware that the *particular patient*, if warned of the risk, would be likely to attach significance to it (ibid., author's emphasis).

The court said that, in Australia, the information to be disclosed is to be determined in this way—that is, from a patient-oriented perspective (pp. 487, 490)—and is not to be determined, as it still is in the United Kingdom, solely or primarily by reference objectively to what doctors normally disclose or regard as acceptable to disclose (the so-called 'Bolam' test in England, p. 484 of *Rogers*).

However, five members of the court (Mason CJ, Brennan, Dawson, Toohey and McHugh JJ) added one qualification—that the doctor can claim 'therapeutic privilege' as a justification for not disclosing a risk (p. 490) where the doctor 'reasonably believed that disclosure of a risk would prove damaging to the patient' (p. 486) and 'there is a particular danger that the provision of all relevant information will harm an unusually nervous, disturbed or volatile patient ...' (p. 490). Gaudron J, while agreeing generally with the majority (p. 492), emphasised that she would give a very restricted ambit to therapeutic privilege, and would restrict its availability to medical emergencies or to circumstances in which the patient is unable to receive, understand or properly evaluate the significance of the information that should otherwise be disclosed to a reasonable person in the patient's position (p. 494). It appears that Gaudron J was concerned that the term 'therapeutic privilege' should not be interpreted so broadly as to undermine the general obligation to disclose material risks to patients or their guardians. The majority did not say whether they agreed or disagreed with Gaudron J's restrictive comments about the scope of therapeutic privilege, but it was unnecessary in the circumstances of *Rogers* to elaborate on that issue as Dr Rogers did not claim that he had relied on therapeutic privilege as his reason for not telling Mrs Whitaker about the risk of sympathetic ophthalmia.

Expert evidence will still be relevant and admissible in any litigation in order to establish, factually, what *were* the risks and the treatment options *at the time* the clinician was diagnosing, advising or treating the patient (see pp. 488–90). Expert evidence will also help to establish, factually, whether or not circumstances existed that could support a valid claim of therapeutic privilege by the clinician as a reason for not disclosing what would otherwise be a material risk.

However, once experts have given courts such factual material, it is then up to the court to balance all considerations to determine whether or not there has been a justified or unjustified failure to warn of any 'material risk'. The High Court (p. 488) specifically approved King CJ who had said in *F v. R* that:

> The ultimate question, however, is not whether the defendant's conduct accords with the practices of his profession or some part of it, but whether it conforms to the standard of reasonable care demanded by the law. That is a question for the court and the duty of deciding it cannot be delegated to any profession or group in the community.[40]

It must be emphasised that even if a breach of duty can be established, in the sense of a failure to give adequate warning advice or information of a material risk, the patient must, *in addition*, establish that it is more probable than not that the breach was *causally* significant; that is, the patient must still persuade the court that it is more probable than not that if the omitted material information had been divulged, the patient would have refused the procedure to avoid running the risk that did in fact occur. If it be assumed that the patient had been informed of the material risk, but that despite such knowledge would nevertheless have undergone the procedure and run the risk, then the doctor's failure to inform the patient did not in fact bring about any change of the patient's behaviour and so was not causally significant, and the patient's claim will be dismissed. This *principle of causation* was applied in the New South Wales Court of Appeal in *Rogers*,[41] and no challenge to the principle was pursued in *Rogers* in the High Court. The test of causation (that is, the question of fact as to whether the patient, if informed, would have refused the treatment) is subjective (whether this patient would have refused) and not objective (whether a reasonable patient would have refused).[42]

Rogers does not appear to disturb the principle in *Chatterton v. Gerson* per Bristow J that:

> ... there is no obligation on a doctor to canvass with the patient anything other than the inherent implications of the particular operation he intends to carry out. He is certainly under no obligation to say that if he operates incompetently he will do damage. The fundamental assumption is that he knows his job and will do it properly. But he ought to warn of what may happen by misfortune however well the operation is done, if there is a real risk of misfortune inherent in the procedure ...[43]

In *Council of the Shire of Wyong v. Shirt*, Mason J (as he then was) said in a well-known and often cited passage that:

> ... a risk of injury which is remote in the sense that it is extremely unlikely to occur may constitute a foreseeable risk. A risk which is not far-fetched or fanciful is real and therefore foreseeable. But ... the existence of a foreseeable risk of injury does not in itself dispose of the question of breach of duty. The magnitude of the risk and its degree of probability remain to be considered with other relevant factors.[44]

In *Malec v. J. C. Button Pty Ltd*, the majority joint judgment of Deane, Dawson and McHugh JJ said that a probability of less than 1 per cent is 'so low as to be regarded as speculative'.[45] However, in *Rogers* the inherent risk of sympathetic ophthalmia that in fact befell the plaintiff in her good eye, and was caused by the operation on her bad eye, was in the order of 1 in 14 000, or slightly more frequently, and this low risk was nevertheless held to be real and foreseeable, and not far-fetched, fanciful or speculative. *Rogers* did not cite *Malec*, but perhaps the two cases are distinguishable—and therefore reconcilable—on the basis that *Rogers* was dealing with an inherent risk in a surgical procedure that had in fact materialised and did eventuate before trial, whereas *Malec* was referring in the quoted passage to inherent risks that had not eventuated at the time of trial and that might or might not eventuate at some future date. Another possible distinction between the two cases turns on avoidability or assumption of risk, because if a risk is avoidable the person with the option of accepting or rejecting such a risk may have a right to more detailed information about inherent risks than a person who cannot by his or her behaviour avoid the risk. Thus, *Rogers* was dealing with a risk inherent in an elective surgical procedure, which risk was avoidable if surgery were refused; Mrs Whitaker had '"incessantly" questioned [Dr Rogers] as to, amongst other things, possible complications' (p. 491) and this included even infrequent risks. But in *Malec* the injury to the plaintiff was not avoidable by any specific behaviour or choice on his part; the illness arose out of a disease, brucellosis, which was contracted at work owing to the employer's breach of duty—without avoidable behaviour having been available to the plaintiff to reduce that risk—and which, having been contracted, then caused a back injury to the plaintiff employee that in turn further caused a depressive neurotic condition that rendered him unemployable.

Breaches of statutory duty

If a patient is injured during medical or hospital care or while using a prosthetic device or medical equipment, a legal claim may be made, alleging breaches of various statutory duties, under the consumer protection provisions of the Commonwealth *Trade Practices Act 1974* and the state Fair Trading Acts.[46] These may be especially important in product liability cases such as the failure of a prosthetic device, although there is presently some reluctance judicially to construe the provisions as applicable to medical treatment.[47] These newer allegations may be made concurrently with more traditional claims for negligence, trespass to the person or breach of contract. Also being pleaded more frequently are claims of discriminatory treatment, contrary to anti-discrimination legislation, that is alleged to have caused refusal of treatment or substandard treatment or wrongful delays in instituting appropriate treatment.[48] These initiatives are relatively new in the specific area of professional liability for personal injury, and there is relatively little case law at this stage.

Breaches of contract

A contract is an agreement that has legal force. Ordinary contracts do not have to be in writing. The relationship between a paying patient and his or her doctor or hospital is usually contractual, based on the patient's agreement to pay a fee (or to sign a Medicare form that authorises the fee) and the doctor's agreement to consult, examine, diagnose, advise and treat the patient.[49]

If a person is a private patient, there may be a number of separate contracts between the patient and each of the senior doctors (the surgeon and anaesthetist respectively) and between the patient and the hospital. Each of those contracts may exist concurrently with the respective duties of the doctors and hospital not to treat the patient negligently and not to treat the patient without consent.

The details of the agreement are known as the 'terms' of the contract. The terms may be expressly written down, may be expressly orally agreed or may arise by implication. For example, the patient and doctor may not expressly discuss the issue of confidentiality, but there would normally be an implied term of confidentiality because it satisfies the criteria for an implied term, namely:

1. it must be reasonable and equitable; 2. it must be necessary to give business efficacy to the contract, so that no term will be implied if the contract is effective without it; 3. it must be so obvious that 'it goes without saying'; 4. it must be capable of clear expression; 5. it must not contradict any of the express terms of the contract.[50]

A patient who has been injured will sometimes allege that the treating doctor had given him or her a contractually enforceable promise that a particular outcome would be achieved. For example, a patient may allege that in exchange for the agreed fee a plastic surgeon had promised that a specific physical defect would be rectified, or a patient undergoing a sterilisation operation may claim that the surgeon had promised that the procedure would be effective in preventing future pregnancy. However, while courts accept that *in theory* a doctor could give such contractual undertakings, *in practice* they seem inclined to regard the doctor's statements of a positive outcome as being merely 'therapeutic reassurance' rather than a legally binding guarantee.[51]

Confidentiality

Practitioners must exercise reasonable care with respect to patient confidentiality. Breaches may give rise to actions for negligence, breach of confidentiality, breach of contract, professional misconduct or criminal prosecution. Restraining orders to prevent threatened breaches, if detected, may be sought in court.

Improper breach of professional confidence need not be intentional. For example, discussion in a corridor of a patient's case and other personal information may be a breach of confidence if it is overheard. The person being discussed does not have to be specified; if enough information is given to allow the person to be identified, then there is breach. Legal action for breach of confidentiality could be brought if it had been possible to foresee that harm or distress might result from this breach of duty. Even if no harm resulted, a registered health professional such as a nurse or a doctor might be reported to the registration disciplinary authority for professional misconduct and/or for breach of confidentiality.[52]

In certain circumstances information of a personal nature about patients may be disclosed provided care is taken to make sure that only those with a legitimate claim to the information are able to have access to it.

Briefly, some of these circumstances are as follows:

> ‹ *Disclosure under authority or on compulsion of law* ... records can be subpoenaed by the courts to be examined as evidence in legal action ...
> ‹ *Consent* ... The resident may expressly consent to the disclosure of confidential information such as the contents of medical records.
>
> Consent such as this is implied to allow access to confidential information only by other members of the health team who are involved in the resident's care or who can demonstrate a 'need to know'. Nurses, physicians and therapists, students, clerical and administrative staff or people to whom the resident is being referred, do not necessarily have a need to know what is included in such records. Valid requests do not automatically include access to everything in the file, therefore the information should be limited to that which is necessary for services to be given ...
>
> ‹ *Disclosure in the resident's interests.* Disclosure of personal information in the resident's interests in order to ensure continuation of care or some welfare or insurance benefit needs to be approached carefully. Any indication that the resident who set this application in motion has withdrawn consent, or would not have consented to the release of the information, must be given legal weight.[53]

Defamation

This is becoming an increasingly important area in practice in Australia, as there seems to be greater willingness to litigate in response to attacks and criticisms affecting professional reputations.

In the course of discussion of medico-legal issues with the author, members of hospital committees and subcommittees have with increasing frequency in recent years raised the general issue of defamation. Anecdotally, it would appear that the general possibility of defamation litigation may deter some persons from accepting appointment to committees if the work of those committees entails making critical judgments about professional reputations of clinical or other staff. However, generally speaking these fears are misplaced in that a defence of 'qualified privilege' would normally succeed in defeating any action for defamation provided that certain procedures were followed by members of committees, namely:

‹ the work of the committee or subcommittee is reasonably within the functions of the organisation—this can be reinforced if the organisation or its senior officials specify the terms of reference and membership of the (sub)committee

‹ the (sub)committee reports up the line to a specified official or higher committee

‹ any critical comments are discussed within the committee and then reported upwards through the line structure and are not disseminated by informal gossip through other channels

‹ any critical comments reflect genuinely held beliefs or conclusions that can be supported as a reasonable interpretation of supporting information.

Sexual relationships between doctors and patients

The phenomenon of sexual relationships beween doctors and patients has traditionally given rise to disciplinary sanctions for professional misconduct, but is also starting to generate civil actions for damages in Australia, as has occurred particularly in the United States and Canada. Canada's Supreme Court has applied fiduciary (that is, special trust) analysis readily to such situations,[54] but the New South Wales Court of Appeal has held by a majority that the concept of fiduciary duty applied by Canadian courts is broader and looser than that applicable in Australia,[55] and the scope of fiduciary analysis is presently unresolved. An 'innominate' claim (that is, a claim presently with no specific name) based on old legal principles of 'action on the case' may, however, also be applicable to allegations of sexual and emotional exploitation and abuse of a patient by a doctor. This type of claim has been developing in the United States, based on alleged wilful and intentional (or, alternatively, reckless and callous) conduct that was calculated to cause—and did in fact cause—psychiatric injury,[56] but its application in Australia in this context is presently untested.

Some issues in criminal legal responsibility: defining death, withdrawal of treatment, 'natural death' legislation, euthanasia[57]

Defining death

It is important to distinguish *concepts* of death of a philosophical nature from technical *criteria* used to assess clinically whether a person is dead. Even if it is not spelt out, a concept of death underlies the choice of appropriate diagnostic criteria to determine whether 'death' has occurred.

Many laws, both today and in the past, have specified legal *consequences* of death (for example, laws of wills, probate and succession; laws of homicide) without saying what death actually is. Even today, the concept of death as an abstract general proposition remains undefined by law and can only be gleaned implicitly.

It is common for laws dealing with homicide, and with related crimes such as infanticide and child destruction, to specify some of the *diagnostic criteria* that are to be used to determine or assess whether a person is alive or dead. The diagnostic criteria specified in these laws have usually included traditional clinical signs such as breathing or blood circulation. For example, the New South Wales *Crimes Act 1900* says that:

> On the trial of a person for the murder of a child, such child shall be held to have been born alive if it has breathed, and has been wholly born into the world, whether it has independent circulation or not.

In *R v. Hutty*, Mr Justice Barry directed a jury in Victoria that:

> Murder can only be committed on a person who is in being, and legally a person is not in being until he or she is fully born in a living state. A baby is fully and completely born when it is completely delivered from the body of its mother and it has a separate and independent existence in the sense that it does not derive its power of living from its mother. It is not material that the child may still be attached to its mother by the umbilical cord; that does not prevent it from having a separate existence. But it is required, before the child can be the victim of murder or manslaughter or infanticide, that the child should have an existence separate from and independent of its mother, and that occurs when the child is fully extruded from the mother's body and is living by virtue of the functioning of its own organs.[58]

More recent laws in the field of organ transplantation and artificial life support systems have supplemented, or supplanted, these traditional criteria with other criteria relating to brain functioning, as discussed more fully in the following subsections. Once again, these laws do not define a *concept* of death explicitly. Such concepts are implicit, however, and guide the selection and development of relevant diagnostic criteria.

Concepts and criteria of 'death'

A number of *concepts* of death may be distinguished in response to the following questions: 'What is it that is so central to your humanity that when you lose it you are dead?';[59] and 'What is so essentially significant about life that its loss is termed *death*?'[60]

Biologically, the *holistic* entity described as a 'person' or 'human being' is to be distinguished from cells and tissues that are merely material components of the person. Even in a healthy and living 'person' there is an ongoing balance between live and dead components; certain kinds of cells (in skin, hair, blood and muscle) are always dying and being replaced by other cells. Other kinds, such as brain cells, die but may not be replaced:

> The total number of neurons in the cerebral cortex has been estimated at between 50 to 100 billion. While there is no truth in the old wife's tale that we only make use of 10% of our brain, there are ample cells available to maintain essential functions if some cells are lost.
>
> Neurons are thought not to be replaced if they die. Neurons are lost during life from a number of causes including innate failure, accumulation of toxins, damage to the vascular supply, and errors of metabolism. Remaining cells increase their connections with other cells as a compensatory mechanism for loss. If sufficient cells are lost, the brain is no longer able to cope with the demands placed on it and reduction of global intellectual capacity results. Focal loss of cells may result in loss of specific functions.[61]

Thus, the 'person' as a *whole* can be alive even if *parts* of his or her body are dead, dying, amputated or in a permanent and irreversible dysfunctional state. Likewise, modern life-support technology gives the capacity to sustain certain bodily functions even after the 'person' is, in some more essential sense, already 'dead'. Different parts of a person's body die at different rates. If a human being is decapitated or hanged, the heart may continue to beat and circulate blood unaided for another 20 minutes or so, and skin and nails may continue to grow for some days. After some point is passed in the process of 'dying', the individual as a 'person' or 'human being' in a *holistic sense* is deemed to be 'dead' *by law* even though parts of the body may be alive. This notion underlies the whole field of legal organ transplantation 'after death'; the donor as a holistic 'person' is legally 'dead', but his or her tissues or organs remain 'alive' for donation to another living person. This has forced society and the legal system to be more precise about what is to be regarded philosophically as essential to the idea of a living *person* as distinct from a mechanically ventilated *corpse*, when the person is already dead.

Older concepts of death formerly dominant in Western societies have included leaving civil society in order to enter certain Christian monastic orders in the Middle Ages, irreversible loss of vital body fluids, and the soul leaving the body.

The more recent idea of 'brain death' has been described and reported in medical literature since 1959. It is not always made clear in this extensive body of literature whether brain death is being considered as a concept of death or as a criterion of death, or as both a concept and a criterion. If one regards a functioning brain as the essence of what it means to be a 'person', then brain death as a concept may be supported. If, however, one rejects materialist conceptions and adheres to a more spiritual or theistic conception of human life, one may be unwilling to support brain death as a concept of death, but still be prepared to accept it as a criterion by which a person is to be diagnosed and certified as alive or dead.

Recent laws in Australia still permit the 'death' of a person to be diagnosed by traditional cardiorespiratory criteria in most situations, but brain death criteria are required to diagnose death where organ transplantation is contemplated or where artificial life support is in place. These laws provide that a person should not be diagnosed or certified or declared to be legally dead unless all brain functions have irreversibly ceased—not only the higher brain functions, but also the more primitive functions associated with the brain stem.[62]

One contemporary school of thought, whose views are not reflected in present laws, advocates that a person in the holistic sense should be regarded as dead if the higher, non-vegetative, neocortical brain functions (including consciousness, self-awareness, personal identity and capacity for social interaction) are permanently and irreversibly absent even if brain-stem functions (such as the capacity to breathe and a beating heart) are intact. For example, Veatch submits that:

> The earlier concepts of death—the irreversible loss of soul and the irreversible stopping of the flow of vital body fluids—strike me as quite implausible. The soul as an independent nonphysical entity that is necessary and sufficient for a person to be considered alive is a relic from the era of dichotomised anthropologies. Animalistic fluid flow is simply too base a function to be the human essence. The capacity for bodily integration is more plausible, but I suspect it is attractive primarily because it includes those higher functions that we normally take to be central—consciousness, the ability to think and feel and relate to others. When the reflex networks that regulate such things as blood pressure and respiration are separated from the higher functions, I am led to conclude that it is the higher functions which are so essential that their loss ought to be taken as the death of the person. While consciousness is certainly important, man's social nature and embodiment seem to me to be the truly essential characteristics. I therefore believe that death is most appropriately thought of as the irreversible loss of the embodied capacity for social interaction.[63]

However, this view is opposed by others; for example, Pallis expresses a more conservative, mainstream opinion favouring sanctity of human life as a more important value than diminished quality of life, when he writes:

> About 10 years ago [a] picture of an unsuccessfully decapitated chicken appeared in a leading magazine. The forebrain ha[d] been amputated and lay on the ground. The brain stem [was] still in situ. The bird, still breathing, was fed with a dropper for several weeks. Was it alive or dead?
>
> The chicken must be considered alive so long as its brain stem is functioning. Let us transfer the argument to a child with anencephaly. There is a spinal cord, a brain stem, and perhaps some diencephalic structures but certainly no cerebral hemispheres. The cranial cavity is full of cerebrospinal fluid and transilluminates when a light is applied to it. The child can breathe spontaneously, swallow and grimace in response to painful stimuli. Its eyes are open. The heart can beat normally for months. No culture would declare that child dead. This emphasises the certainty we instinctively allocate to persisting brain stem function, even in the absence of anything we could describe as cerebration.[64]

Likewise, Mason & McCall Smith are concerned that:

> ... the current 'new wave' of thinking is moving towards the equation of permanent loss of personality with no longer being alive. Such attitudes may be tenable in a general discussion on euthanasia ... but, if related to death, can only confuse the issue and enhance the already strong public apprehension of 'premature grave robbery'. The concept of death must be that of an absolute; there is no place for conditional phrases such as 'at death's door' or 'as good as dead'. The definition of death has not changed; and, if we are to alter our diagnostic methods, the diagnosis of death must be as sure as when using the heart and lungs as parameters.[65]

Brain-death criteria that require proof that all brain functions have been permanently and irreversibly lost have been criticised on technical grounds by some experts who say that it is in fact *impossible* in the current state of knowledge to determine whether *all* brain functions have ceased. 'In a comatose patient there is no way of assessing such important functions of those of the thalmus, basal ganglia, or cerebellum, to mention but a few.'[66] In practice, it appears that the criteria adopted by the medical profession and endorsed by their professional associations focus on higher brain functions and brain-stem functions, from which it is inferred that all remaining functions have also ceased permanently and irreversibly. Accordingly, some experts contend that 'brain-stem death' and 'whole brain death' should in practice be regarded as synonymous.[67]

In murder trials, the accused has sometimes sought to argue for acquittal on the ground that the blows administered to the victim did not cause the death of the person, but that the victim's death was subsequently caused by clinical personnel who disconnected artificial life support in hospital intensive care or surgical units after attempts to save the victim's life were unsuccessful. The courts have found little difficulty in finding that the accused 'caused' the victim's death in these circumstances.[68]

The issue of whether life-preserving treatment can be withdrawn (or not commenced at all) before a person is 'dead' will be considered in the next section, which summarises so-called 'natural death' legislation presently in force in four jurisdictions (SA, NT, Vic, ACT) that allows life-saving treatment to be withdrawn (or not commenced) *with the consent* of either the adult patient (all four jurisdictions) or his or her agent (Vic, ACT).[69]

'Natural death' Acts

Four states and territories in Australia (SA, NT, Vic, ACT) have enacted legislation defining certain circumstances in which life-preserving treatment may—or must—be either *withdrawn* from an adult patient or not commenced. It must be emphasised that this 'natural death'/'medical treatment' legislation does not allow a medical practitioner actively to take a patient's life, but rather allows 'nature to take its course',[70] so-called 'passive' measures.[71]

Reflections for the reader

Can you carefully consider ways in which clinical services, personnel matters and managerial practices at your institution are influenced by—and take account of—legal considerations?

Can you alter the applicable legal framework positively and proactively to support health service goals? Or do your senior personnel and your institution react passively and negatively only when legal crises occur?

Do your legal advisers demonstrate familiarity with and expertise in the special needs and problems of health services? Do they charge reasonably for the quality of legal services delivered? Do you take advantage of the increasingly competitive market in professional legal services to ensure that quality is maintained at a reasonable price—for example, by putting up specified types of ongoing legal services for competitive tender or by seeking independent opinions on important issues?

What methods do you adopt to keep yourself abreast of relevant legal developments? Reading journals or newsletters? Attending talks and conferences? Continuing education arrangements? Speaking to your legal advisers? Other ways?

Health service information systems

Information is a fundamental requirement for good management. Without appropriate information, modern management is impossible. In the health field, knowledge and information are perhaps of greater importance than in many other fields because of the scientific basis of health services.

Health service planners cannot plan without information. Health service accountants cannot balance the books without information. Pharmacists cannot order and dispense pharmaceuticals without information about levels of stocks and the shelf life of products, plus details of the needs of particular patients. Nurses cannot nurse without detailed information about individual patients, workloads and treatment requirements. Doctors cannot make diagnoses or offer treatment without seeking very detailed information about individual patients.

Clearly, health care is a field that is totally dependent on information that is of good quality, detailed and relevant.

Information and data

There are practical advantages in identifying the differences between information and data.

Data may be conveniently defined as the 'new facts', usually numbers that are used for measurement purposes; for example, numbers of people in populations, and of outpatients, pills, blood chemistry tests, meals consumed, characteristics of staff noted, and measurements of linen used, water consumed and money spent. Data provides the components that are processed into information.

Information may be defined as the use of data to create meaning and understanding. In the health field, information is very often created by the use of comparisons: for example, the data indicating that a person's blood cholesterol level is 8 mmol per 100 mL has no meaning unless this level is compared with, say, a population average of 4.5 mmol per 100 mL. Similarly, new data indicating that the cost of maintaining a disabled person at home is $100 per week has no meaning unless this cost is compared with, say, the inpatient cost of $1000 per week for a similarly disabled person.

The term 'related information' is used in the same sense as 'comparisons'. For example, the number of endoscopies performed by a particular physician (the new data) has no meaning unless the data is used with related data, such as the number of endoscopies performed per day or the number performed by other physicians. The new and related data, when compared and analysed, become information.

Data on its own can rarely be used for management purposes. Information can nearly always be used for management purposes. For example, the data indicating that a hospital costs $45 000 000 per year to run cannot be used for any purpose unless this amount is compared with a planned budget figure of, say, $40 000 000 per year. If this were the situation, immediate managerial intervention could begin. Similarly, in the clinical field, raw data indicating a particular patient's temperature of 40 degrees Celsius is of no value without a comparison with the norm of 37.1 degrees Celsius.

Epidemiology and demography

The use of mortality and morbidity information (that is, epidemiology), plus demographic information supplemented by information concerning the effectiveness of treatments (that is, clinical epidemiology), has become the basis for planning hospitals and health services.

Mortality data on a national and state basis is provided by the Australian Bureau of Statistics (ABS) and by similar organisations in other countries. This data can be analysed on a statistical division basis, and is essential for planning purposes.

Morbidity data is collected by way of special surveys, hospital statistics and attendances at health care providers, particularly doctors. Published studies concerning problems and evidence of health problems are also available.

Very detailed information about the numbers and structure of the population, based on the census (conducted every five years, but updated annually) is readily available. The combination of epidemiology and demography provides essential information. The degree of accuracy for some causes of death is very high—as, for example, for histologically proven cancers—but may be 25 per cent in error with respect to coronary artery disease. Similarly, the census can under-count by 3–5 per cent, and population estimates can become progressively less accurate as the period between each census increases.

These inaccuracies are not sufficiently great to cause significant problems, however, as hospital and health service planning is largely 'broad brush' in nature.

The use of statistical techniques for assessing the effectiveness of particular treatments is difficult, but can be rewarding. For example, in Australia intervention rates for discretionary surgery (such as appendicectomy or hysterectomy) have all fallen as a consequence of evaluating outcomes.

Hospitals and clinics need to develop information systems regarding patient characteristics that include detailed diagnoses and treatments. This information

case history very simple and useful epidemiology

Margaret Weddle conducted an inner city clinic for 'skid row' patients in Melbourne. She believed her work was useless—she would patch up her patients, who would then return to their alcohol. However, she began to keep a record of all patients, their ailments and their social backgrounds. When she analysed the data, information began to emerge. Some of the patients were the young, long-term unemployed—people who had given up hope. Weddle began to develop priorities among her patients. She was able to rehabilitate first one young person, then another. Finally, with the help of welfare agencies, she was able to rehabilitate 15 per cent of those she had regarded as hopeless cases. This success was based on simple epidemiology.

is useful for a range of purposes: for example, for clinical evaluation, for assessing the role of the service, for comparing activities with other services and for financial payment purposes. The importance of good medical records as the source of accurate and useful clinical data goes without saying.

Epidemiology and demography provide the fundamental information for public health purposes (public health being defined as the health of populations, as distinct from clinical health, which refers to the health of individuals). Public health information systems most often provide information about trends in morbidity (sickness and handicap) and mortality (death) in populations or communities. Such systems are again dependent on comparative and related data. The number of deaths in a particular population (the raw data) only becomes meaningful information when comparative data is also considered: for example, cause of death, age and sex of the deceased, death rates in other populations.

The use of public health information systems allows priorities to be established for the allocation of resources and for public health programs to be developed. For example, the data indicating that there are 2650 deaths each year due to breast cancer among Australian women has much more value when compared with data on other causes of death. Such a comparison indicates that breast cancer is the leading cause of death due to cancer among Australian women and, therefore, is a major priority. The data has even more meaning when related to data about age, which indicates that 18 per cent of those deaths were among women less than 50 years of age.

While the same principles apply, clinical information systems concern individual patients. These systems predominantly include data and information about diagnostic matters, such as pathology and radiology. However, such systems can also include data and information about treatment matters, particularly about treatment with pharmaceuticals. Such clinical information systems provide the basis for the diagnosis and treatment of individual patients. The care of patients with diabetes provides a good example, since the diagnosis in terms of severity is totally dependent on the patient's blood chemistry as compared with a normal person's blood chemistry. Fine-tuning of such a patient's treatment is dependent on continued monitoring of changes in blood chemistry.

Computers

Computer technology has provided the capacity to process enormous masses of data in health service settings. The value of computer technology is obvious. The need for sensible and cost-effective application is mandatory. However, there are two basic messages.

The first is that of 'garbage in, garbage out'. Regardless of the sophistication of the technology, the quality of the original data will determine the quality and value of any subsequent analysis. The field of biochemistry illustrates this crucial point. The level of blood cholesterol varies in each person throughout the day and night. The variation can be influenced by diet, coffee consumption and even the method of collection of blood. The most sophisticated and accurate computerised technology cannot overcome this biological variation, which has to be taken into account when the data is analysed, compared and converted into information.

The second message is that computer systems are so powerful—they can provide so much data that the recipient is literally buried in computer printouts. Unless there is a capability to analyse this data and to elicit useful information, the computer system has no value. Piles of unread printouts are commonplace in the offices of many busy senior managers. We know the chief executive of a large teaching hospital who uses unread printouts as a doorstop! A less obvious problem is the cost–benefit aspect of computerisation. There are many examples of vastly expensive, centralised computer systems introduced into health care services that in fact provide little information additional to that provided by a calculation made on the back of an envelope. The big issues in health care systems are mostly based on simple information: for example, the geographical distribution of hospital beds, the availability and distribution of general practitioners or the occupancy rates of hospitals. Expensive computer systems are a waste of resources in this area.

On the other hand, some developments are not possible without powerful computer systems. The best example is casemix-based information. 'Casemix' is the grouping of patients according to the similarity of diagnoses or procedures, and is dependent on masses of detailed data that can only be efficiently processed with reasonably powerful computers.

Planning and managing information

Every section of the health service has its own particular requirement for data and information. The clinical services of hospitals need information about patient activities; the accounts department needs information about costs and budgets; diagnostic departments need to know about workloads; all sections need information to measure quality standards. Finally, senior management needs 'global' information about hospitals and health services. If all sections of the hospital and health services required data and information about the system as a whole, they would be swamped with indigestible masses of data. Accordingly, managers must first assess the need for data and information separately and by section, department or clinic, then discard the information that is of lesser value.

Some information systems may originally have been established for good reasons but have since become surplus to current requirements. The problem is that such systems tend to take on a life of their own, and are difficult to discard. People always worry that discarded information may have a future unknown value. In the New South Wales health system, for example, a shortage of nurses led to the creation of information systems aimed at providing details of the shortages in particular geographical areas. When the shortage turned to a surplus, the 'special' nursing staff information systems remained—they had become a standard part of the data collection system, despite the fact that this data was never analysed and used for any purpose. It took twelve months of determined endeavour to abandon the system.

Data and information have a cost. Staff collecting and handling information have to be paid; equipment has to be bought and maintained. As an example, the cost of the Australian census is about $10–15 for each person counted. Yet it is unusual for a cost to be estimated and budgeted in the information field. If detailed costs of each item of information were shown, there would be an incentive to assess the value of such information.

Reflections for the reader

Detailed texts are available in the field of health information systems. We do not recommend any to you, because such texts are written by specialists in the field and the reader becomes swamped in masses of detail. Refer again to our comment about the cost benefit of basing major decisions regarding resources in the health field, such as bed-to-population ratios, on crucial, simple 'back of the envelope' information. When lecturing, we make an attempt to persuade the class to this point of view. On one occasion, a fine member of a class strongly objected—we then learnt her career was as a lecturer in health information management!

We suggest you review the information that crosses your desk, and raise a number of questions.

1 Is the information useful?
2 How much does the information cost?
3 Is the quality of the information appropriate?

Quality management in the health services

It is a fundamental requirement that the community should be provided with high-quality health services. This need has been recognised increasingly in recent years, possibly as a response to the economic success of Japan and Germany, where quality has been a priority. The quality movement, as it has come to be known, has generated its own jargon; the terms used are numerous, and may therefore be confusing. They include 'total quality management' (TQM), 'continuous quality improvement' (CQI), 'quality assurance', 'quality control', 'quality circles', 'quality activities' and simply 'quality'.

In an organisational sense, quality assurance has a very long history and has been widely practised since World War II. However, the setting of standards in the health field has historically been left to the different professional associations and to individuals operating as professionals. The setting of standards has been particularly vigorous in those fields where procedures could be relatively standardised—for example, in obstetrics and in infant care. In addition, quality control has been a stringent requirement for vaccines, pharmaceutical products and infant formulae since their earliest development, for the obvious reason that mass production and use of these substances had the potential to place whole populations at risk unless the highest standards of quality and safety checks were maintained.

It was not until the 1950s that hospitals, as organisations, began to formally assess quality in terms of the hotel services provided and the organisational aspects of clinical services. This was largely initiated in the United States, mainly as a means of ensuring appropriate standards in the voluntary non-government sector. These initiatives were quickly adopted in Australia, and much more recently have begun to be adopted in the United Kingdom and Europe. Typically, most countries with government dominated health service provision have not seen the necessity to introduce formal measures of quality, basically because of the assumption that good standards can be achieved without a formal approach.

Modelled on the Joint Commission on Accreditation of Healthcare Organisations (JCAHO) in the United States, the Australian experience of implementing nationally accepted standards for the management of hospitals and other health care organisations is encapsulated in the history of the Australian Council on Healthcare Standards (ACHS). The mission of the ACHS is to promote, in cooperation with health care professionals, continuing improvement in the quality of care delivered to patients and the community by Australian organisations.

Established in 1974 as an independent, not-for-profit organisation, the Australian Council on Hospital Standards (as it was then known) sought to address observed serious deficiencies in the public hospital system. During the 1980s, in response to increased delivery of health care outside hospitals, it broadened its scope to encompass all health care facilities. The ACHS conducts a voluntary accreditation program, using standards developed in consultation with the health industry and its respective professional bodies. The award of accreditation status signals the ongoing commitment of a health care organisation to providing high professional standards in quality of care.

Quality assurance has been a mandatory standard within the ACHS accreditation program since the mid-1980s. Retitled the Quality Activities Standard in 1994 (to address the confusion in terminology referred to earlier), it requires health care organisations to demonstrate improvement in quality of care and service in significant areas of their operations, especially clinical.

Many countries have employed a wide range of techniques to ensure quality in health care delivery. Greatest success has been achieved with processes such as ensuring that a medical record service is available, that kitchens are clean and that linen services are adequate. It has proved much more difficult to achieve measures of quality and to gain acceptance of quality assurance among clinicians. However, while there is no formal evidence to indicate whether or not these activities have improved standards at population levels, subjective experience and increasing evidence at the local level indicate that they have.

Again, these experiences have been more commonly confined to processes and not to clinical outcomes, which is the reason for having the health services in the first place. It is reasonable to begin a quality assurance plan by concentrating on processes, as indicated above, thus ensuring that basic services of satisfactory quality are provided; for example, by reviewing the standard of documentation in clinical records as distinct from the quality of care reflected in the documentation. As shown, however, by Deming, the father of quality assurance in Japanese industry, actual measures of quality need to be introduced and accepted.[1] Only in this way can true comparisons be made and judgments exercised about what are the appropriate levels of quality. In the 1990s this holistic approach, which includes education, setting of standards and measurement of quality, was commonly referred to as total quality management (TQM). In the health service field, particularly in the United States, the more favoured term was continuous quality improvement (CQI).

The more explicit move to the measurement of clinical outcomes and the development of outcome standards builds on the work of Professor Avedis Donabedian, the respected 'guru' of quality assurance in the health industry.[2] He identified structure, process and outcome as the three basic elements of quality assessment and assurance some twenty-five to thirty years ago, and expressed the fundamental functional relationship that exists between these three elements in the following way:

> The structural characteristics of the settings in which care takes place have a propensity to influence the process of care so that its quality is diminished or enhanced. Similarly, changes in the process of care, including variations in its quality, will influence the effect of care on health status (or outcome).

Both the Joint Commission on Accreditation of Healthcare Organisations and, more latterly, the Australian Council on Healthcare Standards have moved towards more of an outcome focus for their accreditation standards in order to address the need to provide evidence of the end results of the care provided in health care facilities.

The 1990s also saw more explicit acknowledgment that quality is related to cost. Whereas it used to be unacceptable to talk about the quality of patient care in the same breath as discussion of costs, it is now the case that health care managers and clinicians alike ignore the relationship between cost and quality at their peril. However, the provision of high-quality services need not necessarily lead to higher costs; conversely, it is not automatic that low-quality services are cheaper. The key is to achieve the highest possible quality in an efficient manner, within available resources.

Putting quality concepts into action

Pawsey has conducted a review of the key characteristics of quality assurance programs in Australian health care facilities.[3] Some of the following material and conclusions are based on her work.

Quality management programs—whether at organisation-wide or local departmental level—need careful planning to be effective. Plans will vary according to circumstances and settings; it is always appropriate to begin with modest goals that are discrete and measurable. The key to success, however, is to set aside time on a regular basis to discuss quality issues—the setting of standards; the collection of simple, relevant data that can be presented in a meaningful form; and the consistent review of aspects of care and services where improvement may be possible. In addition, there should be regular follow-up evaluation to ensure that ongoing improvement is achieved.

In practice, there are difficulties with each of these steps. The most difficult problem is the natural feeling of insecurity among those responsible for the services. This is particularly noticeable among clinicians because, in addition to worries about peer-group standing, there are concerns about litigation for malpractice.

A further difficulty has been the collection of data. Not only have information systems tended to be poorly organised in many health care facilities, but low priority has been given to the key source of clinical data—namely, the medical (clinical/health) record. Nevertheless, much data is already available in modern hospitals and health services (for example, through the national morbidity data-collection system) and can be used for quality management purposes. Examples of available data are infection rates in elective and emergency surgery, return-to-theatre rates, length of stay of individual patients suffering from similar conditions and the number of surgical interventions for a given number of normal obstetric patients.

Many hospitals and health care facilities appoint a quality manager or quality assurance coordinator to oversee these activities—full-time in larger facilities, part-time in the smaller hospitals. There are arguments against such appointments, mainly on the grounds that quality should be a managerial and professional responsibility for every member of staff, and cannot be delegated to others. It is helpful to have such a resource person, however—someone who can be responsible for coordinating the hospital's quality efforts, keeping them on track, providing expertise where necessary and maintaining enthusiasm for quality among the staff. In some facilities, this task is undertaken by a designated committee. It is also important for resources to be set aside for the collection and analysis of information that can then be made available to the relevant managers and staff members.

There have been some experiences with audit programs in which clinical records have been checked and judgments made about the adequacy or otherwise of treatment. The major problem with such an inspectorial approach is that the review of data by other people causes insecurity and resentment—the very antithesis of the trust required for the open and honest pursuit of quality improvement. A much more fruitful approach involves individual and joint analysis of the same data by interest groups who have been involved in the setting of criteria and/or standards from the outset.

The concept is not one of blame or punishment, but rather of the identification of problems that are to be solved individually and collectively. What must be remembered is that the focus should be on identifying trends in collective practice or performance, not on reviewing the performance of the individual practitioner. The latter properly belongs in the realm of personnel or staff appraisal/performance review.

Hospital-wide clinical indicators

The use of performance indicators is not new in the context of health care. Take, for example, the use of birth, death, disease and complication rates. However, with increasing interest in outcomes, more use is now being made of clinical indicators in hospitals. Hospital-wide medical indicators include those following.[4]

1 *Trauma*
   ‹ delay for trauma patients between presentation and attendance by a doctor
   ‹ delay in craniotomy for patients with head injury
   ‹ missed injuries (cervical spine)
   ‹ audit of trauma mortality.
2 *Pulmonary embolism*
   ‹ development of postoperative pulmonary embolism.
3 *Hospital readmissions*
   ‹ unplanned hospital readmissions.
4 *Return to operating room*
   ‹ unplanned return to the operating room during the same admission.
5 *Hospital-acquired infection*
   ‹ patients having evidence of a wound infection on or after the fifth postoperative day following clean and/or contaminated surgery
   ‹ patients developing hospital-acquired bacteraemia.
6 *Medication prescription and drug monitoring*
   ‹ prescription of drugs for which there is a known previous adverse reaction. Monitoring of toxic drugs (gentamicin).
7 *Hospital throughput/output*
   ‹ average length of stay per top twenty diagnostic related groups (DRGs).

The year 1995 saw the introduction of the first craft-specific clinical indicators—namely, those for obstetrics and gynaecology—developed over the previous five years in conjunction with the Royal Australian College of Obstetricians and Gynaecologists (RACOG). The obstetrics and gynaecology clinical indicator set includes the following.[5]

‹ *Obstetrics*
1 Induction of labour other than for defined indications.
2 The rate of vaginal delivery after caesarean section.

3 Primary caesarean section for failure to progress.

4 Primary caesarean section for fetal distress.

5 Incidence of an intact lower genital tract in vaginal deliveries for other than forceps delivery, breech delivery or vacuum extraction.

6 Apgar score of four or less at 5 minutes.

7 Term infant transferred or admitted to a neonatal intensive care unit for reasons other than congenital abnormality.

8 Postnatal maternal length of stay more than 50 per cent greater than the mean for that hospital for:
   – vaginal delivery
   – caesarean section.

❮ *Gynaecology*

1 Hysterectomy in women below 35 years.

2 Blood transfusion for major gynaecological surgery, other than radical hysterectomy, exenteration or major vulval surgery or radical vulvectomy.

3 Injury, unplanned repair or unplanned removal of an organ or other structure during a gynaecological operative procedure.

4 Unplanned return to operating room during the same hospital stay.

5 Patients having evidence of a wound infection on or after the fifth postoperative day.

6 'Unplanned' hospital readmission.

Individual hospitals have also explored the use of clinical indicators as part of their own facility-wide quality improvement programs. They are usually restricted in number, and measure in quantitative terms the end results of the clinical management and outcome of care in key areas. For example:

❮ unplanned readmission to hospital shortly after inpatient surgery
❮ development of pressure ulcers
❮ development of wound infections after clean surgical procedures
❮ identification of important medication errors
❮ induction of labour outside a range of planned criteria
❮ delivery of infants less than 2500 grams subsequent to a planned caesarean section
❮ delivery of an infant weighing 1800 grams or less in a hospital without a neonatal intensive care unit
❮ dental injury during anaesthetic care.

Depending on the nature and specialty of the hospital, many of these indicators would fall into the rate-based category, although the delivery of an infant weighing 1800 grams or less in a hospital without a neonatal intensive care unit, for example, would always be considered a sentinel event worthy of individual investigation.

Similarly, a series of topics can be reviewed according to specialisation. Examples include the following.

1 *Pharmacy*
   ❮ review of patient waiting times for outpatient medication; audit of

dispensing accuracy; drug utilisation reviews (such as antibiotic prescribing).

2 *Nursing*
   ❮ outcome of patient satisfaction surveys; monitoring of adverse patient incident and accident data; medication errors; decubitus ulcer rates.

3 *Accounting*
   ❮ time and accuracy of reports; internal audit activities.

4 *Cleaning*
   ❮ state of cleanliness; compliance with infection-control requirements.

5 *Food services*
   ❮ conformity to special dietary requirements; temperature of food; patient satisfaction; provision of meals suitable to different ethnic groups.

6 *Linen*
   ❮ handling of dirty linen; client satisfaction.

7 *Supply services*
   ❮ timeliness of service to departments, control of stock levels.

The scope is enormous. Critically important is the identification of indicators that will measure key aspects of performance—whether at facility-wide or departmental level—and provide the opportunity for quality improvement.

Quality and systems

Deming (and other 'TQM gurus' such as Joseph Juran and Phillip Crosby) has drawn attention to the need to review systems when considering quality.[6] A system is the way in which an institution or hospital is organised, including the detailed procedures staff are required to undertake. Individuals within an organisation may not be able to improve the quality of their work, despite their best efforts, because the 'system' prevents them from doing so.

A good example of this in health services has been the requirement to meet traditional 'public service' procedures in mental hospitals. These procedures precisely define roles and staff activities, finance and the purchase of supplies. Within this system, individual staff members cannot reduce obvious waste and inefficiency because to do so would breach service rules and thereby cause punitive action to be brought against them. The only answer where there is a need to improve quality in such a situation is to alter the system and allow individuals to improve their performance—to 'cut the red tape' in order to encourage innovation and creativity among staff. There is a certain risk involved in managers 'letting go', but devolving ownership of quality throughout the organisation is a key ingredient for success.

Steps towards establishing a total quality management program

Regardless of the title used (quality assurance, quality improvement or quality management program), the first step is to set the very clear objective of developing a culture of quality throughout the organisation. This can be achieved by including quality as a formal agenda item on every occasion that the governing board meets. The chief executive officer should formally report to the full board on activities and outcomes in the quality field. The board itself should also be encouraged to lead by example—by formally reviewing the effectiveness of its own activities. Quality should also be a regular agenda item for all other key committees within the organisation.

Step two is to form a multidisciplinary committee responsible for overseeing the organisation-wide quality management program. Committees are an essential tool for bringing together the key members of any organisation—particularly such complex organisations as hospitals and health services, where committees need to include a member of the governing board, the chief executive officer and, above all, the most senior and relevant clinicians. In addition, it is very helpful if key nursing staff are represented, plus those in charge of allied health and hotel services.

Such committees should draw up individual guidelines for achieving a representative and comprehensive quality management program for the organisation. In particular, they should develop guidelines governing the confidentiality of quality data and protect staff against litigation or any sanctions, implied or actual, for perceived failure. Quality management programs can be threatening to staff, particularly to those who carry legal responsibilities, such as the medical staff. To be successful, the issue of intimidation has to be brought out into the open, explored and discussed. Trust is a critical factor in the realisation of quality improvement.

The organisation-wide quality management committee needs to encourage key staff throughout the organisation to develop ideas and suggestions for quality management. They also need to develop guidelines that measure quality, to identify problems and opportunities for improvement and to encourage staff in a decentralised way to document the problems and develop the means of overcoming them.

Step three is the development of standards and measures of quality. It is pointless having a quality management program that simply extols the virtue of quality. There must be some measures of achievement that, in turn, should at least be at two levels: the first is the ideal level of quality to be achieved; the second is an intermediate, practical and achievable goal. A good example concerns wound infection. With respect to clean surgery, the ideal goal is a zero rate of infection; a more practical goal is to have the level below 1 per cent of all patients undergoing clean surgery in a particular hospital or clinic.

Comparison of performance with other facilities of similar size and specialty can also be productive, as shown by the following.

❮ *Patient care*
  – clean wound infection rates
  In a Sydney hospital, clean wound infection rates were reduced from 6 per cent to 1 per cent.
❮ *Efficiency*
  – review of length of hospital stay
  – review of operating theatre use

During the 1980s, a Sydney hospital reduced the length of stay for patients with a fractured femur from five weeks to below eight days.

‹ *Medical records*
  – completion
  During the 1980s, Westmead Hospital in Sydney improved the completion of medical records within three days of discharge from 35 per cent to 90 per cent.

‹ *Pharmacy*
  – dispensing accuracy
  – medication errors
  A Melbourne hospital reduced medication errors from 15 per cent to 2 per cent.

‹ *Dentistry*
  – patient satisfaction
  – waiting time
  A northern Sydney dental clinic reduced the time waiting to be seen by the dentist from nine months to below two months following the implementation of a quality management program.

‹ *Accident and emergency*
  – review of deaths
  – review of documentation
  – waiting times for non-urgent patients
  The waiting time in a western suburban hospital in Melbourne was reduced from 3–4 hours to 30 minutes by the use of a triage system.

‹ *Obstetrics*
  – progress of labour
  – management of haemorrhage
  – management of fetal distress
  At a Perth hospital, operative delivery rates were reduced from 25 per cent to 15 per cent following management review.

‹ *Accounting*
  – internal audit
  – reports on time
  At a Melbourne hospital, late provision of pay for hospital staff had resulted in a major strike. Reviews rapidly overcame the problem.

‹ *Cleaning*
  – measure of cleanliness
  – staff training
  In a Malaysian hospital, following implementation of a quality management program, dirty toilets became as clean as those in any international hotel.

‹ *Food*
  – wastage
  – hot food hot, cold food cold
  At a UK hospital, a waste level of 40 per cent of materials was reduced to 10 per cent.

‹ *Linen*
   – quality
   – cleanliness
   – holes

At a Sydney linen service providing linen for some twenty-three hospitals, the incidence of holes in the linen was reduced from 25 per cent to 5 per cent.

To achieve outcomes of this kind requires a formal approach. In particular, priority should be given to the following procedures:

1 Ensure that there are adequate, reliable and efficient sources of information; for example, routine statistics, medical records and special surveys.
2 Regularly review information related to key performance areas, including the frequency of a problem or unsatisfactory trend, the cost of the problem and its severity.
3 Compare results or outcomes. It is very helpful to compare one experience with another in the same organisation or in a similar organisation. In this way, baseline standards of performance can be developed and used for building acceptable variations and measuring progressive improvement.

A clinical example of particular importance might be wound infection rates. Equally important in non-clinical services might be the time taken to transmit mail between hospital departments. For example, in some hospitals this has been reduced to a matter of 2–3 hours, whereas in others it is days; perhaps an acceptable time is 12–24 hours, depending on the size and complexity of the organisation.

Patient-satisfaction surveys

Many Australian hospitals carry out patient-satisfaction surveys. Their reliability and validity is questionable and there has been limited evaluation of their effectiveness; however, surveys of consumers are sound in principle and have the added advantage of being relatively inexpensive to conduct.

As consumers of the health services are becoming more sophisticated about the type of care they receive, providers are becoming more attentive to their concerns. There is an increasing demand from the public to be allowed to express opinions, and individuals are seeking consultation regarding the course of their own health care.

Added to this is the well-accepted notion that quality is about meeting and exceeding the needs and expectations of the customer. This does not imply the need to call patients 'customers', but rather to treat them as such—and to have in place mechanisms for identifying their needs and expectations and assessing how well these are being met.

It has been well documented and demonstrated that patients do not often use the administrative channels available to them to redress dissatisfaction. Pickering explains this:[7]

Registering a formal complaint and pursuing it, often in the face of considerable hostility, requires perseverance, powers of self-expression and time, to a degree beyond the personal resources of most people. To remedy this situation, service providers need to approach their patients to obtain feedback on the services they provide. By showing an interest in patient opinion and responding to the suggestions, this can improve public relations within the community.

Patient satisfaction has also been linked to improved health outcomes. These include timely attention to the perceived need for comfort, a safe environment, good food and friendly, courteous interaction with health care workers. When these expectations are not met, patients can become frustrated, stressed and unable to respond maximally to the services provided. It has been well established that there is a psychological dimension to recovery from illness. Identification of patient satisfaction is one variable affecting the outcome of care because it influences compliance and cooperation with health care providers.

By obtaining the opinions of patients, health care workers can determine which areas of service are in need of the most attention. Patients' opinions may differ from those of staff, and thus give another perspective. In addition, levels of satisfaction can be used to compare similar services provided by different facilities.

Consumer (or customer) satisfaction is now well established as a legitimate outcome of care and is recognised as a valuable indicator of the quality of facilities and services.

Difficulties with patient surveys

As with any method of measuring quality, there are difficulties in both the definition and the application of this particular measurement. It is difficult to define specific standards for patient satisfaction as an outcome measure for quality of care. The average patient does not have the expertise to evaluate the technical component of medical intervention in the hospital setting; as a result, patients use proxy values that they can understand to evaluate the quality of care and service. Health care professionals also have varied opinions on what constitutes quality care.

It is well recognised that patients are reluctant to report their complaints and genuine feelings, so it is important to distinguish between reported satisfaction and felt satisfaction.

Many authors have questioned the 'positive' findings found in most surveys. They suggest reasons for this are that patients:

‹   are unlikely to complain when they are sick and feel compromised
‹   are afraid of getting staff into trouble
‹   may be afraid of reprisals if anonymity is lacking
‹   feel grateful for their overall care, particularly if their ailment was alleviated.

The timing of the survey also influences the results. In the area of midwifery, it has been found that women's satisfaction with the medical procedures of childbirth, as assessed two years after the event, was significantly lower than assessment at three weeks postpartum.[8] Some hospitals have found it productive to ask a patient to complete a satisfaction questionnaire on the day before the expected date of discharge. This is not appropriate, however, in facilities with a large proportion of day-only or short-stay patients.

It is generally accepted that patient questionnaires routinely left on bedside lockers or tables tend to have a poor response rate unless nursing staff play a role in promoting the value of their completion.

Health care workers' resistance to satisfaction surveys as a method of measuring quality can be an obstacle to implementation. For example, nurses who see their focus as providing professional services only may not always see the importance of meeting the expectations of patients. However, if nursing executives take the initiative in viewing these expectations not as menial tasks but as 'therapeutic intervention', as a means of helping patients to return to optimal states of health, nurses may also view meeting these expectations in the same way.

Analysing the reasons why nurses appear to dislike patient-satisfaction surveys gives some clues for their improved design and use as a tool for quality improvement. First, the design of the questionnaires is sometimes seen as portraying the activities of nurses as menial and does not take into account the higher care duties they perform. Some nurses suggest that these questionnaires give nursing the 'handmaiden' quality of yesteryear. Second, there is no correlation between staffing levels or quality of staff and patient-satisfaction levels. Negative feedback from such surveys is acted on promptly, with little notice given to the staffing level or the workload of the area at the time.

Third, many nurses feel that the way in which patients respond to the nursing care they receive has as much to do with whether their meals were hot when served as with the actual standard of nursing care! As a result, many nurses have no interest in patient-satisfaction surveys or in the data that can be collected.

To remedy this, nurses from the floor level need to be included in the design process and given an opportunity to provide feedback on how the organisation should respond to and use the results. Also, many of the criticisms of or perceived weaknesses in patient-satisfaction surveys would be alleviated by appropriate trialling of the questionnaires in the first place.

Once the difficulties in defining measures of patient satisfaction are identified, and the problems in applying the methods are resolved, some very positive outcomes can develop for the patient group and the health care workers delivering care.

As with the conduct of any quality-improvement activities, the collation and presentation of the results of client-satisfaction surveys must always be done without fear of reprisal and with the assurance that the anonymity of clients and providers will be maintained. Surveys that produce quantifiable results can be reported back to staff on a regular basis (such as monthly) and provide positive feedback as well as the opportunity to integrate appropriate changes to care according to the results. Staff performance ratings can also in part be based on attainment of predetermined standards in measuring patient satisfaction, and recognition mechanisms developed accordingly.

The most consistent finding in the evaluation of patient surveys is that the characteristics of the provider that make for more personal care are associated with higher levels of patient satisfaction.[9] Good communication skills, empathy and caring appear to be the strongest predictors of how a patient will evaluate the care received. Personal care is valued highly and—to the extent that this aspect of care is to be evaluated—more personal care will result in better communication, more involvement and better outcomes, leading to a better quality service.

Reflections for the reader

'Quality' is an excellent starting point for the attention of health service managers. No one can object to the concept of quality, whereas nearly all staff will object to and resent evaluations, audits and inspections.

The search for excellence or quality can, if mishandled, lead to disasters, particularly if the concepts of quality are used to threaten or blackmail staff colleagues. How quality issues are handled is as important as the issues themselves (the art of management again!).

It is reasonable for readers to think about the quality issue in their places of work and to consider opportunities for improvement. Again, trial and error and the gaining of experience are helpful. Begin with an issue that is not difficult, where success can be reasonably assured. Credibility is very helpful when you approach more difficult problems.

Finally, it needs to be remembered that addressing issues of quality is an infinite task. There are issues associated with quality with respect to nearly every aspect of health care.

Think about this statement in terms of a person, soon to become a patient, who is involved in a traffic accident.

1 How long did the ambulance take to arrive?—a quality issue
2 Did the ambulance staff make an accurate diagnosis?—a quality issue
3 Was the resuscitation appropriate?—a quality issue
4 Was there a delay at the hospital emergency centre?—a quality issue
5 Was the care appropriate?—a quality issue.
6 Was there a delay at the operating theatre?—a quality issue
7 Was there a wound infection from hospital sources?—a quality issue
8 Was the rehabilitation appropriate?—a quality issue
9 Were the financial accounts accurate?—a quality issue
10 Was the patient satisfied with the service?—a quality issue

11

Developing trends in management of health services

The purpose of this chapter is to draw attention to some of the more common trends in the management of health services and to review some of the current terminology and jargon. An underlying determinant of many of these trends is the need to control costs.

Casemix

The concept of casemix is simple; namely, to consider diagnoses and procedures in groups that have similar characteristics. In this way, the number of separate diagnoses and procedures has been reduced from around 3000 for a major hospital to less than 500. The value of this grouping is that information is created that allows for comparisons of costs, quality and characteristics of hospitals. However, the best known and most influential use of casemix has been for estimating the cost of hospital services and payment by diagnostic related groups (DRGs—a specific category of casemix). The casemix concept was developed in the United States during the 1960s by Robert Fetter and colleagues at Yale University. The original purpose was to develop better information systems, but the use of DRGs for hospital payment systems in the United States has become the dominant application.

Payment by DRGs has resulted in a reduction of costs by up to 20 per cent in particular hospitals in the United States. However, the overall costs of US health services have continued to rise primarily as a consequence of shifting costs to outpatient care and a continued expansion of services.[1]

The Australian experience of the system of payment by DRGs is currently best developed in Victoria, where public hospitals receive part-payment (approximately 40 per cent) of their overall funds for each patient categorised by DRG. The Victorian experience has been similar to that of the United States—improved productivity and a lowering of costs.[2] As a consequence of this experience, payment by DRGs may be adopted in other parts of Australia.

While payment by DRGs has obvious attractions, the practice is not free of problems. First, both US and Victorian hospitals were more expensive than their counterparts in other countries and other states; hence, improvements in productivity could have been expected. Second, there may be a diversion of funds away from areas where DRG payments are difficult to apply; namely, in psychiatric, paediatric and general preventive services. Third, and perhaps most important, the initial savings gained are a one-off. However, payment by DRGs 'works'. In addition, there are subtle non-financial benefits; for example, bringing antagonistic groups (such as doctors and nurses) together in the common cause of a hospital's long-term survival. However, while payment solely by DRGs may work in the short term, US experience suggests there may not be a long-term effect because of 'cost shifting'. The use of DRG within a global budget context (as in Victoria) may therefore be a better answer.

Payment by DRGs has also been criticised because of the possibility of lowering quality of care. The fear is based on the US-based Rand study, which is the only systematic before-and-after DRG payment study. Close review of this study, however, clearly demonstrates there has been no deterioration in care.[3]

In our view, the funding of hospitals and health services by DRGs as part of a global budget has value. But the development of a global budget needs additional measures; for example, to address the needs of defined populations as well as the needs for services that may not suit DRG concepts (such as prevention, psychiatric or paediatric services). Managers also need to be aware that payments based entirely on DRGs may lead to some difficult problems; for example, hospitals selectively admitting profitable cases, neglect of patients with long-term problems, deterioration of prevention services and DRG 'creep', where hospitals classify patients into DRGs with higher payments.[4]

Donaldson and Gerard of Sydney have reviewed in detail the various methods of financing hospitals; in particular, prospective payments via DRG prepayments through health maintenance organisations and global budgets.[5] They have also reviewed the issue of privatising hospitals. They have concluded that global budgeting based on historical costs is probably the most effective way to control costs, but that such budgets need to be refined by developing 'best practice' clinical standards and 'best practice' costings of clinical care. They also found that competition is only effective if the competing hospitals are in close proximity to each other. Finally, they found that private hospitals are more expensive than non-profit and public hospitals once patient type and severity are standardised.

Purchaser–provider split

This concept was founded in the United Kingdom under the leadership of the then prime minister, Margaret Thatcher. In the United Kingdom, as in many countries with publicly funded and managed hospitals and health service systems, the provider and the funder of the service are the same; namely, the government. The purchaser–provider split concept seeks to separate the provider and the funder, thereby establishing a regulated 'market' that has competition and, therefore, presumably greater efficiency. The concept is based on theories developed in the United States by Alain Enthoven.[6]

In part, the attraction of the purchaser–provider split is the alliteration (it sounds good!). Certainly the concept has been considered on a worldwide basis since the memorable title was created. The reason for such an apparent trivialisation of important concepts is that purchaser–provider splits have been the norm in most Australian states for generations, the major exception being Queensland. The term 'purchaser–provider' was not used, but most Australian public hospitals have been managed by independent boards and have received government subsidies since the nineteenth century! This system has worked well for Australia.

Production line management

This term comes from the manufacturing industry. In the health service context, a production line implies the conduct of many similar procedures at the same place and time—coronary artery bypass surgery provides an example. Attempts to organise hospitals into units that provide health services along product lines appear to have failed in Australia because of the difficulty in attracting the relevant medical staff to the concept. On the other hand, specialised units and hospitals are commonplace, and are a form of product line. There are many specific instances of such management in Australia; for example, all tonsillectomies at the Royal Children's Hospital in Melbourne are performed by the same team of surgeons on Mondays and Wednesdays. The patients are admitted and discharged on the same day. Dilation and curettage procedures, endoscopies and ECT (electroconvulsive therapy) are other procedures that lend themselves to this approach.

Where product line management can be achieved, there appear to be advantages in terms of lower costs and enhanced quality.[7]

Area health services

The development of area (or district/regional) health services has previously been discussed. In essence, the concept is to provide hospital and health services by way of a coordinated network of services on behalf of a defined population.[8] A single health authority is charged with responsibility for the provision and coordination of all health services, both public and private, for this population.

There is a range of advantages that result from providing health services in this way; namely, continuity of care for long-term patients, coordination instead of fragmentation, the acceptance of responsibility for the health of the whole community and not just those who seek care, and the possibility of planning a balanced health service—that is, a balance between institution-based and community-based care and a balance between treatment and prevention services. The term 'area' is interchangeable with 'region' or with the international term, 'district'.

Although the development of area health services has been of advantage to the community, the details of their organisational management need careful consideration. Where the concept of areas has not been implemented with care, some disadvantages have been identified. These include the loss of identity of individual services, such as hospitals and clinics, where they have been incorporated in a large area; and area management becoming quite remote from the action, resulting in loss of morale among some staff.

There are answers to these problems in the area context, including the creation of meaningful (not just token) local committees of management with substantial delegation of authority.

Internal markets

Again this concept evolved in the United States largely through the work of Alain Enthoven.[9] The aim is to have separate parts of a health care system compete for patients and services on the basis of price and quality. However, there appears to be no evidence supporting the value of this concept except where hospitals are in close geographical proximity.[10]

Health outcomes

'Health outcomes' is an attractive concept that proposes that all activities in the health field, whether they be clinical, managerial or financial, should be evaluated in an effort to determine their value or otherwise.[11] The concept is familiar to clinical researchers. In our view, the main value of the health outcome concept is to keep health issues on the agenda of health authorities, instead of having a total focus on finance—an important means to an end. Government health departments have, for the past decade, been forced to give overwhelming priority to financial matters. If the concept of health outcomes can shift this focus, it will be of great benefit to the community.

Managed care

'Managed care' is a term mainly used in the United States to describe health service products and health services provided in the context of a defined financial contract.[12]

The main aim of managed care is to control costs. It seeks to establish definitions of care to be provided at an agreed cost. Both elements are included in any contracts prior to the service being offered.

Managed care tends to be a confusing concept because it has become part of 'managed competition' and 'health maintenance organisations'. Managed competition is a concept that encourages 'purchases' of services; that is, individuals or members of a health insurance fund plan to seek the best contract for the provision of health services from competing providers. The providers may be, for example, hospitals and doctors who are willing to enter into contracts to provide defined services at defined costs.

Health maintenance organisations (HMOs)

The essential concept here is for the prepayment by individuals and families of a fee to a health maintenance organisation in return for comprehensive health care. There is a long-term experience of this concept in the United States.

The care offered within HMOs appears to be of high standard and the costs lower than fee-for-service systems.[13] The reason is mainly that there is less hospital-based care and there are fewer interventions for discretionary surgery (such as hysterectomy, appendicectomy or tonsillectomy).

In view of the success of this concept, it is surprising that it is confined to less than 25 per cent of the US population. Australia's universal health care system has removed incentives for the local introduction of HMOs.

Benchmarking and best practice

Benchmarking (the term has carpentry origins) and best practice are methods of improving performance.[14] Indeed, the quality movement is entirely dependent on developing criteria, norms or standards that are measurable.

There is a difference between best practice and total quality management (TQM) in the sense that concepts of best practice imply an active search for the very best procedure or intervention, whereas TQM can imply measurement as a means of ensuring adherence to best practice.

Best practice involves an active search for examples in which the best quality at an affordable price has been achieved. This search may involve organisations not involved in the health field as well as local and international health service experiences. Best practice may apply to the systems affecting the whole of the organisation or to a specific technique.

It is now accepted in the business world that top-class organisations have a major emphasis on continuous improvement and customer service that can only be achieved with full involvement of the workforce. Demonstration projects have been useful in achieving these aims. For example, the demonstration by the Eastern Sydney Area Health Service that multiskilling of the workforce is practicable has led to widespread adoption of the concept among nursing, catering, portering and cleaning assistants.

Best practice concepts have been usefully linked with amounts and methods of pay to staff—more commonly referred to as 'enterprise bargaining'. While it is highly probable that progress in multiskilling and in linking pay with quality, cost and needs of patients could only have been achieved in a climate of economic difficulty, progress has been sufficiently rewarding that it is likely to continue regardless of the economic situation.

Best practice concepts are not new to clinicians. Indeed the practice of adopting world standards has long been a normal one, particularly in surgical fields where newly developed techniques can be readily evaluated and adopted. A current example is the widespread adoption of endoscopic surgical techniques that are clearly superior to many traditional procedures.

Quality of care

By far the most important trend is the new emphasis on quality of care. Quality of care is a long-standing issue but it has never, until recently, been THE issue.

Quality issues have been explored by Ian O'Rourke in Chapter 6. We commend his work to you.

Reflections for the reader

Trends are just that—trends. They come and they go. Few trends become permanent fixtures. Many are merely new names for old ideas. For example, purchaser–provider splits, which make sense in the United Kingdom, have long been established in Canada and Australia.

Product line management is thirty years old in some Australian hospitals, although the name is new for the health services.

Readers are well advised to consider carefully the old and well-tried ways of managing before adopting any new fashion.

References

Chapter 1

1   PR Torrens, in SJ Williams & PR Torrens (eds), *Introduction to Health Services*, 2nd edn, John Wiley & Sons, New York, 1984.
2   RW Revans, *Standards for Morals,* Oxford University Press, Oxford, 1964.
3   C Craig, *Launceston General Hospital—First 100 years, 1863–1963*, Launceston General Hospital Board of Management, Launceston, 1963.
4   JS Lawson, 'Difficulties in the transition from clinician to manager', *Executive Physician,* vol. 20, 1994, pp. 19–21.
5   A Daniels & D Daniels, 'The psychiatrist as administrator and organisational leader', *Social Psychiatry and Psychiatric Epidemiology,* vol. 24, 1989, pp. 295–300.
6   G Prideaux, *Making Management Development Relevant for Health Service Managers,* Centre for Health Services Management, Royal Melbourne Institute of Technology, Melbourne, 1990.
7   H Mintzberg, *The Nature of Managerial Work*, Harper & Row, New York, 1973.
8   RE Boyatzis, *The Competent Manager,* John Wiley & Sons, New York, 1982.
9   J Dwyer & SG Leggat, 'Innovation in Australian hospitals', *Australian Health Review*, vol. 25, 2002, pp. 19–31.
10 Lawson, op. cit.

Chapter 2

1   World Health Organization, *Health Systems Reform,* WHO, Western Pacific Regional Office, Manila, Philippines, 1994.
2   JS Lawson & AE Bauman, *Public Health—Australia,* 2nd edn, McGraw-Hill, Sydney, 2001.

3   JW Farquhar, N Maccoby, PD Wood et al., 'Community education for cardiovascular health', *Lancet*, vol. 1, 1977, pp. 1192–5.

4   JT Salonen, P Puska, TE Kottke & J Tuomilehto, 'Changes in smoking, serum cholesterol and blood pressure levels during a community-based cardiovascular disease prevention program—the North Karelia Project', *American Journal of Epidemiology*, vol. 114, 1981, pp. 81–94.

5   World Health Organization, Health Statistics Annuals 1980–2000, WHO, Geneva.

6   ibid.

7   J Braithwaite, L Lazarus, RF Vining & J Soar, 'Hospitals: to the next millennium', *International Journal of Health Planning Management*, vol. 10, 1995, pp. 87–98; J Braithwaite, 'Organisational change, patient focused care: an Australian perspective', *Health Services Management Research*, vol. 8. 1995, pp. 172–85; P Lloyd, J Braithwaite & G Southon, 'Empowerment and the performance of health services', *Journal of Management in Medicine*, vol. 13, 1999, pp. 83–94.

Chapter 3

1   J Braithwaite, 'Identifying the elements in the Australian health service management revolution', *Australian Journal of Public Administration,* vol. 52, no. 4, 1993, pp. 418–30.

2   RJ Maxwell, 'Hospitals at a cross-roads', Paris Conference Paper, WHO, Geneva, 1994.

3   'Future of the acute hospital', *King's Fund News,* vol. 16, 1993, p. 4.

4   D Jolly, *The Hospital of the Future—What Will It Look Like?*, Assistance Publique Hopitaux de Paris, monograph, 1993.

5   JS Lawson, 'Decentralizing health services in Australia', *World Health Forum,* vol. 12, 1991, pp. 96–8.

6   Australian Bureau of Statistics, *National Health Survey 1989–1990, Australia*, cat. no. 4364.0, Canberra, 1991.

7   EG Dax, 'The evolution of community psychiatry', *Australian and New Zealand Journal of Psychiatry,* vol. 26, 1992, pp. 295–301.

8   *First National Mental Health Report*, Commonwealth Department of Health, Canberra, 1993.

9   J Hoult, A Rosen & I Reynolds, 'Community oriented treatment compared to psychiatric hospital oriented treatment', *Social Science and Medicine,* vol. 18, 1984, pp. 1005–10.

10 J Hoult, *Mental Health Services in Australia,* Australian Schizophrenic Foundation, Melbourne, 1994.

11 E Shanley, M Jubb & P Latter, 'Partnership in coping: an Australian system of mental health nursing', *Journal of Psychiatric Mental Health Nursing*, vol. 10, 2003, pp. 431–41.

12 J Hoult, I Reynolds, M Charbonneau-Powis et al., 'Psychiatric hospital versus community treatment: a randomised trial', *Australian and New Zealand Journal of Psychiatry,* vol. 17, 1983, pp. 160–7.

13 MG Marmot & GD Smith, 'Why are the Japanese living longer?', *British Medical Journal*, vol. 299, 1989, pp. 1547–51.

14 JS Lawson, C Leaver & EK Cullen, 'The successful development of co-ordinated rehabilitation and geriatric service in North Sydney', *Australian Health Review*, vol. 4, 1979, pp. 1–10.

15 E Smith, S O'Malley & JS Lawson, 'The costs and experiences of caring for sick and disabled geriatric patients—Australian observations', *Australian Journal of Public Health*, vol. 17, 1993, pp. 131–4.

16 EB Chain, *Social Responsibility and the Scientist in Modern Western Society*, The Council of Christians and Jews, London, 1970.

17 JH Brown & JS Lawson, 'The dental health revolution: the dramatic improvement in dental health of school children in the Northern Metropolitan Region of New South Wales', *Medical Journal of Australia*, vol. 1, 1978, pp. 124–5; VJ Burton, MI Robb, GG Craig & JS Lawson, 'Changes in caries experience of 12-year-old Sydney school children between 1963 and 1982', *Medical Journal of Australia*, vol. 140, no. 7, 1985, p. 405; VJ Burton, L Pryke, MI Robb & JS Lawson, 'Traumatized anterior teeth amongst high school students in Northern Sydney', *Australian Dental Journal*, vol. 30, no. 5, 1985, p. 346.

18 WW Holland, *The Oxford Textbook of Public Health*, vol. 3, 2nd edn, Oxford University Press, Oxford, 1991, p. 48.

19 JS Lawson & JC Blatch, 'Early progress report on practical lifestyle problems in a suburban population', *Medical Journal of Australia*, vol. 2, 1981, pp. 119–21.

Chapter 4

1 H Mintzberg, *The Nature of Managerial Work*, Harper & Row, New York, 1973.

2 F Luthens et al., 'What do successful managers really do?', *Journal of Applied Behavioural Science*, vol. 21, no. 3, 1985, pp. 255–70.

3 PD Degeling, *The Management of Organisations*, School of Health Services Management, University of New South Wales, 1993.

4 ibid.

5 JS Lawson, 'Clinical managers—difficulties in the transition from clinician to manager', *Physician Executive*, vol. 20, 1994, pp. 19–21.

6 D Ulrich, J Zenger & N Smallwood, *Results-based Leadership*, Harvard Business School Press, Boston, 1999.

7 LG Bolman & LG Deal, *Reframing Organisations: Artistry, Choice and Leadership*, 2nd edn, Jossey-Bass, San Francisco, 1997.

Chapter 5

1 *Fortune Magazine*, February 1994, p. 1.

2 ML Holle & ME Blatchley, *Introduction to Leadership and Management in Nursing*, Jones & Barlett Publishers, Inc., Boston, 1987.

3 JB Miner, 'The real crunch in managerial manpower', *Harvard Business Review,* November–December, 1973.

4 M Walsh, 'What you need for the throne of power', *Sydney Morning Herald*, 15 May 1992.

5 J Pfeffer, *Managing and Power, Politics and Influence in Organisations*, Harvard Business School Press, Boston, 1991.

6 HJ Eysenck, *Uses and Abuses of Psychology,* Penguin, London, 1953.

7 J Carlopio & L O'Donnell, ch 5 in R Collins (ed.), *Effective Management*, CCH, New Zealand, 1993.

8 H Mintzberg, *The Rise and Fall of Strategic Planning,* The Free Press, Macmillan, New York, 1994.

9 A Rotem & P Manzie, 'How to use small groups in medical education', *Medical Teacher*, vol. 2, no. 2, 1980.

10 R Likert, 'The nature of highly effective groups', in DA Kolb et al. (eds), *Organizational Psychology*, 3rd edn, Prentice-Hall, Englewood Cliffs, New Jersey, 1979; I Rubin, 'Team development', in R Schenke (ed.), *The Physician in Management*, American Academy of Medical Directors, Washington, 1983.

11 A Maslow, *Motivation and Personality*, Harper & Row, New York, 1954.

12 F Hertzberg, B Miausner & B Synderman, *The Motivation to Work*, John Wiley & Sons, New York, 1959.

13 DC McLelland, *The Achieving Society,* Harvard Business Company, New York, 1961.

14 CP Alderfer, 'A new theory of human needs', *Organisational Behaviour and Human Performance*, vol. 4, 1964, p. 142.

15 D McGregor, *The Human Side of Enterprise*, McGraw-Hill, New York, 1960.

16 P Dewe, 'Content and process theories of motivation: a review and critique', in M Thomson (ed.), *Management: A Source Book*, The Dunmore Press, Palmerston North, NZ, 1989.

17 EA Locke, 'Toward a theory of tasks, motives and incentives', *Organisational Behaviour and Human Performance*, vol. 3, 1968, p. 157.

18 J Adams, *The Diary and Autobiography of John Adams*, Belknap Press, Cambridge, Massachusetts, 1962.

19 I Mangham, *The Politics of Organisational Change*, Greenwood Press, Connecticut, 1979.

20 JH Jackson, *Organisation Theory: A Macro Perspective for Management,* Prentice-Hall Inc., Englewood Cliffs, New Jersey, 1978.

21 R Plant, *Managing Change and Making it Stick,* Gower Publishing Company Ltd, Aldershot, UK, 1987.

22 JS Lawson, 'Success and failure among senior public administrators', *International Journal of Career Management,* vol. 6, 1994, pp. 10–13.

Chapter 6

1 RM Wilson, G Runciman et al., 'The Quality in Australian Healthcare Study', *Medical Journal of Australia*, vol. 163, 1995, pp. 458–71.

2 L Armstrong & S Jenkins, *It's Not About the Bike*, Allen & Unwin, Sydney, 2000.

Chapter 7

1 RG Evans, J Lomas, ML Barber et al., 'Controlling health expenditures—the Canadian reality', *New England Journal of Medicine,* vol. 320, 1989, pp. 571–7.

2 P Hjortdahl & E Laerum, 'Continuity of care in medical practice: effect on patient satisfaction', *British Medical Journal*, vol. 304, 1992, pp. 1287–90.

3 JW Peabody, SR Bickel & JS Lawson, 'The Australian health care system: are the incentives down under the right side up?', *JAMA*, vol. 276, 1996, pp. 1944–50.

4 MW Raffel, *Comparative Health Care Systems,* Pennsylvania State University Press, University Park, 1984.

5 ibid.

6 R Gilbert, B Gibberd & J Stewart, 'The New South Wales resource allocation formula: a method of equitable health funding', *Australian Health Review,* vol. 15, 1992, pp. 6–17.

7 Australian Health Insurance Commission, Annual Reports, 1990–2002, AHIC, Canberra.

8 ibid; J Richardson, 'Is 8 per cent of GDP enough?: the future direction of Australia's health care system', *Australian Quarterly*, summer 1990, pp. 314–36.

9 OECD, *Measuring Health Care 1960–1986*, OECD, Paris, 1989.

10 S Domberger & L Piggot, 'Privatisation policies and public enterprise—a survey', *Economic Survey*, 1986, pp. 145–62.

11 P Yang, V Lin & JS Lawson, 'Health policy reform in the People's Republic of China', *International Journal of Health Services*, vol. 21, 1992, pp. 481–91.

12 A Enthoven, 'What can Europeans learn from Americans?', *Health Care Financing Review,* Annual supplement, 1989.

13 G Egger, *Pathways to Better Health: The National Health Strategy*, AGPS, Canberra, 1993.

14 A Williams, *200 Years is Not Enough,* Special monograph 1/89, Australian Hospital Association, Canberra, 1989.

15 MC Weinstein & WB Stason, *Hypertension: A Policy Perspective,* Harvard University Press, Cambridge, Massachusetts, 1976.

16 S. Hurley, 'A review of cost-effective analyses', *Medical Journal of Australia,* vol. 153 (supplement), 1990, pp. S20–3.

17 PE Fidler, 'A comparison of treatment patterns and cost for a fluoride and non-fluoride community', *Community Health,* vol. 9, 1977, pp. 102–13.

18 D Cohen, 'Marginal analysis in practice: an alternative to needs assessment for contracting health care', *British Medical Journal*, vol. 309, 1994, pp. 781–5.

19 R McEwin, *Personal Communication,* Health Commission of New South Wales, Sydney, 1982.

Chapter 8

1 World Health Organization, *Evaluation of Recent Changes in the Financing of Health Services,* Technical Report Series 829, WHO, Geneva, 1993.

2 WW Holland, *The Oxford Textbook of Public Health,* 2nd edn, Oxford University Press, Oxford, 1993.

Chapter 9

1 This section draws in part on PW Bates, 'The role of legislation in health services development (with particular reference to China and Australia)', *Medicine and Law*, vol. 13, 1994, pp. 433–49.

2 World Health Organization, *Health Legislation: Technical Discussions,* WHO, Western Pacific Regional Office, Manila, 10–14 September 1990 (WPR/RC41/Technical Discussions/2).

3 ibid., p. 8.

4 G Pinet, 'The WHO European Program of Health Legislation and the Health for All Policy', *American Journal of Law and Medicine*, vol. 12, 1986, pp. 441–60. Also see the forum, to which a number of authors contributed, entitled 'The future of international health law', *International Digest of Health Legislation,* vol. 40, 1989, pp. 1–29.

5 World Health Organization, *Report: Regional Workshop on Legal and Ethical Aspects of AIDS and HIV Infection, Seoul, Republic of Korea, 23–25 July 1990*, WHO, Western Pacific Regional Office, Manila, April 1991, pp. 4–5, paragraph 2.1.2 (Report no. (WP) CDS(P)/ICP/GPA/001-E). The author was present at the workshop as a WHO consultant.

6 ibid.

7 PW Bates & JC Dewdney (eds), *The Australian Health and Medical Law Reporter,* CCH Australia, Sydney, paragraphs 22-600 to 22-730. (This is a one-volume looseleaf service, first published in 1988 and updated approximately every two months since then.)

8 World Health Organization, *Report: Regional Workshop on Legal and Ethical Aspects of AIDS and HIV Infection,* op. cit., pp. 24–5.

9 ibid., p. 26.

10 See the examples discussed in A Allott, *The Limits of Law,* Butterworths, London, 1980, pp. 174–236.

11 World Health Organization, *Report: Regional Workshop on Legal and Ethical Aspects of AIDS and HIV Infection,* op. cit., pp. 4–5, paragraph 2.1.2.

12 World Health Organization, Technical Report Series, no. 766, WHO, Geneva.

13 ibid., pp. 15–6, paragraph 2.2.4; pp. 91–4, paragraph 5.3.

14 ibid., pp. 104–5, paragraph 6.11.

15 This section and the following one draw in part on PW Bates, 'Introducing the law', in PW Bates & JC Dewdney (eds), op. cit., paragraphs 220–420.

16 *Wyong Shire Council v. Shirt* (1980) 146 CLR 40, 47–8. (A list of abbreviations used in citing law reports is given at the end of these notes.)

17 MA Somerville, 'Rights to, in and against medical treatment: increasing conflicts of personal, professional and societal interests', *Bioethics News* (Monash University), vol. 5, no. 3, April 1986, p. 13.

18 A Stone, 'Law's influence on medicine and medical ethics', *New England Journal of Medicine*, 1985, pp. 309–12.

19 Department of Human Services and Health, *Compensation and Professional Indemnity in Health Care: Interim Report*, Ms F Tito, Chairperson, (Review

of professional indemnity arrangements for health care professionals), AGPS, Canberra, February 1994, chs 2, 5, 6, 7.

20 United States, Secretary Commission on Medical Malpractice, *Report,* Department of Health Education and Welfare, Washington DC, 1973, DHEW Publication no. (OS) 73-88, pp. 25, 67–71.

21 LD Wardle, 'Protecting the rights of conscience of health care workers', *Journal of Legal Medicine*, vol. 14, 1991, pp. 177–230.

22 See further Bates & Dewdney (eds), op. cit., paragraphs 420, 440, 60-000 to 60-480.

23 *The Macquarie Dictionary,* Macquarie Library, Sydney, 1981.

24 See further Bates & Dewdney (eds), op. cit., paragraphs 27-750 to 27-890.

25 For more detail, see Department of Human Services and Health, *Compensation and Professional Indemnity in Health Care,* op. cit., ch 8. See also *New South Wales Medical Defence Union Ltd v. Crawford* (1993) 31 NSWLR 469.

26 *R v. Adomako* [1994] QB 302.

27 *Wyong Shire Council v. Shirt* (1980) 146 CLR 40 at 47-8; *Rogers v. Whitaker* (1992) 175 CLR 479.

28 *Alrighton v. Royal Prince Alfred Hospital* [1980] 2 NSWLR 542; *Rogers v. Whitaker* (1992) 175 CLR 479.

29 B Bromberger, 'Patient participation in medical decison-making: are the courts the answer?', *University of New South Wales Law Journal*, vol. 6, 1983, pp. 1 ff.

30 For example, *Henson v. Board of Management of Perth Hospital* (1939) 41 WAR 15.

31 *Minors Property and Contracts Act 1970* (NSW), s. 49.

32 *K v. Minister for Youth and Community Services* [1982] 1 NSWLR 311 at 323.

33 *Secretary, Dept of Health and Community Services (NT) v. JWB & SMB* ('Marion's Case') (1991–92) 66 ALJR 300 at 305B–G, 329A, 330D, 337G–338B, 339A–B.

34 *Gillick v. West Norfolk & Wisbech Area Health Authority* [1986] 1 AC 112 at 174, per Lord Fraser.

35 cf. 'Marion's Case', op. cit., (note 33), p. 241.

36 *Chatterton v. Gerson* [1981] 1 QB 432.

37 T McDonald & PW Bates, *Commonwealth Nursing Homes Outcome Standards: A Practical Guide to Duty of Care,* AGPS, Canberra, 1989, pp. 36–7.

38 ibid., p. 36.

39 *F v. R* (1983) 33 SASR 189 (Full Sup Ct); *Battersby v. Tottman* (1985) 37 SASR 534 (Full Sup Ct); *Cover v. State of SA* (1985) Australian Torts Reports 80-758; *H v. Royal Princess Alexandra Hospital for Children* (1990) Australian Torts Reports 81-000; *E v. Australian Red Cross Society* (1991) 105 ALR 53 (Full Fed Ct).

40 (1983) 33 SASR 189, 193–4.

41 (1991) 23 NSWLR 600.

42 *Ellis v. Wallsend District Hospital* (1989) 17 NSWLR 553.

43 [1981] 1 QB 432 at 444.

44 (1979–80) 146 CLR 40 at 48.

45 (1990) 169 CLR 638 at 643.

46 *Fair Trading Act 1987* (NSW), *Fair Trading Act 1989* (Qld), *Fair Trading Act 1987* (SA), *Fair Trading Act 1990* (Tas), *Fair Trading Act 1985* (Vic), *Fair Trading Act 1987* (WA), *Fair Trading Act 1992* (ACT).

47 *E v. Australian Red Cross Society* (1991) 105 ALR 53 (Full Fed Ct).

48 For example, *Ferguson v. Central Sydney Area Health Service* (1990) HOC 92-272.

49 See generally PW Bates, 'Contract law for the hospital and health administrator', *Australian Health Review,* vol. 9, 1986, pp. 294–310.

50 Endorsed in *Mann v. Capital Territory Health Commission* (1981) 54 FCR 23 at 32.

51 *Thake v. Maurice* [1986] 2 WLR 337 at 354; *Eyre v. Measday* [1986] 1 All ER 488.

52 McDonald & Bates, op. cit., pp. 22–3.

53 ibid.

54 *Norberg v. Wynrib; Women's Legal Education and Action Fund, Intervener* (1992) 92 DLR (4th) 449; *McInerney v. MacDonald* (1992) 93 DLR (4th) 415.

55 *Breen v. Williams*, NSW Court of Appeal, CA no. 40600/94 decided on 23.12.94 (Mahoney & Meagher JJA; Kirby P dissenting); the High Court of Australia agreed to hear an appeal from this decision.

56 See generally NJ Mullany & PR Handford, *Tort Liability for Psychiatric Damage,* Law Book Co., Sydney, 1993, pp. 48–9.

57 This section draws on and updates PW Bates, 'Defining death, natural death legislation and withdrawal of treatment', *Australian Health Review,* vol. 15, 1992, pp. 392–421; 'Legal criteria for distinguishing between live and dead human foetuses and newborn children', *University of New South Wales Law Journal,* vol. 6, 1983, pp. 143–51, also published in *Bioethics News* (Monash University), vol. 3, no. 4, 1983; 'Foetal and neonatal life, death and the law', *Legal Service Bulletin,* vol. 9, no. 1, 1984, pp. 40–3, published simultaneously in *New Doctor,* vol. 31, 1984, pp. 17–20.

58 [1953] VLR 338 at 339.

59 C Pallis, 'ABC of brain stem death', *British Medical Journal,* vol. 2, 1976, pp. 1–4, reprinted in I Kennedy & A Grubb (eds), *Medical Law: Text with Materials*, 2nd edn, Butterworths, London, 1994, pp. 1370–3.

60 RH Veatch, *Death, Dying and the Biological Revolution*, rev. edn, Yale University Press, 1989, reprinted in Kennedy & Grubb, op. cit., pp. 1373–93.

61 H Dickson, 'Rehabilitation', in PW Bates (ed.), *Brain Damage: Medico-Legal Aspects*, Blackstone Press, Sydney, 1994, pp. 105–6.

62 See further Bates & Dewdney (eds), op. cit., paragraph 19-200.

63 Reproduced in Kennedy & Grubb (eds), op. cit.

64 Reproduced in Kennedy & Grubb (eds), op. cit.

65 JK Mason & RA McCall-Smith, *Law and Medical Ethics*, 3rd edn, Butterworths, London, 1991, p. 292.

66 Pallis, in Kennedy & Grubb (eds), op. cit., pp. 1370–3.

67 Parliament of Victoria, Social Development Committee, *Inquiry into Options for Dying with Dignity: Second and Final Report,* Parliament of Victoria, Melbourne, April 1987, pp. 147–51. This seems to be confirmed by the UK case of *Re A* [1992] 3 Medical Law Reports 303, which focused on brain-stem death.

68 *R v. Kinash* [1982] Qd R 648.

69 See also Bates & Dewdney (eds), op. cit., paragraphs 22-200 to 22-390.

70 *Natural Death Act 1983* (SA) and Natural Death Regulations 1984 (SA); *Natural Death Act 1988* (NT) and Natural Death Regulations (NT); *Medical Treatment Act 1988–94* (Vic) and see also *In Re Graham Michael Kinney; Application by Talila Kinney*, Supreme Court of Victoria, unreported judgment of Fullagar J, proceedings no. M2/1989, judgment delivered 23 December 1989; *Medical Treatment Act 1994* (ACT).

71 Additional legislation concerning *active* voluntary euthanasia in the Northern Territory in certain circumstances is considered in the *Rights of the Terminally Ill Act 1995* (NT).

Abbreviations

AC	Appeal Cases;
ALJR	Australian Law Journal Reports;
All ER	All England Law Reports;
ALR	Australian Law Reports;
CLR	Commonwealth Law Reports;
DLR	Dominion Law Reports;
EOC	Equal Opportunity Cases;
FCR	Federal Court Reports;
NE	North Eastern Reporter;
NSWLR	New South Wales Law Reports;
NZLR	New Zealand Law Reports;
QB	Queen's Bench;
Qd R	Queensland Reports;
SASR	South Australian State Reports;
WAR	Western Australian Reports;
WLR	Weekly Law Reports

Chapter 10

1 A Gabor, *The Man Who Discovered Quality*, Random House, New York, 1990.

2 A Donabedian, 'The quality of care: how can it be assessed?', *Journal of the American Medical Association*, vol. 260, 1988, pp. 1743–8.

3 M Pawsey, *Quality Assurances for Health Services*, New South Wales Department of Health, Sydney, 1990.

4 Australian Council on Healthcare Standards, *Care Evaluation Program—Clinical Indicators: A User's Manual—Hospital-wide Medical Indicators*, ACHS, Sydney, 1994.

5 ibid.

6 Gabor, op. cit.

7 E Pickering, cited by V Maher, *Consumer Satisfaction in Health Care*, Planning and Service Development Unit, Central Sydney Area Health, 1991.

8 A Bennett, 'The birth of a first child: do women's reports change over time?', *Birth*, vol. 12, 1985, pp. 153–8.

9 PD Cleary & BJ McNeil, 'Patient satisfaction as an indicator of quality care', *Inquiry*, vol. 25, no. 1, 1988, pp. 25–36.

Chapter 11

1 C Donaldson & K Gerard, 'Minding our P's and Q's? Financial incentives for efficient hospital behaviour', *Health Policy,* vol. 17, 1991, pp. 51–76.

2 Department of Health and Community Services, *Momentum: Case Mix— Performance and Funding*, DHCS, 1994, pp. 2–4.

3 JM Duggan, 'Quality of care under case mix', *Medical Journal of Australia,* vol 161, no. 5, Supplement, p. 18.

4 ibid.

5 Donaldson & Gerard, op. cit.

6 AC Enthoven & R Kronick, 'A consumer-choice health plan for the 1990s: universal health insurance in a system designed to promote quality and economy' (in two parts), *New England Journal of Medicine,* vol. 320, 1989, pp. 29–37, 94–101.

7 MP Charns, 'Product line management and clinical costing systems', *Australian Health Review*, vol. 9, 1986, pp. 396–405; MP Charns & LS Tewksbury, 'A model for product line management in health care', *Australian Health Review,* vol. 14, 1991, pp. 65–82.

8 JS Lawson, 'Decentralised health services in Australia', *World Health Forum*, vol. 12, 1991, pp. 96–8.

9 Enthoven & Kronick, op. cit.

10 Donaldson & Gerard, op. cit.

11 H Wetzler, 'Outcomes: a way to measure value', *Healthcare Forum Journal*, vol. 37, 1994, pp. 43–50.

12 R Baldwin, *Managed Care,* College monograph 4.1, Australian College of Health Care Executives, 1994.

13 W Manning, A Leibowitz, G Goldberg et al., 'A controlled trial of the effect of a prepaid group practice on use of services', *New England Journal of Medicine*, vol. 301, 1984, pp. 1505–10.

14 PW Haserot, 'Benchmarking: learning from the best', *CDA Journal*, vol. 63, 1993, pp. 81–93.

Index

health care professional education, **110**
health care professionals, 110, 112, 114
health drivers, **12–18**
health economics v. national economics,
    125–6
health hazards, **38**
health insurance, 14, 20, 57, 123, 124, 129
health legislation, **151–92**
health maintenance organisations, 124, **214**
health outcomes, 12, **15**, 102, 207, **213**
health problems, **144**
health professional management, **43–4**
health professionals, **42–4**
health promotion, 27, 29, **33–4**, 39, **40–1**, 82,
    104, 126
health service finance, **119–41**
health service management trends, **210–15**
health service managers
    job description, **46–9**
    skill requirements, **73–107**
    survival tips for, **102–7**
health service management context, **142–50**
health service provision objectives, **151–3**
health status, 13, 102, **125–6**
health task changes, 12, **15–18**
health threats, **54–5**
health transport systems, **36–7**
hearing loss, 14
'hearsay' evidence, 169
heart disease, 15, 16, 17, 41, 133, 144, **145**,
    194
Hemphill, Dr Woodrow, 147
hepatitis B, 89
hierarchical culture, 4
High Court of Australia, 154, 182, 183,
    184
HIV/AIDS, 15, 16, 17, 26, 40, 41, 144, 146,
    152, 159
home-based geriatric programs, 83
home nursing services, 36
honesty, **106**
Hong Kong, 15, 44, 144, 145
honorary medical staff system, 21, 76
hope, **148**
hormone treatment, 34
Hornsby Hospital, Sydney, 31
hospital bed numbers, 23, 129
hospital closures, 16, **22**, 23, 81, 99
hospital culture, **4–5**
hospital divisions, **25**
hospital inspections, **116–17**
hospital planning, 194
hospital siting and development, **22**, 146
hospital-wide clinical indicators, **201–3**

hospitals
    amalgamation of, 25
    assets of, 79, 137, **138**
    clinical indicators &, **201–3**
    creation of, 19, 22–3, 125
    development of, **22**, 146
    future &, **26–7**
    infection acquired in, 201, 202
    internal organisation of, **20–1**
    length of stay in, 26, 129, 144, 201,
        204, 205
    operating room returns to, 201
    operation of, **20–7**
    organisation and management of, **23–6**
    psychiatric units in, 31
    quality management &, **193–209**
    readmissions to, 201, 202
    restructuring of, 25
    role of, 21, 23, 24, 142
    size of, **25**, **26**, **148**
    trends in, 26, 129, **144**
    tripartite organisation of, **24–6**
    see also private hospitals; public hospitals
hostels, 28, 34
hotel services, 198
Hoult, Dr John, 31, 32
human error *see* adverse incidents
human factors, **114**
human resource function, 77
human resources management, 8, 77
human rights, 160
Hurley, Susan, 132
husband and wife communications, 170

identification, 94
ignorance of the law, **155**, 158
incentives to spend, **120–2**
India, 28, 144, 162
individualists, 90
Indonesia, 144, 162
industrial disputes, 43, **44**, 91, 101
industrial relations, **87**, **100–1**
inflation, 60
information, 48, 49, 51, 61, 87, 97, **135**,
    193–4, 195
information analysis, 181, **102–3**
information channels, 48
information demands, **15**
information disclosure, **182–5**
information gathering, **51–4**, **69**, 70, 81, 87,
    102–3
information planning and management,
    196–7
information sharing, 47, 87, 88, 98, 106

obstetrics and gynaecology clinical indicators, **201–2**, 205
occupational health services, **37–9**
occupational therapy/therapists, 5, 34
OECD countries, 16–17, 44, 124, 125, 126, 127
official v. unofficial rulings, **154–5**
open-ended finance, **122–3**
opinion, 47, 64, 98
opportunities, 50, 51, **81**
opportunity costs, 55, 134
organisational issues, 50
organisational performance evaluation, **67–70**
organisational reframing, 50–1
organisational structure, 58
osteoarthritis, 14
osteoporosis, 33, 34
'out of court' settlements, **167**
outcome improvement desire, **15**
outreach campaigns, 55
outsourcing, **128**, **129**, 131

parental consent, 178–9
parental leadership style, 75
paternalism, 182
Paterson, John, 105
pathology services, 122
patient care errors *see* adverse incidents
patient-centred care, 9, 113, 121
patient compliance, 6
patient consent, 154, 174, **178–85**, 186
patient-doctor relationships, 169–70, 171, **187**
patient expectations *see* consumer expectations
patient needs, 21
patient restraint, **180–1**
patient-satisfaction surveys, **206–9**
peer interaction, 8
people management, **77–9**
performance evaluation, organisational, **67–70**
performance indicators, **201–3**
personal appraisals, **66–7**
personal ego, 76
personal injury litigation *see* litigation
personal interaction, 48
personal relationships, **84**, **85–6**, **90**, 98, 99, 100
personal survival, 48
personality and management, **73–5**, 91, 93, 94
Peter Principle, **74**, 75
Pfeffer, Jeffrey, **76–7**
pharmaceutical services, 27, **35–6**
pharmaceuticals, 14, 126, 127, 135, 195, 201, 202
pharmacies, 124, 202–3, 205

Philippines, 28, 144
physical asset assessment, **79**
physiotherapists, 5, 7
physiotherapy, 34
plaintiffs, 172, 173, 182
plan development, 49–50, **57–8**
planning, 3, 6, 8, **23**, **67**, 73, 193, 194
politeness and courteousness, **103**
political agendas, 12, 27, 28, 47
political changes, 80
political interest, 56
political patronage, **22**
politician, acting as a, **100**
population-based health services, 26, **27–8**, 91, 212
positioning, 80
positivism, **153–8**, 160, 161, 162, 171
postoperative wound infections, 18
power, 8, 73, 75, **76–7**, 83, 87, 88, 89, 91, 94, 97, 100, 103
power sharing, 78
praise, **96**
precedents, 154, 165
prevention measures, 12, **16**, 17, 27, 29, **33–4**, 35, 36, 39, 53, 82, 126, 129, 132, **133–4**, 135, **146–7**
Prideaux, Geoffrey, 8
Prince of Wales Hospital, NSW, 23
priorities, 49, 51, 52, **54–6**, 78, 123, 130, 134, 135–6, 195, **206**
private health insurance, 14, 20, 57, 123, 124, 129
private health sector, **129**, 136
private hospitals, **20**, 24, 26, 41, **129**, **142**, 211
private international law, **163**
privatisation, **127–9**, 211
privilege, **169–70**
problem anticipation and response, **81**
problem identification, 6
problem solving, 8, **90**, 99–100
procedural fairness, 171
product liability cases, 185
production line management, **212**, 215
productivity, 43, 57, 77, 81, 95, 99, 119, 127, 149, 211
professional indemnity insurance, 172, 173
professional liability, 157, **171–87**
professional misconduct, 186, 187
professional organisations, 77
professionalism, **4**, 12, 94
profit and loss statements, 137, 138
progress measurement indicators, **69**
prostate cancer, 17
psychiatrists, 31